The Calling of
Congregational
Leadership

BOOKS BY
The Columbia Partnership Ministry Colleagues

George W. Bullard Jr.
Every Congregation Needs a Little Conflict

FaithSoaring Churches
Pursuing the Full Kingdom Potential of Your Congregation

Richard L. Hamm
Recreating the Church

Edward H. Hammett
Making Shifts without Making Waves:
A Coach Approach to Soulful Leadership

Reaching People under 40 while Keeping People over 60:
Being Church to All Generations

Spiritual Leadership in a Secular Age:
Building Bridges Instead of Barriers

Key Leadership Books

Gregory L. Hunt
Leading Congregations through Crisis

Cynthia Woolever and Deborah Bruce
Leadership That Fits Your Church: What Kind of Pastor
for What Kind of Congregation

Penny Long Marler, D. Bruce Roberts, Janet Maykus, James Bowers,
Larry Dill, Brenda K. Harewood, Richard Hester, Sheila Kirton-Robbins,
Marianne LaBarre, Lis Van Harten, and Kelli Walker-Jones
So Much Better: How Thousands of Pastors
Help Each Other Thrive

Larry McSwain
The Calling of Congregational Leadership:
Being, Knowing, Doing Ministry

For more leadership resources, see
TheColumbiaPartnership.org
ChalicePress.com

The Calling of
Congregational
Leadership

Being, Knowing, Doing Ministry

Larry L. McSwain

CHALICE
PRESS
ST. LOUIS, MISSOURI

The Scripture quotations contained herein, unless otherwise designated, are from the *New Revised Standard Version Bible*, copyright © 1989 by the Division of Christian Education of the National Council of the Churches of Christ in the U.S.A., and are used by permission. All rights reserved.

Selected biblical quotations are Scripture taken from THE MESSAGE. Copyright © 1993, 1994, 1995, 1996, 2000, 2001, 2002. Used by permission of NavPress Publishing Group.

Taken from the *Cotton Patch Version of Matthew and John*, by Clarence Jordan, published by NuWin Publishing, Inc., Clinton, N.J. Copyright ©1970. All rights reserved.

Figure of "Concentric Circles of People Groups in a Congregation" on page 58 is from George W. Bullard, Jr., *Pursuing the Full Kingdom Potential of Your Congregation* (St. Louis: Lake Hickory Resources, 2005), 44. Used by permission. All rights reserved.

Permission to quote from Jackson W. Carroll, *God's Potters: Pastoral Leadership and the Shaping of Congregations* (Grand Rapids: William B. Eerdmans Publishing Company, 2006), 143, Figure 4.2 granted by Copyright Clearance Center

Cover design: Scribe, Inc.
Cover art: iStock

www.chalicepress.com

Print: 9780827205314 EPUB: 9780827205321 EPDF: 9780827205338

Library of Congress Cataloging-in-Publication Data

McSwain, Larry L.

  The calling of congregational leadership : being, knowing, doing ministry / Larry L. McSwain.

    pages cm

  Includes bibliographical references.

  ISBN 978-0-8272-0531-4 (pbk. : alk. paper) — ISBN 978-0-8272-0532-1 (epub : alk. paper) — ISBN 978-0-8272-0533-8 (epdf : alk. paper)

1. Christian leadership. I. Title.

  BV652.1.M435 2013

  253—dc23

2013006100

Contents

Editor's Foreword

Inspiration and Wisdom for Twenty-First-Century Christian Leaders

You have chosen wisely in deciding to study and learn from a book published in **The Columbia Partnership Leadership Series** with Chalice Press. We publish for

- Congregational leaders who desire to serve with greater faithfulness, effectiveness, and innovation.
- Christian ministers who seek to pursue and sustain excellence in ministry service.
- Members of congregations who desire to reach their full kingdom potential.
- Christian leaders who desire to use a coach approach in their ministry.
- Denominational and parachurch leaders who want to come alongside affiliated congregations in a servant leadership role.
- Consultants and coaches who desire to increase their learning concerning the congregations and Christian leaders they serve.

The Columbia Partnership Leadership Series is an inspiration and wisdom-sharing vehicle of The Columbia Partnership, a community of Christian leaders who are seeking to transform the capacity of the North American church to pursue and sustain vital Christ-centered ministry. You can connect with us at www.TheColumbiaPartnership.org.

Primarily serving congregations, denominations, educational institutions, leadership development programs, and parachurch organizations, the Partnership also seeks to connect with individuals, businesses, and other organizations seeking a Christ-centered spiritual focus.

We welcome your comments on these books, and we welcome your suggestions for new subject areas and authors we ought to consider.

George W. Bullard Jr., Senior Editor
GBullard@TheColumbiaPartnership.org

The Columbia Partnership
332 Valley Springs Road, Columbia, SC 29223–6934
Voice: 803.622.0923, www.TheColumbiaPartnership.org

Foreword

What you are holding in your hand or observing on your favorite digital reader or computer screen represents the pinnacle of the ministerial and academic career of a person deeply committed to excellence in ministerial leadership and congregational vitality.

Larry McSwain has been my teacher, mentor, supervisor, colleague, and friend throughout the past 40-plus years. We initially encountered one another during my first semester at the Southern Baptist Theological Seminary in Louisville, Kentucky, in the fall of 1971. We have most recently experienced one another in his role as professor of leadership at McAfee School of Theology at Mercer University in Atlanta, Georgia.

In between have been an enormous number of delightful, yet challenging, engagements with a person truly dedicated to helping ministerial students, congregational leaders, denominational executives, and academic professionals soar in Christian ministry with Christ-centered faith and academic competence.

Hardly anyone is better equipped, better trained, or better qualified through personal experience to share perspectives on issues surrounding leadership and congregations. Larry has studied countless volumes of academic and research documents about leadership and congregations. He has taught thousands of students in academic and field seminar settings about leadership and congregations. He has been in, observed, or read about a multitude of congregations in several denominations. He has conducted numerous original research projects on leadership and congregations. In the intersection of these various endeavors is a synergistic understanding of leadership and congregations that is invaluable and is now recorded in this high-quality volume of work.

McSwain as Urban Strategist

For me personally, the high point of Larry's integration of academic insight with original field research came during the 1980s. While serving in a denominational agency dedicated to missional work throughout North America, I had the privilege to be on a team that sponsored his sabbatical. He and his family moved to Houston, Texas, for the academic year of 1983–84 to study the religious life patterns of Houston and Harris County, Texas, and to suggest those strategies that might be most effective in fulfilling the Great Commission in the spirit of the Great Commandment in that setting.

True to the theme of this book, now more than a quarter of a century later, much of what Larry discovered during his sabbatical focused on leadership and congregations.

At that time Southern Baptists, the denomination of heritage for both Larry and myself, had around five hundred congregations in Houston and Harris County, one of the largest megalopolitan areas in North America. My personal role was as leader of Mega Focus Cities, an emphasis on missional work in the fifty largest urban areas in the United States. The strategic question for us was, "With the resource base we have in Houston and Harris County, if we cannot reach that setting for Christ, what makes us think we can reach any urban setting anywhere for Christ?"

While Houston and Harris County have not been fully "reached," the work Larry did on the religious life patterns in a Sunbelt city had an immediate and tremendous impact on Christian ministry in that setting and inspired numerous new missional strategies that are still impacting the quality of Christian work in that setting.

McSwain as Community Context Interpreter

Long before sophisticated computer and web-based graphic information systems (GIS), Larry would have his students diving into various government and business reports to discover the underlying statistical trends in a community context. He found it important to know the past, present, and future projected trends in any context where leaders anticipated engaging in relevant Christian ministry.

Way beyond statistics was the need to experience the context in a manner that would cause the learners to move outside their comfort zones. Larry was a big advocate of getting out into the community—on foot rather than by car—to experience real people in real life situations. His strongest call was for participation in at least a 24-hour plunge in which students would live on the street for a full day in places such as New York City, but especially in Louisville, Kentucky.

I must admit I resisted these teaching methods. As an alternative, I offered to let people come live with me in the inner city of Louisville, Kentucky, where I served as a pastor.

That was a permanent urban plunge!

Yet Larry's insistence that students get out of the classroom and experience real ministry with real people in real life settings set him apart from many of his colleagues. At the same time, Larry could pull the learning experience back into the classroom with the full rigors of academic requirements and formal documentation of reading sources.

McSwain as Conflict Minister

Anyone who observes or engages the front line of congregational and community ministry will eventually have to address in a serious way the issues of conflict and how they impact both church and community. In their book *Conflict Ministry in the Church*, Larry and his colleague in ministry, William C. Treadwell, Jr. addressed in an in-depth manner the issues and processes of conflict in congregations.

This provided another intersection for our mutual ministries. In a denominational role I related to regional and local denominational staff leaders who needed to be possessed by the knowledge and skills of conflict ministry. It was an easy move—in the category of *no-brainer*—to ask Larry and Bill to become the trainers of these denominational staff persons. Once again, Larry's insight into leadership and congregations played a key role as over 750 denominational leaders were trained in conflict ministry skills over multiple years.

For me personally I have always seen Larry as one of the people I could talk to about conflict situations I was addressing. He has been a great outside third-party with whom to discuss the dynamics of various congregational situations, or leadership situations in which conflict arose. At the same time both Larry and I are probably seen in some quarters as being "carriers" of the conflict virus, as we have not been afraid to confront injustice and inadequacy in leadership when and where we see it. That at times has been very helpful. At other times it may have gotten us in a lot of trouble. Yet, life and ministry go forward.

What Will You Learn from This Book?

The bottom line you probably want to know is not these anecdotal insights into Larry McSwain and our long-term relationship—although I hope they will give you insight into the significant contributions he has made to Christian ministry in general and my life specifically. You want to know what you are going to get out of the time you will invest in reading this book. Here is a selected list of things I believe you will gain that will cause your investment to be of great value.

1. *Calling.* Leading in Christian ministry is a calling from God. Without a deep and abiding sense of call to Christian ministry leaders can find themselves emotionally and spiritually drained without any centering points to help them move forward.
2. *Self-Knowledge.* We must know who we are as leaders in the Christian arena: when we are healthy and when we are unhealthy; when we are

x The Calling of Congregational Leadership

excellent and when we are mediocre; when we are inspiring followership and when we are antagonizing followers; and when we have a synergy of spiritual gifts, strengths and skills, and preferences versus when we are functioning outside of these characteristics.

3. *Doing.* Leadership is not about improving ourselves alone. It is about doing the work of leadership. While being is of extreme importance, if you cannot do the work of leadership then the congregation God is calling you to serve cannot thrive.

4. *Dreaming.* Leadership is as much about that which is unseen as it is about that which is seen. What can you imagine as a leader? What dream is God giving you for a vital and vibrant congregation?

5. *Proclaiming and Caring.* This book will share perspectives both about preaching and teaching as you proclaim the Word of God and about caring for the people. A critical component of leadership is that you figure out how to do both with excellence, rather than one to the exclusion of the other. Leaders figure out how to develop systems to empower and improve both proclamation and caring even when they are not gifted and skilled in both.

6. *Management.* Unfortunately for some people, leadership is also about managing the strategies, structures, and systems of congregations. I hope you will pay careful attention to the sections on generosity, legal issues, and developing and relating to staff.

My prayer for you is that you will be informed and inspired by this book to become an exceptional leader in congregational settings. The work of the kingdom of God needs your very best efforts. Whether you are beginning your ministerial journey, a few years in, at a midpoint reassessment, reaching your full potential, or thinking about finishing well, use this book to remind yourself of those key aspects of being centered on God's leading in your ministry and the practical things you need to be reminded of on a daily basis.

George Bullard
Strategic Coordinator,
The Columbia Partnership at www.TheColumbiaPartnersip.org

General Secretary,
North American Baptist Fellowship of Baptist World Alliance

Acknowledgments

A community of friends and colleagues shape the writing of any book, and this one is no exception. I have been given the gift of time, work, and review by a host of persons for whom I am grateful. R. Alan Culpepper, dean of the McAfee School of Theology, is a long-time friend and colleague with whom I have worked at two seminaries. His creation of an atmosphere of support for research and writing, amidst the myriad of teaching and administrative responsibilities, has made possible time for completing this long project.

The resources of The Louisville Institute and the support of James W. Lewis made possible the field research during a sabbatical leave that undergirds many of the ideas presented here. Brian Wilson provided necessary and superb support for the transcription of interviews, bibliographic materials, and assistance with congregational surveys. Erica Geralds Washington served as my student assistant during much of the writing and provided library research and proofreading of sections of the manuscripts. Multiple individuals read sections of the drafts and offered suggestions for improvement, including Davis Byrd, Michael Gregg, Valarie Hardy, Ercil Harrison, Anthony Lankford, Neal Schooley, Walter Shurden, and Brett Younger. James Lamkin, my pastor, has been gracious to allow use of his sermon material to illustrate some of my insights. My colleague in the teaching of leadership at McAfee, James N. (Dock) Hollingsworth, offered helpful suggestions in the classroom trials of some of the material, and also read through the manuscript. Lamar Barden is gracious to visit McAfee classes to discuss clergy finances and assisted in the development of Appendix C. My sister, Sharon McSwain Monroe— a former English teacher—provided helpful proofreading and offered a lay view of overly ponderous theological concepts. Daniel Vestal offered encouraging support from his reading of the manuscript.

George Bullard gave early encouragement and assistance for publishing with Chalice Press, as well as writing the foreword. We have worked together for decades on multiple projects, and I am grateful for his commitment to strengthening churches, denominations, and seminaries for the missional journey. Brad Lyons, publisher at Chalice Press and the editors Gail Stobaugh, Trent Butler, and John Carey have been superb guides in the editorial and publication process. I assume full responsibility for any errors in content, however.

I am especially indebted to the ten pastors from whom I learned congregational leadership on the "front lines" in Spring 2010. They gave of their time in interviews and group conversation, and opened their congregations to my scrutiny. They are:

Rev. Benjamin Barnett, Senior Pastor of the Atlanta Metropolitan Christian Church, Atlanta;

Rev. Steven Dial, Pastor of the Rainbow Park Baptist Church, Decatur;

Dr. Gerald Durley, retired Pastor of the Providence Missionary Baptist Church, Atlanta;

Rev. Dr. William E. Flippin, Senior Pastor of the Greater Piney Grove Baptist Church, Atlanta;

Rev. Dr. Cynthia L. Hale, Founding Pastor and Senior Pastor of Ray of Hope Christian Church, Decatur;

Rev. David Lambert, Pastor of the Cellebration Fellowship, Clarkston;

Rev. Tony Lankford, Lead Pastor of the Park Avenue Baptist Church, Atlanta;

Rev. Dr. William L. Self, retired Senior Pastor of the Johns Creek Baptist Church, Johns Creek;

Rev. Melanie Vaughn-West, a member with Dr. Lanny Peters of the pastoral team, Oakhurst Baptist Church, Decatur;

G. Bryant Wright, Senior Pastor of Johnson Ferry Baptist Church, Marietta.

Finally, and most importantly, my wife, Sue, provided encouragement, patience, and sometimes insistence to take a break from the tasks of the project.

Introduction

Thinking about the future is done on the scaffolding of a narrative.
RICHARD HESTER & KELLI WALKER-JONES[1]

At the conclusion of World War I, William Butler Yeats wrote a poem, "The Second Coming," that is among the one hundred most anthologized poems in English literature. In part, he wrote:

Things fall apart; the centre cannot hold;
Mere anarchy is loosed upon the world,
The blood-dimmed tide is loosed, and everywhere
The ceremony of innocence is drowned;
The best lack all conviction, while the worst
Are full of passionate intensity.

And then he concludes with a question:

And what rough beast, its hour come round at last,
Slouches towards Bethlehem to be born?[2]

Pessimism is natural during times of war and violence, global economic upheavals, shifting currents of social values, or unprecedented change. Remember Psalm 137:1, 4? "By the rivers of Babylon— / there we sat down and there we wept... / How could we sing the LORD's song / in a foreign land?" Or Job 7:1, "Do not human beings have a hard service on earth...?" Or Revelation 13:4b, "Who is like the beast, and who can fight against it?"

The same difficult questions as Yeats and the biblical witnesses raised are being lifted up today by pastors, denominational leaders, congregational researchers, and leaders in the pews as attendance declines, income stagnates, and the typical Protestant congregation ages at a rate far faster than the population of the United States. One could easily propose the death of the American Church in the twenty-first century if the voices of doom and despair are the primary ones to whom we listen. Such a case would not be a difficult one to make.[3]

When we examine the kinds of changes that have swept across the landscape of our community lives of the past several decades, it would be easy to give in to the negative moods of the naysayers on the future of the church. To do so would overlook the essence of the gospel, which proclaims the good news of the promises of God in Jesus Christ as the abiding *hope* of the Church and human life. The theme of this book will be to reverse the pessimism of Yeat's poem written during the crises of World War I. I would reinterpret that theme as: *Things do fall apart;...the center can hold.* The foundation of that hope is the activity of God who continues to call women and men to embody in the world a life commitment to fulfilling a new order of God's Spirit in their daily lives and congregational gatherings.

Audience for the Book

Three audiences are the focus of this book: pastoral leaders of congregations with a focus on those in the Free Church tradition, Protestant seminarians, and laity who seek understanding of their call to congregational leadership. I need to be specific about who I mean as "pastoral leaders," (the *first* audience). I am using this term to describe all of those engaged in ministry as employees of a local congregation. My assumption is that all ministers must relate pastorally to congregants if they are to participate fully in God's new order of the Spirit. Churches with multiple staff members have the additional challenge of seeking a team approach to the work of that staff. This understanding in no way alters the importance of the central "pastoral leader." This is the pastor, senior pastor, lead missionary, elder, bishop, or whatever title is assigned to the one who is understood by the congregation as "the" leader. But our approach does suggest "the" leader is a member of a team of ministers and laity who must engage in collaborative work in the context of the twenty-first–century church.

Regarding the *second* audience, as a seminary professor teaching students in the practice of ministry that focuses on congregations, I have discovered a perennial search for textbooks to provide a resource for the student. While the bibliography on both ministry and congregations is long, the limitations are significant. I hope to address in this work a young generation that mirrors much of the tension of the contemporary congregation. It is a seeking generation for which "going to seminary" is as much a quest for vocation as a response to a decisive call. Present-day seminarians are incredibly open to the Spirit. They are also more limited in their experience in the work of congregations than past generations. When the idealism of being an open, postmodern student encounters the reality of a church as it is, a reality that often occurs two to three years after graduation, the personal and spiritual resources for survival in ministry may seem inadequate. It is my hope this book can tap the youthful idealism of a new generation of church leaders while preparing them for the realities of human congregational systems.

Brian McLaren makes the provocative suggestion that churches need to develop openness to the creative, even entrepreneurial, insights many recent seminary graduates bring to ministry. Rather than squelching the enthusiasm and the new learning they bring, affirming their insights into critical recent biblical and theological research could be a source of renewal for congregations. McLaren reminds us of the price all good leaders have experienced for change in the church:

> But recalling that Jesus himself was unable to transform the Temple establishment of his day, and remembering that Paul was run out of a good many more synagogues than he was welcome in, I'm not sure that any amount of training can equip seminarians for transformation in churches that are quite happy with how they are—or were, thank you very much. It may sound harsh for me to say, but I think it is unethical to send gifted, idealistic, and high-potential young leaders into intractable, dysfunctional congregations that will grind them up, disillusion them, and damage them for life.[4]

McLaren's solution is either to create new congregations by seminary graduates for a postmodern generation, or work more effectively with first placement churches to support the graduate in achieving change. In either case, he assigns the burden of such a vision to the seminaries.

Concerning the *third* audience, the vital congregation of the twenty-first century will never fulfill its potential without a dynamic cadre of lay leaders who understand congregational life and partner with others to provide the leadership churches need to fulfill their mission. Congregational leadership is a calling to the whole congregation and not just its clergy leaders. So, here is an effort to create a dialogue within congregations that will encourage the next generation of lay and clergy leaders God calls to become church. Understanding the cadre of new ministers who will serve the Church in the next several decades will be a critical agenda for laity rooted in traditions that may not be known nor accepted by today's youthful leaders.

Definitions

A few definitions are in order for developing the themes of this book. Who are the people who shall participate in this partnership? The responsibility for fulfilling this divine-human partnership belongs to *all* the people of God. Leadership for the Church is never a singular vocation. It belongs to no one person, but can be accomplished only as all who claim obedience as disciples of Jesus Christ seek a common destiny. The Reformation principle of the "priesthood of all believers" is foundation for congregational vitality. All who respond affirmatively to the invitation to "follow Jesus" are leaders of the Christian community.

Yet, every fellowship of grace needs those who have a primary responsibility, a vocational calling, to participate in guiding the whole people of God to accomplish the mission of the rule and reign of God. A calling from God comes to the few who are set apart by the power of the Holy Spirit and their congregations to provide the environment in which people fulfill the potential of their leadership as a community. These vocational persons are pastoral leaders and may include the individual pastor of a specific community of faith or the collective group of ministry staff who work as a team to accomplish their visions. The primary leader of any such team is the pastor, who leads with unique responsibilities for the vitality of the whole. But the pastor never functions alone. Pastors have a unique role. Theirs is a calling to take primary responsibility for the mission of God, motivate others to participate with them in that calling, and provide specialized skills to accomplish it. While the focus of this book is on these responsibilities, pastors never function in isolation from a tightly woven web of relationships with all disciples of a congregation to fulfill that mission.

There is another critical definition. *Church* is the universal community of all believers whose collective partnership with God transforms the world "that the creation itself will be set free from its bondage to decay and will obtain the freedom of the glory of the children of God" (Rom. 8:21). Whenever this understanding of the Church is used in this work, it will be a capital "C" Church.

The Church is first and foremost a creation of the Holy Spirit. Jesus defined the foundation of the Church as a confession of his identity as Messiah (Mt. 16:13–20) and called forth gatherings of disciples with a promise of his presence in their midst (Mt. 18:20). He established no human organization or institution. The birthplace of the Church was Pentecost, where the prophetic promise of the outpouring of the Spirit on all flesh manifested by a community of vision (Joel 2:28–29) was fulfilled. Wind and fire were the signs of spiritual presence that unified a gathering of diverse ethnicities that Peter could only understand as the manifestation of that promised day:

In the last days it will be, God declares,
that I will pour out my Spirit upon all flesh,
  and your sons and your daughters shall prophesy,
and your young men shall see visions,
  and your old men shall dream dreams.
Even upon my slaves, both men and women,
  in those days I will pour out my Spirit;
   and they shall prophesy.
           (Acts 2:17–18)

But none of us lives in a universal fellowship, except conceptually. We live in families and neighborhoods of towns and cities; we partake of sociological categories of race, ethnicity, class, and gender. Consequently, we gather in smaller networks of people most often reflective of individual values that evolve into core values of congregational identity. These communities of faith meet together in local environments and have themselves unique qualities and characteristics. These churches (small "c") will never embody the fullness of the Church. But they can be called *church* only to the degree the presence of the Holy Spirit guides through human struggle, difference, and discernment to mirror that universal community of faith called Church.

This is a book about these small reflections of the fire of the Holy One who often filter the light of such holy moments through darkened lenses. Churches are undeniably "treasure in clay jars" because they are human entities, which possess all the frailties of the human family. Otherwise, they would claim the source of their power within themselves, denying "that this extraordinary power belongs to God and does not come from us" (2 Cor. 4:7).

To make the distinction clear, *congregation* or *church* will be the term used to describe these faith communities and how they may aspire to embody the fullest meaning of the community of faith we call Church. This is a book about congregations and their leaders with the belief that vital congregations seek to fulfill the mission God has for the Church.

Purpose

The purpose of this book is to propose positive and life-giving understandings for how local Christian bodies of believers can model communities of obedience to the lordship of Jesus Christ in who they are and what they do. This is not a roadmap to success in the market-driven, entrepreneurial arena of popular American Christianity. It can be suggestive of some specific ways pastoral and lay leaders can do a better job of leading their communities of faith to be more like the master of the Church.

Personal Background

I bring to this work nearly forty years of participating in congregations as a consultant in planning new directions for their ministries, or in helping conclude difficult conflicts they had within their fellowships. My primary vocation during this time has been teaching prospective ministers the realities of what they might face in congregational ministries. I have been blessed to have opportunities for service beyond any I imagined as a seventeen-year-old making a public commitment of my calling from God to be a "minister of the gospel." Mine is a pilgrimage from a small rural church in a farming community in northern Oklahoma to working and living in urban America. The sociological changes described in this text have been experienced personally as I have participated as a member of thirteen different congregations, served many others as interim pastor or consultant, and worked in multiethnic, multicultural, multiracial contexts.

I bring to this task a certain set of values and commitments that shape what I think and how I express those thoughts. With all of their diversity and the many differences in understanding their meaning, I affirm the biblical texts as the foundation for the Church's identity. Vital churches root themselves in a biblical narrative that defines their practices of faith—the confession of Jesus Christ as Lord of life and the Church, baptism as a sign of that confession, and discipleship as a search to live out faith as a vocation from God.

I am also a Baptist. This identity roots me in a historical tradition that emphasizes the authority of Scripture for faith and practice, the priesthood of believers to interpret that authority for themselves with the guidance of the Holy Spirit, the practice of faith in a local congregation that is responsible for its own governance, and an unswerving commitment to religious liberty and the separation of church and state in a civil society.

What Baptists can claim clearly is that the commitment to a locally autonomous form of polity or governance makes a difference in how one leads in the congregation. Sherwood Lingenfelter summarizes four theological and structural variations of governance in the history of the church: apostolic authority, Reformation confession, voluntary organizations, and the Free Church movement. Baptists' heritage includes elements of each of them, but primarily derives from the Free Church movement. Lingenfelter writes of that tradition:

> The Free Church Movement rejected the state and its religious hierarchy and gave much more privilege to the communion of

the saints. Known as the Radical Reformation, the Free Church Movement emphasized the redeemed community. Focusing on personal conversion and believer baptism, the redeemed community lived transformed lives in response to the call of God. Asserting the priesthood of all believers, many empowered mature believers to offer communion, baptize new believers, teach Scripture, and participate in any of the other sacramental activities of the worship of the church.[5]

Focus

These kinds of congregations function differently from many that are more connected to hierarchical and connectional structures of resources and guidance. Locally autonomous congregations are like pilgrims in a foreign land who must forge their own way in doing God's work, as they perceive it best done. Pastoral leaders of these kinds of congregations often function with fewer resources than those of more connectional traditions. Consequently, they often rise to the heights of creativity and energy, or descend to the depths of unbridled authoritarianism and relational failure. This book is an effort to call forth the best of pastoral leaders in their callings to these "independent" and "free-thinking" congregations. The vast majority of Baptist, nondenominational, independent, and some Pentecostal congregations fit within this category. These congregations ordain their clergy, own their own property, and call their leadership without associational, denominational, or network control.

The very independence of these congregations makes the lack of understanding beyond them understandable. Generally, they fit into more conservative theological perspectives with Fundamentalist, Evangelical, or Pentecostal approaches, whose scholars are more interested in theology than sociology. Given the individualism of clergy in this tradition, the leadership of the Spirit is often more important than the insights of social scientists when it comes to leadership philosophy and practice.

As a subset of this grouping, most African American congregations fit this understanding of church, even when the congregation is affiliated with a denomination, especially those in the Baptist tradition. No area of pastoral leadership studies receives less attention than does the distinctive role of the pastor in the African American church.

According to the National Congregations Study (Wave 2-2006/07, the second group of congregations studied, 20.4 percent of congregations in America are unaffiliated with any denomination/convention/association.

If you add the congregations that are affiliated with a denomination/convention/association that practice congregationally based polities, as many as 53 percent of all congregations function as locally autonomous entities.

During the spring of 2010, with support from a research grant from The Louisville Institute, I had the privilege of engaging in interviews with pastors of ten very different, but all vital, locally autonomous congregations in the Atlanta, Georgia, region. It was important for me as an academic to test my own ideas in light of the realities of contemporary congregational life. What I learned brought awe for the depth of commitment from the ten leaders to the vitality of their churches, as well as the numerous challenges they face in a radically changing context. While there was considerable diversity in these churches, five primarily African American and five primarily Caucasian, eight led by male pastors and two by female pastors, few of them fit the dominant theories of multiple scholars of how to lead a church. They were more organic in their styles; and the congregations responded more to the pastors' personalities and individual uniqueness than to any systematic, rational, or logical approach of how they accomplished their respective ministries. Perhaps it has always been so, but one could hardly imagine such from the multitude of published materials on the work of church leaders. Such insight has forced me to revise my own approach to understanding the work of congregations in the twenty-first century. This book is an effort to fashion a different leadership language that is verbal, open, and organic in its style.

This is not a book that proposes to suggest ways for all churches to prosper in terms of the institutional measures of success—bodies, budgets, baptisms, and buildings. This would perpetuate the use of an understanding of the church as an institution with measurable outcomes as the only true measure of effectiveness. This book suggests that the authentic ministry needed is possible in every congregation, no matter its size, affluence, or influence.

Thesis

The thesis of this book is that Christian congregations are community organisms with the potential for conveying the power of God in the lives of all they touch.

Every thesis has an antithesis. Those same organisms can be the agents of hurt, pain. and darkness to those they touch. Like cancerous cells in the human body, diseased churches can grow toxic feelings and behaviors that destroy God's intention for the church.[6]

Leaders of congregations, whether clergy or lay persons, have choices about what their congregations will believe, how they will organize themselves for effective ministry, and how they will serve the settings of which they are a part. Further, when they make those choices as a disciplined search for the will of God in their midst, no human standards of measurement can assign to them a designation of "failure."

I am convinced by both the theological moorings and sociological insights of my lifelong study of fragile communities of faith that congregations are the heart of where God's work in the world is best accomplished. I believe in the power of participation in vital churches that seek God in what they do to change human life, the communities of which they are a part, and ultimately this world God has created.

Yet, the churches I know need help. They have always needed the helpful insights of leaders who love them—from the apostle Paul with his nurture of small cells of believers within the Roman Empire, through more than twenty centuries of theologians, mystics, pastors, and devoted laity who have invested themselves as servants in the work of churches. Their collective wisdom makes real the Church of Jesus Christ in human history. Consequently, this work will seek to be faithful to that collective wisdom. It will be more practical than theoretical. However, it should be obvious to the reader that it is undergirded with thorough research in congregational studies, my own field research, and personal experiences of observing and working with congregations.

I have been blessed to spend the latter years of my pilgrimage in a new seminary, the James and Carolyn McAfee School of Theology at Mercer University in Atlanta, Georgia. McAfee Seminary was created out of the controversies within the largest Protestant denomination in the United States, the Southern Baptist Convention. This new venture in theological learning was designed by its founding faculty to focus on practices of *being*, *knowing*, and *doing* in an open environment of searching for truth that would embrace students with gender, racial, and theological diversity. Thus, every course taught in the curriculum is reviewed by the faculty as a whole to ensure consistency with this verbal expectation of a threefold understanding of ministry.

This insight has proven to be so important to me in conceptualizing the nature of ministry that I have organized this book on leadership around this threefold emphasis. Part I explores the most essential aspect of leading—*being*. Who we are is more important than anything we do. Leading grows out of the personhood and character of the leader. Part II identifies the essential *knowing* needed by the congregational leader. This part develops an exploration of a mission theology for congregational leaders, an understanding of the cultural and community context within which congregations work, and a summary of the organizing dimensions of congregational life. Part III is the most practical of the sections, with a description of tasks at work in congregations. This is the managing or *doing* side of ministry leadership. I have sought to propose practical best practices for congregational leaders. A holistic approach to leading churches will involve all three dimensions.

Some readers may be most interested in a facet of the overall work of ministry in contemporary churches and choose to read first those chapters that address specific tasks of ministry such as planning, raising the funds to support ministry, or addressing issues of conflict. This is not a mystery novel in which a sequential understanding of the narrative is essential to understand the conclusion. I would, however, encourage you to begin with the first chapter, with its emphasis on the calling to leadership as foundational for each of the three sections of identity, knowledge, and practice of ministry.

It is my hope that this book may be an instrument of grace to those who seek to enlarge the understanding of their leadership to make their communities of faith more vital and more reflective of the mission of God in the world. Lingenfelter's summary captures well the hopes of this book:

> The critical factor in healthy, growing churches is Christ-centered leadership. When leaders are passionate about their faith in God and follow Jesus in their love and care for their people, when they are motivated by the mission of God and bring this vision to their people, when they commit to covenant relationships with those who follow and give away power rather than seek it, the people follow as the leader follows Christ and the church becomes a powerful force of the transforming mission of God in their world.[7]

Reflections on What You Have Read

It helps to apply your own experience to what you have read. Take a few moments and record the major events of your life experience that shape the kind of leader you are becoming. What major changes in where you have lived have you experienced? What is your experience in the church? Are you a lifelong participant in a congregation? A recent convert to Christ? Are you a member of a specific congregation? Describe a pastor who has influenced who you are today.

PART 1: Being
The Identity of the Congregational Leader

Leadership flows from the heart. In the contemporary congregation leaders bear the responsibilities of providing vision, giving encouragement, and extending personal care. Leaders accomplish these responsibilities best when they have a clear understanding of self in relationship with congregants. Our identity grows within the self, combining the totality of genetic inheritance, life experience, and faith realities.

Leading is a calling from God. Chapter 1 guides the reader through understandings of the meaning of calling in the biblical narrative by emphasizing the multiple ways in which God is experienced as a calling Holy One. The chapter will explore both the transcendent and the immanent aspects of the meaning of calling, with illustrations from the biographies of the called in the biblical story.

To understand how one lives out the calling that is experienced, the leader must claim certain dimensions of identity. Chapter 2 explores the contributions of family systems and several measures of self-knowing to our identities. Among these measures are the Myers-Briggs Type Indicator, Emergenetics®, and the Enneagram. These instruments can help a leader enlarge one's personal awareness of primary strengths and weaknesses. Revealing one's self to others is an essential quality of the mature leader. A guide in practicing revealing identity to others concludes this discussion of leadership identity.

Equally important in the quest for clarity in identity is an understanding of the several forms of intelligence that are a part of our natural styles of leading. Chapter 3 devotes attention to emotional and mystical intelligence. Primary for congregational leadership is awareness of the Spirit's leadership, with an emphasis on practices of spiritual disciplines to enhance one's growth in mystical intelligence.

The essence of leading lies in how you integrate these multiple aspects of identity. Chapter 4 discusses how knowing what kind of leader you are is a consequence of understanding your sense of calling, your multiple intelligences, your depth of awareness of the presence of God in life and ministry, and identification of the uniqueness of your gifts for ministry inspired by the Holy Spirit. Congregational leading is a consequence of being who you are as God's gift, knowing the content of the congregation's challenges, and shaping how you do the work of ministry based on the effectiveness of your interaction with all of the leaders of the congregation. Ministry leadership integrates the central themes of the book: being, knowing, and doing.

1

Calling

Your Mission here on Earth can be defined generally as follows:

To seek to stand hour by hour in the conscious presence of God, the One from whom your Mission is derived.

To do what you can, moment by moment, day by day, step by step, to make this world a better place, following the leading and guiding of God's Spirit within you and around you.

To exercise that Talent which you particularly came to Earth to use—your greatest gift, which you most delight to use, in the place(s) or setting(s) which God has caused to appeal to you the most, and for those purposes which God most needs to have done in the world.

RICHARD BOLLES[1]

Calling is essential to being in ministry, whether that ministry is leading a congregation or serving others—whatever the context. Every follower of Jesus Christ does so in response to an invitation to follow. Each of the four gospels identifies Jesus as an invitation giver, centered in the word "follow." It means to walk behind, to walk alongside, to imitate, to respond to. The essence of calling is following Jesus:

- "Follow me." (Mt. 8:22, 9:9; Mk. 2:14; Lk. 5:27, 18:22; Jn. 1:43; 12:26)
- "Follow me and I will make you fish for people." (Mt. 4:19; Mk. 1:17)
- "If any want to become my followers, let them deny themselves and take up their cross...and follow me" (Mt. 16:24; Mk. 8:34; Lk. 9:23).
- "I am the light of the world. Whoever follows me will never walk in darkness but will have the light of life" (Jn. 8:12).

I have a fascination with the biography of the called. That interest begins with the call stories of people in the biblical texts. Through the years of my teaching, I have often asked students to write summaries of their understandings of their callings to ministry. I asked each of the ten pastors interviewed in the Atlanta region in Spring 2010 about their sense of why they were ministers. Calling was crucial to their stories.

One reality becomes clear when you listen to people of Christian faith. No two believers describe their experience with God the same. Some would even say they are not called. They think calling is a special experience that is only for those few who serve the church as a job or profession.

The biblical stories of faith would suggest otherwise. All who choose to say "yes" to the invitation to follow Jesus Christ belong to the community of the called. How that response is made and what it means is different for each person.

Calling and leading go hand-in-hand, because faith and community belong together. Following Jesus is a calling to share his ministry with other followers. All who claim faithfulness to Jesus Christ are called to live out their whole lives as reflections of his life and teachings. This means you cannot have a congregation of Jesus followers unless they are called to engage in ministry in the world. Understanding calling as essential for all ministry is foundational to vital congregational life. What, therefore, does it mean for the call of God to so infuse one's being that we can say one's identity is "being called"?

Unique, Not Uniform

Vocation is an ancient religious concept, especially in the religions of Judaism and Christianity with their concepts of God as an active revealer of divine will in human experience. In a biblical sense, the concept of vocation is always communitarian, as it applies to a people. In summary:

> Vocation [Lat. *vocatio*]. The biblical doctrine of God's call to his people to become instruments of his purpose at work in history and to be the recipients of his grace and salvation. In the OT, vocation is the calling of Israel to be the people of God; and in the NT, the doctrine refers to the calling of men [people] to follow Christ, to become incorporated in the fellowship of the church, and to share in the Christian hope. Strictly speaking, these biblical ideas are quite different from the modern understanding of vocation as a job, position, or profession.[2]

H. Richard Niebuhr's classic description of the meaning of calling includes four dimensions. The *universal* call is the call to be a Christian, the call to follow Christ in all dimensions of one's life—the calling to service, whatever may be the form of work one does. One may receive the *secret* call or that inward feeling of God's invitation to the work of ministry as service to others. The *providential* call includes the circumstances of guidance and awareness of talents one has—the sense that one is endowed with the gifts for leadership and ministry and chooses to exercise them through the church. Finally, the church issues the *ecclesiastical* call as a congregation/denomination recognizes people as gifted for ministry and eventually ordains and/or employs them for a particular understanding of ministry leadership.[3]

Can you imagine the transformation in your congregation if each participant were aware of a calling in his or her life to serve as a follower of Jesus? For many, faith is a verbal acknowledgment of belief without an accompanying commitment that such faith makes a difference in how one serves. R. Paul Stevens emphasizes the call of the laity in his thoughtful emphasis on the "universal" call. He identifies the call of Christ to become a disciple; the providential inheritance of family, education, personality, and opportunities; the gifts of the Holy Spirit as a charismatic call; and the heart call of inner desire for service all as dimensions of the call to "everyone" who claims Christ as Savior.[4]

You may understand the experience of calling in two essential ways. The first view may be best identified as the traditional Christian understanding of calling as a clear encounter with God. Calling comes from beyond the self in this view. James Fowler describes it as a response a person makes of *"total self to the address of God and to the calling to partnership."*[5]

Some of us have experienced dramatic encounters with God that defy explanation. Like ancient patriarchs, prophets, priests, and missionaries, we live with an experiential reality of calling rooted in the mystery of a very personal encounter with the holiness of God. Congregations in the Free Church tradition tend to emphasize this view of calling, especially for their clergy. Calling is transcendent.

Calling from Beyond

You must explore the biblical view of calling as beyond the self to understand fully this concept. When one reads the accounts of key leaders called in both the Hebrew and Christian Scriptures, an interesting congruence emerges. The same elements tend to appear in the biographies of the called. These include summons, identity, community, and mission.

The Call of Abram. Abram is the prototypical individual of calling in the biblical story. God initiates a covenant with him. Abram responds positively and becomes the father of a nation. The story of the people of faith begins. "Now the LORD said to Abram, 'Go from your country and your kindred and your father's house to the land that I will show you. I will make of you a great nation, and I will bless you, and make your name great, so that you will be a blessing'" (Gen. 12:1–2). We have no more content than that Yahweh directs him without specific detail. Abram becomes a wanderer toward a land of promise and with the implication he will recognize this land when he sees it. The essential element of the call is submission to the Divine Will accomplished by movement toward a mission. Abram, with his wife Sarai, are to become parents of a people in spite of biological conditions that indicate such a mission is impossible.

The details of the story are fascinating—Abram and Sarai leave the security of their homeland and spend years in search of the goal of this pilgrimage, with wanderings in the lands of Sodom and Egypt before agreeing on a settlement with Lot. Abram fathers Ishmael with the slave Hagar, and sends the mother and child away. Eventually, he and Sarai fulfill their destiny with the birth of Isaac.

The call transforms Abram and Sarai. Their identities are rooted in obedience to the One who summons. Abram's identity (Hebrew for "the Father exalts") changes to Abraham (Hebrew for "father of a multitude"). Sarai's identity becomes Sarah, meaning "princess." All of the multitude born of this family belong to their calling. Abraham and Sarah are claimed as parents by both the people of the Hebrew covenant and the people of the Christian covenant (Gen. 17:4–5; Heb. 11:8–22). They are the parents of all who through faith follow God, not just those who are genetic children.

The Call of Moses: a prototype of transcendence. The call of Moses incorporates all of the elements of the biblical concept of calling as transcendence. First comes the Holy encounter. "God called to him out of the bush" (Ex. 3:4). The dialogue that follows covers each of the four elements suggested above—summons, identity, community, and mission. Most significant is the personal nature of the encounter between Yahweh and Moses. The mysterious caller identifies with the heritage of Abraham, "I am the God of your father, the God of Abraham, the God of Isaac, and the God of Jacob" (Ex. 3:6). When the purpose of the encounter is revealed, Moses asks the name of the One with whom he was speaking. "I AM WHO I AM" (Ex. 3:14). The mysterious, indescribable, otherness of the Divine (YHWH) is made clear. No longer would God be identified with the namable aspects of his character *el*, but this one who calls is unnamable mystery. Consequently, no one will ever create a total description of one's encounter with a call from beyond; it defies understanding. The mysterious calling is grace, presence, holiness. In its presence one stands in vulnerable openness with awe. Moses is commanded, "Come no closer! Remove the sandals from your feet, for the place on which you are standing is holy ground" (Ex. 3:5). In the face of such an experience, a divine summons is difficult to resist.

The second element of Moses' experience is the identity recognized in him. The divine caller addresses him by name, "Moses, Moses!" (Ex. 3:4). For the Hebrews, one's name is an expression of essential character, of one's identity. Calling is synonymous with naming. In the creation account, naming is an activity of Yahweh, and the naming of creation by Adam is an evidence of humanity's likeness to the Creator. Cities and places are named to communicate a destiny or event of significance.

Moses' name, given him by Pharaoh's daughter when he is discovered as an infant, means "draw out." "She named him Moses, 'because', she said, 'I drew him out of the water'" (Ex. 2:10). Unlike other biblical characters, Moses' name never changes. He lives with the character of his birth gift, to be one who is drawn out—by the circumstances of history and by the call of Yahweh. Not only is he drawn from the river, but he becomes one who "draws out" the gifts and the potential of others. He draws out the people of Israel from their slavery. He draws his brother Aaron and sister Miriam into partnership with him as, respectively, a priest and prophetess to the people. He draws out Joshua and a host of others to engage their skills in leadership of a wandering Israel.

Yahweh knows Moses better than Moses knows himself. When God issues the mission mandate to become a deliverer to his people, Moses protests that he does not have the verbal skills or the status necessary to draw his people out of their bondage. "Who am I that I should go to Pharaoh, and bring the Israelites out of Egypt?" (Ex. 3:11). God assures him that he will not go in his own strength or solely out of his identity. "I will be with you" (Ex. 3:12a).

The biblical understanding of calling is contextual. It occurs in the context of the needs of the people who are the focus of God's concern. Calling does not occur in isolation from a tribe, nation, people, or church. This calling is not to a person to explore exclusively his or her individual goals or purposes. The idea one could be an autonomous self and fulfill the call of the Divine in isolation from the world's alienation from God, social disparities, economic injustices, or class inequities is foreign to the biblical meaning of vocation.

In this regard one must deal with several questions related to the specialness of calling. Yahweh clearly chooses some persons for exemplary leadership within the community, but the reality of biblical faith is that the patriarchs, matriarchs, prophets, influential priests, and apostles constitute a small minority of the people of the story. The quiet summons to the masses is important, yet often not recorded in Scripture.

The Hebrew understanding of corporeality may offer some explanation. The call to the one with a mission that is indeed empowered by the Almighty is a call to all who become recipients of the benefits of the actions of the individual who leads. The call of Moses to be a deliverer was a call to Hebrew slaves to respond to the leadership of Moses as deliverer. The special call to the individual is successful only to the degree the community acts in reciprocity to the called.

The relationship of Moses and Aaron, his brother, shows this most clearly. Yahweh sends Aaron to Moses in the wilderness, and Moses tells him the story of God's plan (Ex. 4:27–31). When Moses protested he did not have the gift of speech, Yahweh responds in anger to point out the availability of Aaron to assist him. "He indeed shall speak for you to the people; he shall serve as a mouth for you, and you shall serve as God for him" (Ex. 4:16).

By the period of the New Testament, vocation is a nearly universalized invitation rather than a prophetic, charismatic summons. The invitation to follow Jesus is extended to all who will respond. The invitation of the kingdom of God is to any who will accept it. The called of the church are all the saints who live in obedience to the universal mandates of the Risen Lord: make disciples, teach them all I have taught you, baptize them (Mt. 28:19–20). Consequently, Paul, who himself claimed the calling of an Old Testament prophet, could address all Christians in Rome as persons "called to be saints" (Rom. 1:7).

When one views the broad scope of salvation history, most of the called are nameless. It includes: (1) all of those women, men, and children who follow the leadership of voices of justice and mercy; (2) the kings who act for the welfare of the nation in the face of political intrigue and international chicanery; (3) those who die in sacrifice for the cause of the reign of God; and (4) those who live to bear witness to the truth of the good news of such a kingdom. In the listing of the exemplars of faith in Hebrews 11, the giants through whom the story of redemption was told are named—Abel, Cain, Enoch, Noah, Abraham, Isaac, Jacob, Sarah, Joseph, Moses, Rahab, Gideon, Barak, Samson, Jephthah, David, and Samuel. But the unnamed heroes of faith who suffered unspeakably for the causes of faith are not forgotten (Heb. 11:32–40).

Calling from Within

The second understanding of calling arises from within—an immanent experience of one's purpose and passions. Paul Minear describes this more universal view, "Vocation is no esoteric matter, important to only a few extraordinary individuals; it is an everyday source of energy that determines the health of all. Ordinarily it is less like a bolt of lightning than like a daily sunrise."[6]

The more inward view of calling is best expressed by Parker Palmer when he suggests the gift of God comes as a voice from within calling each to become the person one is born to be at birth.[7] This view of calling is more typical for contemporary Christians, especially for those in more mainline Protestant congregations or those with less focus on biblical language in their worship and educational practices. Some traditions such as Quakers, which is Palmer's tradition, emphasize the inward approach exclusively. It is certainly more typical of most of the students I teach than the charismatic, transcendent view of calling.

The biblical stories of the called are as likely to be imminent and inward as otherworldly, especially in the biographies of women. Sarah was as important as Abraham in the story of his calling; however, no narrative relates a direct calling for her. Sarah is the willing partner who follows the uncertain Abraham for years, cooperates with him in deception before Pharaoh in Egypt, responds in normal jealousy to Hagar, and in the midst of her laughter at the irony of pregnancy beyond menstrual years bears a son from whom a nation will grow. Their progeny become the lineage for an entire community, sons and daughters of Abraham, Isaac, and Jacob.

For all of the attention focused on those with a charismatic calling—such as Mary as the angel Gabriel confirms to her that she will deliver Jesus as a gift of the Holy Spirit—most of the servants of God in Scripture are described by what they do rather than how they decided to serve. Their calling to act grew out of circumstances and opportunities to which they responded with faith. If Moses experienced calling from beyond, his brother Aaron and sister Miriam lived out of the giftedness of their personalities. Aaron became the voice for the stuttering Moses, while some have suggested Miriam was the poet who composed the song of Moses (Ex. 15: 1–18). She was surely the worship leader for the women of the exodus as she led them in dance and singing to celebrate their deliverance (Ex. 15:20–22). Even when judged for her resistance to Moses' leadership by being inflicted with leprosy, she had to experience healing before the people would move forward (Num. 12:15). Barbara Essex summarizes her importance:

> Miriam emerges as an able, capable mediator, prophet, musician and leader among the Hebrew people. She is a strong personality, rivaling that of the more dominant Moses. Where Moses is slow of speech, she is eloquent. Where Moses is reluctant and hesitant, she is energetic and lively. Where Moses seeks to pass the leadership

baton to someone else, she takes on the leadership role with gusto…
she sings and dances and praises God for triumph in the face of
formidable odds![8]

Esther clearly had no otherworldly call in her deliverance of her people
in Babylon. Becoming the queen of the empire, she immediately faces danger.
Her cousin and guardian Mordecai confronts her with the reality of Haman's
plans to destroy the Hebrew people in the 127 provinces of the kingdom of
Ahasuerus. She takes Mordecai's advice and acts courageously, approaching
the king to appeal for a reversal of the decrees Haman got from the king
by manipulation. The name of God appears nowhere in the Hebrew text;
however, Esther prays to God for help in the Greek additions of the book. In
spite of fainting before the king in terror of his reactions, she saw God alter
the king's demeanor as he encouraged her to speak (Add. Esth. 15:8–10).

That same inward responsiveness characterizes multiple characters
of the New Testament. Whether it is the widow Anna praising God at the
dedication of Jesus in the temple or the long list of house church leaders
thanked by Paul in Romans 16, most of the saints of God's mission are
relatively unknown followers. They serve faithfully out of their inward sense
of calling. Their names are many, but their stories are largely unknown. Gregg
Lavoy states the meaning of calling in more practical terms:

> Living out a calling may mean living an unspectacular life, a life of
> quiet ministry, steadfast backstage work, politicking without renown;
> it may mean a life unknown to fame. Even the highest calling entails
> the unremarkable tasks of licking stamps, stuffing envelopes, and
> tacking up flyers. It asks that we do our homework, sweep the front
> porch, sock away pennies, and knock on wood.[9]

The Ecclesiastical Call

Calling to ministry leadership is more than a person's recognition of
or declaration of his or her intention to engage in ministry. Calling may
begin with such, but until one's community of faith affirms the gifts and
character of the one called, a person has no opportunity for either clergy
or lay leadership. Stevens suggests the biblical expectations for pastoral
leadership are all related to character (1 Pet. 5:1–10). "There is no ontological
difference," he writes, "between leaders and people. The call to leadership
in the church comes from the church!"[10]

North American Protestantism extends that call to leadership in quite
diverse ways. The process in the hierarchical denominations is prescribed in
clear and legal canons of church practice. Clergy leadership involves multiple

steps in education, experience, and evaluation that may lead ultimately to ordination. Connectional bodies have processes that may be less structured, but require approval outside that of the congregation.

No such canons or processes are normative for the more than half of North American congregations that are autonomous. Some, such as the Disciples of Christ, maintain congregational governance, but also include regional church participation in the decision for ordination.

Autonomous congregations generally have the sole authority of affirmation for ministry leadership, including the granting of a church license to preach or serve, ordination, and employment. One of my colleagues in the past, Clyde Francisco, often quipped, "Not even God can tell a Baptist church what to do."

Such a system offers the opportunity for affirmation of highly gifted individuals as well as the potential for "laying hands" on those who prove to be an embarrassment to the affirming body. Most congregations require at least a testimony of calling and the observation of commitment to ministry to affirm a candidate for ordination. African American congregations tend to require a one-to-two-year apprenticeship prior to ordination.[11]

Employment to engage in ministry is a more structured reality. The responsiveness of the pastoral leader to leading a congregation or ministry organization is more than the negotiation of a job with a salary, job description, and benefits package. Few congregations in the autonomous tradition employ their ministerial leaders on the basis of a contract. Many in more organic congregations may not have so much as a letter of employment. They accept the verbal invitation of a group of people based on the trusting dependence of the leadership of God in bringing together parties in a mutual fashion. We name whatever process is at work at the congregational level "a call from God." Without that spiritual dimension of belonging to one another so that leader and people "fit," the leader can exercise little claim of authority in calling the church to God's mission.

Such a theology can be problematic when encountering the human nature of some congregations and the failure of some ministers. What happens when the "called" encounter so much resistance and failure in congregational life? Or, they make ethical mistakes or fatal judgments for that setting? Is the call "null and void"? Certainly the ecclesiastical call may be. Some must experience their lack of skill or character for this work before they can understand employment may best be fulfilled outside the church. This does not eliminate them from continuing within the church as laity. According to Palmer, calling may lead to the affirmation of either light or darkness.[12] No greater tragedy for the church exists than for those who claim the mantle of leadership but live out of the dark side of their character. Given the growing body of lawsuits against church bodies spurred by the sexual abuse crisis in churches, the Free Church tradition needs to do some rethinking of the practice of ordination.[13]

One of the questions I asked the ten pastors who helped shape many of the ideas in this work was, "Have you ever had an experience in your ministry that was so discouraging you seriously considered leaving ministry as your primary vocation? Can you describe it?" Some of the responses were humorous: "Every Monday," or, "Today!" One pastor of an exceptionally large and effective African American congregation stated the general consensus of the group: "No. Leaving the church, yes. But leaving the ministry, no." All but one could describe a specific challenge during ministry so discouraging that serious consideration was given to leaving a specific congregation for fear of termination. One of the more insightful responses was given by one of the female pastors in the group:

> No, I don't think I can say there is any experience that has been that challenging or disappointing. My continual struggle with this vocation is how do I do it and get a decent amount of sleep, eat well, and not exhaust myself. It's less of some issue or place that I can point to and more of a continual sense of how can I do this and find balance in my life. I think if I left the ministry it would be from not being able to find that balance. The call to ministry is enduring even when a change in ministry setting may be needed or demanded.

For all of the literature bemoaning the stresses and challenges of congregational leadership, the vast majority of ministers find deep satisfaction and abiding purpose in their ministries. According to an eighteen-year-long study on job satisfaction and general happiness by the National Opinion Research Center completed in 2007, "An overwhelming 87.2 percent of clergy described themselves as 'very satisfied' with their jobs; in contrast, only 47 percent of the general population described themselves this way."[14] The same survey listed clergy as the most highly rated career of all options in spite of rating second from the bottom of the top ten careers in income and second in the highest number of hours worked weekly.[15] William L. Self, retired senior pastor of the Johns Creek Baptist Church and the longest tenured pastoral leader of my interviewees, responded to a recent review in the Christian Century by G. Jeffrey MacDonald documenting the disappointments in pastoral ministry, "I've done it for 55 years, and I've seen all that MacDonald talks about and more—but the church is still the best thing God has going in the world. I'll listen to MacDonald when his opinions bear the stain not of his wounded idealism but of his tears mixed with his lifeblood."[16]

Calling is the foundation of effective leading. Palmer states it clearly, "Vocation at its deepest level is not, 'Oh, boy, do I want to go to this strange place where I have to learn a new way to live and where no one, including me, understands what I'm doing.' Vocation at its deepest level is, 'This is something I can't not do, for reasons I'm unable to explain to anyone else and don't fully understand myself but that are nonetheless compelling.'"[17]

The Ministry of Vocational Exploration

Vocational understanding is a forgotten emphasis in too many congregations. The loss of involvement in Christian education by many adults and the growth of an activity-oriented approach to children and youth ministries mean that God's call for one's life is too seldom mentioned in the church.

The church has multiple practical means for addressing this concern. An adult study of selections from the bibliography at the end of this book, especially the work of Parker Palmer, can be helpful to those living with a sense of unfulfilled expectations in their places of work and living. Finding one's calling may be a mid-life or even later experience. It may not happen without attention.

One of the questions I have posed for years to ministers and seminarians is, "At what age did you first sense the stirrings of a calling from God?" The response has been overwhelming. Adolescence and college years are the primary years for such exploration and decision-making. Because of this, my friend Kay Shurden and I collaborated on a book for teenagers to help them in this discernment process.[18] Youth ministers and adults working with teens have found it a helpful resource as curriculum for Sunday school or youth discussion groups. The book offers readable discussions of the meaning of calling, and guides for using the book in a variety of settings. Remember, the vitality of the congregation is rooted in the commitment of its people. Imagine the future of congregational leadership when teenagers understand and affirm their calling for service to Jesus Christ. We can be instruments of God's calling to others as we explore together what it means to write our life stories as partners with the Holy One who calls.

Applications for Learning

How is calling discussed in your congregation? Consider collecting stories of vocation within your church. An Advent or Lenten Guide that includes reflections on vocation from members can inspire others with personal stories. Collections of call experiences, whether video recorded or written in a booklet, can be useful curricula for Christian education. Imagine the impact on younger participants if they heard testimonies of calling in worship from congregational leaders representative of multiple generations in the church.

2

Self-Knowing

Leadership development is self-development... It's about leading out of what is already in your soul. It's about liberating the leader within you. It's about setting yourself free.

JAMES M. KOUZES AND BARRY Z. POSNER[1]

Leading begins as a process of introspection: self-analysis and feedback from others about their perceptions of who you are. No leader finds him- or herself only from the study of the concepts and understandings of a book like this—or from many others, as helpful as they may be. Leadership does not emerge only from experience, though the practice of leading is essential in the growth process of knowing one's self. Leading is first and foremost a matter of identity.

One of the major misconceptions in the popular mindset about leaders is that they are born rather than formed. Without a doubt, inherent in the human psyche some of us have a kind of natural attractiveness that makes it easy for others to respond to us. Even the most gifted learn through self-examination, study, and practice of the skills of connecting to Jesus Christ, other people, and developing working teams for effective ministry. This chapter will explore avenues for growing in one's identity as a leader.

Self-Awareness of Personality Factors

What is the identity of a leader? If that question were posed to twenty-five people in a given congregation, we would expect considerable diversity in the responses. Most would likely respond, "A leader is charismatic." Others would suggest, "I want a leader who has a magnetic personality," or, "The leader is someone who knows me and understands me." Each of us will respond to others based on our own personalities and experiences as well as those qualities needed in the role of the person identified as our leader.

No leader personality type is normative. If that were true in congregations, we would have to finds ways of identifying the select few who meet our criteria for leading and find ways of eliminating all others from any opportunity of ministry. Congregational leading is rooted in the theological affirmation of the strength of the body of Christ in the collective diversity of the people who make up that body. The apostle Paul's teachings of the church as a collective unity whose strength is in its diversity affirm the richness of personality differences. All have the potential of leading; the question is, "Who will lead out of the strength of their individual identities?" Read carefully 1 Corinthians 12:12–31. Each member of the body has the personal gifts for specific roles of leadership, but the kinds of leading are different. All can lead; but each must lead in ways consistent with his or her gifts. The challenge is for each of us to become adequately aware of our personalities and natural and spiritual gifts so that we can fit the call of God to specific forms of leading. Now, what are the practical aspects of making such personal judgments?

Family of Origin

The self is rooted in family. Until I understand the shaping influences of the generations of my family, I cannot know myself. Multiple resources developed for the church and rooted in the family systems theories of Murray Bowen are useful foundations for self-awareness.[2] Each of us is shaped in our relationships to others by the quality of relationships in our family system. Patterns can be understood more clearly by constructing a three-generational analysis of the family relations in a genogram.[3] Some families have strong and healthy relational bonds, and others highly dysfunctional ones. A review of a personal genogram may reveal repeated forms of illnesses, addictions, cut-offs in relationship, or healthy interactions that shape personal identities. You are not determined by these patterns, but you are certainly influenced by them. Understanding that is a key step in self-knowing. Sharing your genogram with a peer group or family systems specialist can be among the most helpful growth processes in which you can engage.

Your birth order within your family of origin can be a source of insight in how you interact with others as well. First-born children tend to function differently from the youngest or middle children in their families. Those characteristics affect relationships within the church. Ronald W. Richardson provides helpful summaries of the differing relational styles of leaders based on the order of their birth.[4] Such knowledge can provide useful insight into why a given lay leader seems to be competing with you. Why not explore your birth order in relation to the lay leaders' birth order and ask, "Am I relating to this person as a younger sister when she is the eldest in her family, as am I?"

Leading and Personality Types

A second helpful resource for understanding identity is an assessment of your personality type. The Myers-Briggs Type Indicator (MBTI) is a standard instrument for exploring self-understanding for personality characteristics. The McAfee School of Theology requires each student in the first year course in spiritual formation to complete the indicator and interpret it with the guidance of a specialist. Congregational staff and key laity would enhance their abilities to understand each other and work more effectively as teams if such a resource were used in the local church.

The MBTI, a well-established instrument for use by individuals and organizations in personal understanding, is based on Carl Jung's archetype theories and applies four basic measures to how individuals order their worlds and behaviors. A brief summary will be offered here, but the resources for understanding the MBTI are vast. Explore the information at http://www.personalitypathways.com for an introductory examination. By measuring two types of mental processes and two types of mental orientations, sixteen types of personalities can be identified. Each personality type has its particular strengths and weaknesses. To know your MBTI type can be a source of identifying ways to enhance your strengths, minimize your weaknesses, and recognize how you can best relate to other types.

The first mental process of the MBTI identifies how people take in information, based on being one of two types:

1. The *sensing* (S) type. One type of person prefers information rooted in facts, data, or measurable information. Sensing types look at the details when collecting information.
2. The *intuitive* (N) type. The second type prefers more abstract, conceptual information. Intuitive types like to look at the "big picture" in making their decisions about reality.

The second mental process identifies how people make decisions or form judgments with the information they collect:

1. The *thinking* (T) type prefer to think through their decisions in rational ways with objective, logical, analytical processes. They make decisions based on what their heads tell them is important.
2. *Feeling* (F) types make their decisions based on visceral reactions that are value-laden and measure the impact on other people. They decide with their hearts.

There are also two mental orientations measured by the MBTI.

The first examines the sources of energy that guide the way we function:

1. *Introverted* (I) types find their energy internal to themselves. The introvert gets energy from time alone, when there can be internal thought processes that sort out how they will react. A high introvert will feel exhausted after attending a large social event and will have to engage in solitude to regain a sense of energy for tasks that need accomplishing.

2. The other type, *extroverted* (E), finds energy external to the self. These types thrive on interaction with other people or outside influences. The more people or external stimuli there are, the merrier they are. Extroverts can find solitude draining.

The majority of Americans are extroverted; about 60 percent of all women are extroverts, and 60 percent of men are introverted. You can imagine the role expectations for laity toward their clergy based on their type. The extroverts have difficulty with what they perceive as distance or perhaps unfriendliness from their introverted clergy. Introverted laity can be overwhelmed by the attention given them by extroverted clergy. Awareness of the needs of those with either of the two basic energy sources is helpful for relating to others effectively.[5]

The second mental orientation addresses the ways in which both energy types deal with the outside world:

1. The *judging* type (J) seeks to organize the outside world in an organized, planned way that emphasizes closure for decisions. The J types rely either on their dominant thinking (T) or feeling (F) skills to make decisions. They may be aggressive or gentle in their conclusions, but they seek an ordered response to the outside world.

2. The *perceiving* (P) type relies on his or her sensing (S) or intuitive (N) styles in making sense of the outer life. Perceivers seek to experience the external rather than order it.

Have you ever attended a meeting where a high P individual is repeatedly late for the meeting or shows up without a calendar for planning future events, and you are a high J who is constantly organized in doing your work? It's frustrating, isn't it? Or, if you are the high P, you may chafe at the constant demand for quick decisions and decisive action from the J leader! What if you learned to balance individual preferences by drawing on the strengths of all types in the room? Appendix A provides a summary of the approaches to leadership of each of the sixteen types of the MBTI. A study of this resource can enhance your understanding of yourself and those with whom you work. Remember! You will not change the basic type of the person with whom you interact. You can understand her and adapt your own behavior to him, but you will not transform an ISTP individual into an ENFJ or any other type. We are who we are.

Leaders can be any of the sixteen types identified by this approach. But they will function in roles that are most comfortable for their personality types. An INFP leader will not be comfortable in the dominant role of the strong, driving person and will seek a more "behind the scenes" approach to accomplishing work with effectiveness. The ENTJ, on the other hand, is more likely to be aggressive, decisive, and emerge as a directing leader of an organization.[6]

Brain Structure and Personality

A relatively new approach to understanding human behavior is rooted in insights from brain research that identifies the preference for colors as clues to how one behaves. The organization Emergenetics®, Inc., has developed a fascinating instrument that measures four thinking attributes and three behaviors that are both inherited and learned in one's environment. The instrument is based on the theory derived from brain research by Geil Browning and Wendall Williams, a theory tested since 1991. The principles of their approach are quite simple. Each person has four thinking modes that are primarily genetic, one of which is dominant for most people—though some people have more than one primary mode and may be bi-modal or even tri-modal. A color preference is assigned to each mode. The thinking modes are analytical (blue), structural (green), conceptual (yellow), and social (red).

- Analytical thinkers are logical, rational, objective, factual, and skeptical.
- Structural thinkers are practical, cautious, predictable, and methodical.
- Conceptual thinkers are imaginative, creative, innovative, visionary, and intuitive.
- Social thinkers are sympathetic, connected, socially aware, and intuitive about other people.[7]

I participated in a training session on this approach at the Pastoral Institute in Columbus, Georgia, led by Kelvin Redd with the Center for Servant Leadership.[8] Each of us in a group of about twenty-five people had completed the Emergenetics® profile. Redd divided us into groups based on our dominant thinking preference. His assignment was for us to meet in groups of our dominant preference and describe to each other how we shop for groceries. It was amazing how similar each member of the group approached such a task, yet how differently the four groups shop. The green group (structural) agreed that they made detailed lists in the order of where each item could be found in the store when they shopped. Some even had computer lists with the location of their needed items. They did not purchase items not on the list. The blue group (analytical) got a general idea in their heads of what they needed, scribbled a quick list of items, knew generally where items could be found, and walked back and forth until each was located. If they saw a needed item not on the list, they purchased it. The red group (social) would drive to stores where they knew the employees, ask store personnel where they could find their needed items, check out in lines where they knew the name of the person serving them, and enjoy the interaction with other people shopping. The conceptual (yellow) group would imagine a picture of the store layout and "feel" their way through the aisles, imagining where they would find specific items.

The more we shared, the more we laughed at our differences. Now imagine planning a church retreat with a church team meeting in which each of these preferences is present. Understanding the differences can make the process more productive than getting bogged down in an argument between those who want to develop a detailed agenda and those who want to gather and let the Spirit lead in what they do. Of course, the socials will want to spend most of their time in conversation and play with each other.

Three behavioral attributes measure how we interact with others. The instrument charts the degree of expressiveness, assertiveness, and flexibility employed by an individual. By examining these seven characteristics together, one can understand the patterns of thought employed as well as preferences for interaction. The instrument requires a trained interpreter for adequate understanding, but can be a most useful way for training leader teams better to understand each other.[9]

The Enneagram for Understanding Self

A third resource for self-knowing is the Enneagram. It is an instrument designed to measure the strength of nine personality types. There are variations of the interpretation of the earliest form of the concepts developed by Oscar Ichazo in the 1970s. His application was connected to the classic Christian seven capital sins, plus fear and deceit, and the system is widely used by spiritual directors within multiple spiritual traditions. Don Rico and Russ Hudson of the Enneagram Institute developed the most useful form of the enneagram, a symbol of nine interrelated personality types. They have a test online for a cost of $10, with a written interpretation of the results of the instrument.[10] The instrument provides a measurement of the strengths of each of nine personality types:

Figure 2.1: the Enneagram Symbol

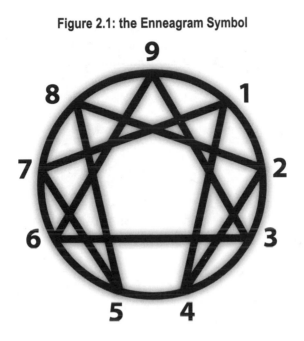

Type 1: The Reformer possesses a high level of ethical consciousness, sensibility, idealism, and self-discipline with the goal to improve the world and self. Negative attributes include impatience, perfectionism, judgmentalism, and tendencies toward anger.

Type 2: The Helper is other-directed, cares for others, willingly sacrifices self, and is nurturing. Negatively, the helper can be possessive, manipulative, intrusive, and easily deceived.

Type 3: The Achiever is ambitious, seeks self-improvement, excellence in tasks, and self-distinction. The achiever can be perceived as arrogant, exploitative, calculating, and hostile toward those opposed to his or her drive to achieve.

Type 4: The Individualist has great potential for intuition, sensitivity, self-expression, and individualism. The negative side of the type is self-absorption, self-consciousness, self-doubt, and depression.

Type 5: The Investigator is curious, perceptive, and original. This type seeks knowledge and technical expertise. The negative side is emotional detachment, social isolation, speculative theorizing, and mental projections.

Type 6: The Loyalist bonds easily with others, is sociable, industrious, deeply committed to larger efforts, and is loyal to others. There is potential negatively for dependency, ambivalence, rebellion, anxiety, and inferiority feelings.

Type 7: The Enthusiast is seen as enthusiastic, productive, achievement oriented, flexible, and as one who seeks change. Negative tendencies include hyperactivity, impulsiveness, excessiveness, and escapism.

Type 8: The Challenger is self-confident, a strong leader who is self-determined and aggressive. Challengers may become dominating, insensitive to others, combative, or ruthless.

Type 9: The Peacemaker seeks harmony with others, has emotional stability and endurance, and is not self-conscious. The peacemaker may become passive, disengaged, neglectful, and mentally dissociative.

The Rico-Hudson instrument provides a numerical score of the strength of each of the nine personality types. Each of us, according to the theory, possesses characteristics of each type. What is important is to develop awareness of the primary strengths among them. Normally, one will have tendencies to live out of one of the types on the wing of a dominant type. If you are a Type 2 (Helper) on the enneagram, the wings are Type 1 (Reformer) and Type 3 (Achiever). The stronger of the wings is a backup type. A leader who is a Helper with a strong Reformer wing will be an activist seeking to help others with considerable aggressiveness. She or he may appear to some to be a crusader for whom the cause is more important than people who do not share the same ethical sensibilities.

Conclusion

Personality is a crucial aspect of self-understanding. Our basic personalities are a combination of genetics, family upbringing, life experiences, the gifts of God, and psychological growth. The challenge of leading is to be sufficiently aware of self that the primary strengths of personality can be claimed and shared in consort with the leading of the Spirit. Claiming your strengths recognizes the limits of your approach to adapt to the specific needs of a given context for ministry.

Intelligence and Leadership

Understanding the multiple forms of intelligence is a useful resource for how we lead. The standard measure of knowledge in the form of Intelligence Quotient (IQ) has long been used and misused to assess the potential for learning and performance. When 95 percent of the population of the U.S. has IQ scores in a range of 70 to 130, the primary usefulness is to identify the limitations of those with very low scores on the IQ test. A small segment of the population has such limits that the forms of work in which they can engage successfully either do not exist or require very specific tasks with considerable supervision in their completion.

Intelligence and Skills

The role of IQ is largely being replaced in the leadership arena by exploring the multiple skills of intelligence. Howard Gardner identifies eight human intelligences important for understanding how people approach solving problems:

1. Linguistic (involving language)—reading, writing, and speaking are preferred approaches to solving problems.
2. Logical-mathematical (concerning numbers and logic)—reasoning, critical thinking, and mathematical problem solving are your talents.
3. Spatial—thinking in pictures, patterns, and images using shapes and colors to envision the world around you.
4. Musical (dealing with rhythms and melodies)—singing in tune, keeping time to rhythms, and having an ear for music are your preferred abilities.
5. Bodily-kinesthetic—using one's whole body or parts of the body to handle objects, demonstrating athletic prowess or hands-on problem solving.
6. Interpersonal—tuning into the needs, feelings, and desires of others; understanding and working effectively with others.
7. Intrapersonal—being self-directed; aware of the inner self and inner feelings.
8. Naturalistic—sensing, understanding, and systematically classifying the natural world/environment.

Gardner explored the possibility of adding "spiritual" and "existential" intelligence to his theories, but chose not to formalize them given the difficulty of fitting them into logical criteria.[11]

Most of us discover something of our natural intelligence in school. We may excel in math and dislike social studies, or find that we learn biology better by roaming the woods than reading descriptions in a textbook. Knowing your natural intelligences will guide your choice of vocation and employment fit.

Emotional Intelligence

The work of Daniel Goleman and his associates in understanding emotional intelligence and its impact on leadership is among the most helpful developments for understanding congregational leadership.[12] Goleman's work stresses four dimensions of emotional intelligence. The first is *self-awareness*, which Goleman describes as "having a deep understanding of one's emotions, strengths, weaknesses, needs, and drives. People with strong self-awareness are neither overly critical nor unrealistically hopeful. Rather, they are honest with themselves and with others."[13]

The second key concept is *self-management*. Goleman assumes humans are capable of controlling their negative impulses and relating to others with healthy control of feelings. When anxiety is replaced by self-control, leaders are more likely to act with integrity because their actions are thoughtful and comfortable with ambiguity and change.[14] Have you ever worked with a congregational leader who had unusual abilities but could not control his anger? The lack of self-management in ministry is a major source of congregational conflict.

Goleman's third dimension is *social awareness*. Pastoral leaders will identify readily with this emphasis. Empathy with others is the primary indicator of social awareness—decisions are made with regard for the feelings of others.

The fourth emphasis of emotional intelligence is *social skill*—the managing of relationships with social awareness. The socially skillful understand the goals of any entity require working with and through other people.[15]

Most of the work on emotional intelligence and leadership focuses on corporate settings. However, the insights of this understanding are transferable to the church and can be helpful to church leaders.

Goleman suggests the most essential quality of effective leaders is motivation to achieve "beyond expectations—their own and everyone else's."[16] The first sign of such is passion for the work they do. A passion for one's calling generates the energy and enthusiasm needed for effectiveness.

The motivation to lead manifests itself in utilizing a variety of leadership styles based on the needs of the context of the work being done. No one leadership style will work in all settings—the emotionally intelligent leader has an intuitive sense of the context that calls for a leading response. Goleman summarizes:

Authoritative leaders mobilize people toward a vision. Affiliative leaders create emotional bonds and harmony. Democratic leaders build consensus through participation. Pacesetting leaders expect excellence and self-direction. Coaching leaders develop people for the future, and coercive leaders demand immediate compliance.[17]

The challenge of leading is to help develop a climate in which an organization achieves its goals; in the case of the church, it is achieving its mission. The most effective of these six styles is the authoritative leader—a visionary who motivates others to achieve a collective vision. The affiliative style is essential in congregational life, for it values people and their emotions, creating harmony and loyalty. The least effective is the coercive leader. Such a style should be used only in crisis moments that require decisive action. Knowing which style to employ is the sign of deep emotional intelligence. Such a leader has the flexibility to respond to meet the demands of the context.

Transparent Self

Openness to others is difficult for ministers. Pastors especially feel that too much revelation of self creates the potential for resisters to leadership or opponents in the congregation to capitalize on pastors' weaknesses. Power struggles among the people are especially difficult, for an antagonist to the pastor will use his or her power to create dissension and questioning of the pastor's motivations or approaches to leading. Craig Barnes describes the pressures on the pastor from parishioners who "assume that the pastor has no calling other than to create satisfied customers, or they can always take their tithe dollars to the place down the street. This has reduced the pastor to a store manager to whom one complains when the service is not satisfactory."[18] This consumerist mentality of laity; books that describe pastors as therapists, that offer family systems diagnosis of congregations, or that encourage pastors to be entrepreneurs building megachurches and leading like a business executive; plus denominational expectations for avoiding scandals create a legacy "that has been to make pastors afraid of both their congregations and themselves."[19]

Transparency is one of the risks of authentic ministry. To do other than to be oneself is to live as a quivering mass of insecurity rather than on the path of a follower of Christ to which pastoral leaders are called. Family systems theory calls this process of openness "differentiation." As long as an individual is so connected to the family (whether one's own or the church family) that he or she feels no identity apart from the expectations of the family, that person cannot live as a true self. On the other hand, one does not sever the connection with the family to be a true self. James Lamkin defines self-differentiation as *"an organism's ability to 'define itself' apart from, yet staying connected to, its surroundings."*[20] To reveal who you are does not require others to agree with who you are. But they will take heart in witnessing the openness of an authentic self, though struggling that self may be.

The Johari Window is a long-used visual picture of the relationship between knowing ourselves and others knowing that self first developed by Joseph Luft and Harry Ingham. Different models by team development consultants have been adopted as tools for individuals to understand the levels of their interactions with others. I prefer the helpful instrument available from Teleometrics International, Inc., http://www.teleometrics.com/programs/partNumber_1010I/info.html, that can be used for identifying one's quadrants on the model.

Figure 2.2: The Johari Window Model

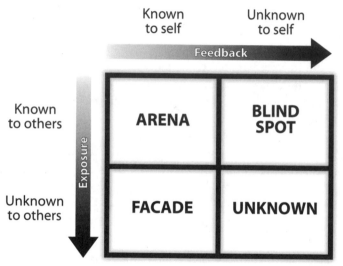

The advantage of this model is its ease of use. The "arena" is that part of the self that we know, and that others know as well. It is the quadrant of the model that reveals the degree of openness and transparency you have with others. The larger the arena the more your life is an "open book."

Everyone has "blind spots," however. We may have no awareness of parts of the self that are readily apparent to those with whom we live and work. The proportion of the blind spots we have can only be reduced by the "feedback" we receive with openness to others. You have to listen to how you are being perceived to understand your personal self.

The "façade" is the part of the self of which you are aware but keep hidden from others. These are secrets, habits, life experiences, and painful realities you know well, but which you do not want to be known. This is a presentation of the self as façade. Living out of a façade causes us to pretend to be together when we are riddled with anxiety. The façade is a like an internal voice that whispers, "Don't let them know you or they will not like you!" Only by exposure to others, as gradual as it may be, can a fuller understanding of who you are be known by others.

Finally, a part of our selves is "unknown." We have a "deep self" within that is a true "hidden" self. Only by exploring the unconscious in psychotherapy, dream analysis, spiritual meditation, or other transpersonal disciplines can the unconscious dimensions of self-awareness emerge.

Why are these multiple understandings of self so important? The two most essential values for congregational leaders are character and trust. Character is who you are in terms of the consistency with which you function in relation to your deepest self—core moral and theological values, relationship with God, genetic attributes, and learned behaviors. Alan J. Roxburgh and Fred Romanuk write persuasively of the importance of character:

> Character is a matter of personal habits, skills, and behaviors that engender confidence and credibility. It also involves a leader's motivation, values, and sense of life purpose. Character requires self-knowledge and clear evidence that Jesus Christ is the center of the leader's life, meaning, and call. Character is the place where one's deep hunger, personal identity, and calling merge to generate the confidence that allows people to trust a leader and agree to journey together in a new direction. Such character is observed in four personal qualities: maturity, conflict management, personal courage, and trustworthiness and trusting.[21]

Trust is the outcome of character in relationship with others. It is the personal authority one is granted as a kind of "second ordination"[22] by the congregation as a result of observing effective ministry. When a congregation perceives its leaders as persons of character who minister to others with honesty about who they are, trust grows. As trust grows, anxiety within the congregation diminishes and energy flows. Energy stimulates creativity and attractiveness from newcomers. Commitment deepens, and the congregation demonstrates vitality in its primary ministries. Kouzes and Posner suggest the "first law of leadership" is, "If you don't believe the messenger, you won't believe the message."[23] The corollary to the first law is, "You can't believe in the messenger if you don't know what the messenger believes."[24]

When the character of a leader is questioned or the leader demonstrates inconsistency in her or his presented self, mistrust is planted like a seed that flowers into anxiety, questioning, rumor and innuendo, resistance, and control. Energy slumps into apathy and withdrawal. The church finds itself in the crisis of mistrust.[25]

Applying Self-Knowing

How might the insights of the learning from this chapter be helpful in congregational leadership? Let me describe a staff development process. Richard Youngblood is the pastor of Riverside Church, a relatively large nondenominational congregation of eight hundred active participants. He is a Doctor of Ministry graduate of a well-known evangelical seminary, is in the second year of his call to the congregation, and works with a staff of:

- Cynthia Montell, the worship leader responsible for planning worship with the pastoral team, assembling musicians, and guiding the worship service. She is a graduate of a well-known university music program with an emphasis in contemporary music. Cynthia completed her third year of ministry in the congregation last month.
- Steven (Skip) Williams is the minister to youth. He completed an M.A. in Christian Ministry with a specialization in youth ministry from a nearby seminary. He is responsible for the youth ministry in which eighty-five students of high school age participate as well as a small group of college students. He has been on the staff for six months.
- Monique Blackstone is the senior educator of the staff, responsible for the development of the Sunday school program of the church and small group Bible studies during the week. She works with the lay leadership to determine and order curriculum, organize classes, and recruit new teachers and group leaders. Monique's tenure on the staff will be fifteen years her next anniversary of employment. She has a Master of Divinity degree in Christian Education.
- Gretchen Higgins serves as a part-time children's coordinator who works with Monique by providing learning opportunities for the children. She has no formal training in working with children and was recruited as a layperson from the congregation five years ago. Gretchen loves children, and they love her.

Richard is feeling well connected to the congregation but senses a need for more quality interaction with the staff if they are to become an effective team. He decides to gather the staff together weekly for two hours of team building for six months, using the resources he learned about in seminary. He chose to ask each staff member to complete a Johari Window, followed by the MBTI and Emergenetics® instruments. The following profiles were evident:

Figure 2.3: Profiles of Riverside Church Staff Johari Windows

Richard   Cynthia   Skip   Monique   Gretchen

	MBTI	Emergenetics
Richard	ENTJ	Strong Conceptual Relatively Strong Social Moderately Expressive Moderately Aggressive Low Flexibility
Cynthia	ESFP	Strong Social Very High Expressive High Aggressive High Flexibility
Skip	ISFP	Strong Analytical Low Expressive Low Aggressive High Flexibility
Monique	ESTJ	Strong Conceptual Moderate Expressive Moderate Aggressive Moderate Flexibility
Gretchen	ENFP	Strong Social Moderate Expressive Low Aggressive High Flexibility

When Richard reviewed the profiles of the staff he had inherited and selected, he understood more clearly some of his concerns that had begun to develop. Cynthia's tendency to alter the worship planning decisions of the staff irritated him. She often changed the selection of music after meeting with the musicians, with the result of the loss of a strong theme in the worship experience. Her high expressiveness meant she often voiced her opinions about Richard and the church in ways that did not seem helpful to him. Older members expressed concern about the dominance of her leadership in worship, and he knew she did not listen very well to the feedback he offered at times. Her "blind spot" was large and her "unknown" even larger. The profile that gave him the greatest concern was Skip's. He wished he had known more about him six months earlier when he was chosen to work with the students in the church. It was clear that in spite of his handsome physical appearance, he was not very interactive with the youth. Richard was hearing complaints about him being distant, though he seemed to excel in one-on-one conversations.

Monique's profile helped him understand her tenure better. She seemed to fit her responsibilities well and the congregation was quite affirming of the steady and thorough work she did in education.

Gretchen's profile reaffirmed the congregation's selection of her to work with children. She was caring, loving, and parents and children alike responded to her with affection.

The next six months of staff meetings were among the most productive since Richard's arrival. They began conversations by discussing together their self-interpretations of their profiles, gradually revealing more of themselves to each other. Richard chose to work privately with Skip. After several conversations, Skip confided he had been sexually molested by an uncle in his childhood. Then Richard better understood Skip's closed personality. He arranged for personal counseling with a skilled therapist, and Skip began sharing more of himself with the group. As he did so, his connections with the youth improved. He would never be the life of the party; but, as he opened himself to others, a trust developed with youth and parents that resulted in a growing gathering of teenagers in the youth group.

The conversations also gave the group opportunities to communicate frustrations with Cynthia about her maintaining commitments to staff planning. She was able to hear their feedback and gradually began to exercise more discipline in expressing her opinions that some found irritating.

The most valuable learning for Richard was the atmosphere of trust that allowed staff to communicate some their frustrations with him. They challenged his low flexibility, which they experienced as a need to control them and decisions in the church. He felt his confidence as a leader grow as he "let go" of his anxiety about success and allowed staff and lay teams more freedom in their work. Within six months of conversations, the staff meetings were marked by more laughter and spontaneity. Energy emerged that changed weekly meetings from calendar and planning meetings to explorations of visionary directions they could embrace together in their common work. The fifth month proved to be decisive when Gretchen suggested to the group that they move from talking about themselves and spend more time in prayer together and working on their relationships with God as a group. So they agreed that for the next six months they would incorporate into their meetings discussions and sharing of their experiences in spiritual disciplines.

3

Growing in Spiritual Disciplines

Most healthy trees have a root system that's three times the diameter of their canopy of branches and leaves.

ROBERT D. DALE[1]

The constancy of the demands for ministry tests the hardiness of congregational leaders. Most leaders can draw on their reserves to find energy for a special event or exhibit passion in the early years of their work. After a few disappointments, a couple of church fights, the experience of entering the pulpit with the drained feeling of dryness, conducting four funerals in one week, and repeating the cycle of weekly sermon preparation, pastors will come face-to-face with their humanity. Staff employees will have a different litany of tasks to perform each week, but their burdens may be no less demanding. Associate pastors who serve in a "second chair" of leadership often work more demanding schedules than their senior pastors. Laity go through the same sense of endless demand—another lesson preparation, visitors to contact, hospital visits, preparing a casserole for the grieving, or attending another committee meeting. The constancy of the mundane is the long-term enemy of leading with energy and momentum.

Leaders' humanity is a reminder of dependency. Anyone who thinks he or she can go to school, develop some people skills, and serve a congregation for a few years living only out of personal knowledge and experience will discover a major reality. It takes the form of a "crash" into loneliness, disappointment, physical illness, or depression. It is the widely claimed phenomenon of "burnout," which Anthony Robinson addresses directly: "'Burnout,' the word and the lament, is symptomatic of the absence of a reasonably clear and compelling purpose. Lacking clear and compelling purpose, congregations (and clergy) tend to become reactive: they try to respond to every need, itch, hurt, and crisis that comes along. And *that* is a recipe for burnout, because people's needs, itches, and hurts are limitless and endless."[2] I would add to his antidote of a "clear and compelling purpose" an unspeakable sense of Divine Presence.

The refreshing streams of God's Spirit must flow through the soul of a congregational leader or aridity as dry as the barren desert will overwhelm the soul. There is refreshing water for the dependent soul, however. The psalmist said: "O God, you are my God, I seek you, / my soul thirsts for you; / my flesh faints for you, / as in a dry and weary land where there is no water" (Ps. 63:1).

This thirst of pastoral leaders is for the presence of God within the leader's self and in the church community. When such is evident, little else matters. How do you experience it? God's Spirit must be sought in the practice of openness to the Presence. It is what Brother Lawrence called the practice of the presence of God.[3] The behavior of seeking God is rewarded with the presence of God, which stimulates a greater thirst for "those who drink of the water that I will give them will never be thirsty. The water that I will give will become in them a spring of water gushing up to eternal life" (Jn. 4:14).

Growing in Mystical Intelligence

The descriptions of intelligences in Chapter 2 are limited in that they do not include one of the most important forms of intelligence for the congregational leader. This is what Graham Standish calls "mystical intelligence." He describes it as a "deeper level" of intelligence than other approaches such as IQ or emotional intelligence. It "has to do with how aware we are of God's purpose, presence, and power."[4] Mystical intelligence includes "an intuitive, integrative awareness of God's presence... An acceptance and expectation of providence... A passionate desire to make God's will a priority."[5]

The ministry leader lives out of realities that may be important to other leaders in their work environments. To the minister of the gospel, the practice of the presence of God is not optional. The disciplines of growing in spiritual awareness and revealing such to others is the mystery for which the Church of Jesus Christ hungers and thirsts. Ministers are not only called to complete the tasks of the church, but also to engage them in a way that reveals an underlying holiness. The pastoral leader is God's representative and unless recognized as such will have little authority as a leader. Craig Barnes calls this reality "*gravitas*" and says, "It refers to a soul that has developed enough spiritual mass to be attractive, like gravity... It has everything to do with wounds that have healed well, failures that have been redeemed, sins that have been forgiven, and thorns that have settled in the flesh."[6] Standish identifies the same reality as "humble leadership," which he defines: "To be a humble leader means to follow willingly wherever the Spirit leads, and to make following the Spirit, even into times of struggle and dryness, the ground from which we lead others to follow the Spirit."[7]

Disciplines of the Spirit

Mystical intelligence is not a natural gift; it is available to any who are open to receive the presence of God. This reality of transcendence is a matter of the integration of the personality factors described previously with a lifelong growing awareness of the grace and gifts of God. It requires practice. No formulas can be offered that fit every person. Each of us brings our own life with its pain and joys, its challenges and opportunities, and its skills and limitations to the Spirit with a vulnerable receptivity. That is what Moses experienced in the theophany of a burning bush when Yahweh proclaimed, "Remove the sandals from your feet, for the place on which you are standing is holy ground" (Ex. 3:5). Spiritual practice that transforms is rooted in awareness of our truest selves in communion with the Spirit.

Urban Holmes explored the spirituality for ministry profoundly. His definition of spirituality captures the elements important to the spiritual journey: "I am defining *spirituality* as (1) a human capacity for relationship (2) with that which transcends sense phenomena; this relationship (3) is perceived by the subject as an expanded or heightened consciousness independent of the subject's effort, (4) is given substance in the historical setting, and (5) exhibits itself in creative action in the world."[8] The means of such spirituality are varied; there is no one path to the presence of God. I have identified four primary forms of spirituality, drawing from the work in spirituality by Corrine Ware.[9]

Mystical Spirituality: The Journey of the Heart

The journey of the heart is an inward movement into solitude and prayer. Ware calls this *affective* or *heartfelt* spirituality. People who are more introverted, such as the prophet Elijah, thrive on the prayer of the heart. After Elijah's dramatic encounter with the priests of Ba'al, he had to withdraw from interaction with people and retreat to a cave of solitude. The description in 1 Kings 19:11–17 of his encounter with the Holy taught him that the "sheer silence" was a source of God's renewal for action that the dramatic power of wind, earthquake, and lightening could not provide.

The practices of observing silence, long periods of meditative prayer, quietly praying through the pathways of a labyrinth, or dwelling alone with God are ancient and cherished disciplines. Monastics and mystics have demonstrated the power of the Spirit in the "sheer silence" of solitude. We are indebted to them for nourishing our lives through their prayers for the world and through their writings.

Conceptual Spirituality: The Journey of the Mind

Henri Nouwen, one of the true mystics of the twentieth century, said, "the spiritual life can be lived in as many ways as there are people."[10] The spiritual discipline of thinking with concentration on the words of Scripture, of devotional literature, or of writing in a journal the thoughts, feelings, and expressions of the sense of God are activities of the mind. Ware designates this *speculative* spirituality. Thinking spirituality may not find its roots in deep feelings or emotions, but can be the conduit of the Spirit in shaping an understanding of God's will. The discipline of *lectio divina*, the reading and rereading of a passage of scripture until it has been infused into your being, plants words of faith into the mind and heart. Reading the biographies of Spirit-led leaders can be a source of nourishment to the bedraggled follower, for all of them struggled to find their way. Probing the deep thinking of theologians can enlarge your understanding of God in profound ways. The brain is an organ of the Spirit as much as the heart. Thinking is a spiritual discipline as much as is feeling.

Activist Spirituality: The Journey of the Hands

Elijah experienced the "sheer silence," but David encountered God on the battlefield and in the multiple decisions of his kingly rule. The crowds engulfed Jesus, among whom he engaged in multiple tasks of healing, exorcism, teaching, and demonstrating the nature of the reign of God. His was a spirituality of doing, "for whatever the Father does, the Son does likewise" (Jn. 5:19b). True, he also retreated into solitude: in the crisis of Gethsemane, Jesus found his most poignant discernment of God's will (Mt. 26:36–46). Still, the active life was his primary demonstration of the kingdom of his heavenly Father. Ware calls this *apophatic* or *imaging* spirituality, in which deeds reveal God's presence in a kingdom spirituality.

Let us not overlook the presence of God in the multitude of tasks that encompass our lives. Working on a Habitat project, drilling for water in arid Africa, serving the hungry in a soup kitchen, attending to the paraments for the celebration of the Eucharist, or teaching children in a Sunday school class is working in Holy space. Our hands become God's hands as we do the work of God's will in the Church and world. Engaging with God in service to the world may enliven the high extrovert who goes to sleep when seeking God in silence.

Journey Spirituality: The Movement of the Feet

It may sound strange to some, but God is moving within us as we walk. The Spirit led Jesus on his multiple journeys. The gospels speak repeatedly of his walking from place to place to encounter the people who needed his comfort and challenge.

God is my partner in a daily walk that is a personal routine of the early morning. In the solitude of the quiet daybreak the cool oxygen of the air clears my mind and stimulates my body for the tasks of the day. Most of my conversations with God occur on these walking ventures. Some of the most critical decisions of my life were clarified in the light of the rising sun as the inaudible voice of the Spirit guided and confirmed important tasks or directions. For Ware, this is an *apothetic* or *mystic* spirituality in which God is experienced as spirit.

Every form of spiritual venture is valid. In reality, God works within us through all of these multiple avenues of revelation. We have those times when we need the quiet of reflection alone in the closet of prayer. We think carefully in search of God's will that we might understand and decide wisely. We incarnate that presence as we engage the world in deeds of kindness, mercy, and grace, attending to what T. S. Eliot called the small gestures "measured out in coffee spoons."[11] We journey through life walking through doors of opportunity because God leads. When the leader lives out of Spirit-reality, the work of God is accomplished with *gravitas*.

Knowing the Dark Side

A dark side lives within each of us, which has the potential to dominate how we lead. The temptation to sin cannot be overlooked in Christian faith. The power of the "evil one" is too often overlooked in the liberal-prone theologies of the contemporary world. A healthy dose of realism about the tendency toward hubris or pride is necessary to understand the extraordinary leadership of tyrants and dictators, murderers and exploiters. How else does one explain the captivating power of the emperors of Imperial Rome whose system of domination crucified Jesus? What about Hitler and the Holocaust, Stalin and the killing of ten million Ukrainians, Pol Pot and the massacres of a million people in Cambodia?

Living out of the dark side can infect the pastoral leader as well. When pride replaces humility in leading the church, manipulation, self-centered narcissism, exploitations of feelings, and domination define the leaders' qualities.

Holmes identifies the dark side of ministry leadership as the "sins" of the clergy. By sins he is not referring primarily to the "warm" sins of moral failures so much as the "cold" sins of indifference. The root cause of such sins the desert fathers called *accidie*, which Holmes called "spiritual boredom, an indifference to matters of religion, or simple laziness."[12] His list of the consequences of such sins is telling: the lust for power, insulation, evasion, the confusion of means and ends, the fear of failure, and extramarital genital relationships.[13] He described what have become the headlines of the news media consumed with the failures of pastoral leaders!

Living the Spiritual Disciplines

When the staff of Riverside Church made the decision to engage in a process of spiritual practice, Pastor Youngblood had learned enough about himself and the identities of the ministry team he led to know they needed to shape how to implement their decision to engage spiritual disciplines together. The agenda of their next staff meeting focused on essential tasks of the week's activities. They completed that point in thirty minutes. Two hours more were spent in conversation together about how they would proceed. It soon became clear that among the five people in the room were six different opinions of how they might experience God together. By the end of the session, they concluded that each person would lead in a time of meditative prayer and devotion at the beginning of each staff meeting. Each would reflect personal study, daily devotional practice, and styles of spirituality comfortable to him or her. Second, they concluded it would be helpful for the group to agree on a common book on spiritual practice they could read together so they might have some common language for their conversations. Third, they decided that a spiritual retreat led by the prayer minister of a nearby church trained in spirituality could provide a more focused effort to explore the varieties of God's presence in their lives.

It took several weeks to work out the details for the retreat. Joseph Santiago, the prayer minister they knew, readily agreed to work with the group and asked them to identify the three key concerns of the group. Two staff meetings were needed to provide definitive responses:

- We want to experience a variety of approaches to understanding God's presence in our lives during our time together.

- We would like to see suggested resources from which we can select a choice for our common reading.
- We want to leave the retreat with a sense that each person has experienced soul nourishment, so we want there to be an evaluation of the experience before we leave.

The church did not provide adequate budget to afford an expensive venture, so they decided to gather at Celebration Cathedral, the congregation where Santiago served. The congregation was a large charismatic congregation in the Anglican tradition that sought to incorporate a rich variety of worship and learning traditions in its ministry. The facilities, located on a wooded area of land, offered walking areas and trails with convenient seating. A labyrinth had been constructed in a clearing in the trees. A section of the educational space served as plain sleeping quarters to house youth and mission groups who visited the congregation. So the staff decided to spend the night at the church and bring simple food for their meals together.

When the team arrived for their twenty-four hours of time together, they discovered a meeting space that was large enough for fifty people with a small communion table, a circle of six chairs, and interest stations placed around the room. Several books on spiritual practices were stacked on a small table for examination by the group for common reading.[14] A prayer station was set up with three chairs and a mat for those who preferred to pray prostrate. Candles perched in various locations around the room stood ready for an experience of Taize worship. Of course, the trails outside enabled walking, meditation, and praying the labyrinth.

Joseph Santiago introduced the weekend with an emphasis on the diversity of the Early Church. He asked the group to read silently and together Ephesians 3:14—4:16. He engaged in a brief discussion of the idea that conceptual unity is the foundation of functional diversity. "As a group shares in common the understanding that the body of the congregation is a gift from God," he suggested, "the variety of expressions of how we experience God and do God's work can be affirmed and celebrated." The following discussion made it apparent the staff was already translating ways they could bring a sense of the Spirit to their respective areas of ministry.

Ninety minutes into the process, a break was declared. The energy in the room seemed to grow as individual conversations continued the group discussion. Cynthia Montell, the ever-expressive music leader, approached Joseph with a suggestion. "I wish you had challenged us to identify our spiritual gifts as a staff. Maybe if we were more aware of our strengths, we could balance our differences more effectively." She did not know she had identified the agenda for the next session of the evening!

Rev. Santiago was not sure he could get the group back together, they seemed so engaged with each other. After about twenty minutes of conversation, he announced that the next session would take place in the church's resource room down the hallway from their first meeting. There they found five desktop computers running, each connected to a Web site with a Spiritual Gifts Inventory.[15] "I want you to take your time and slowly work through this inventory of your individual gifts of the Spirit," instructed their leader. "When you finish, please print your personal profile and return to our gathering space. If you need any help, just let me know."

By the time the group completed this task and assembled again, fatigue was becoming apparent. They had been thinking together for more than two hours, and it was time to conclude the evening. "Thank you for being such a cooperative group," intoned Joseph. He then explained that he had prepared a brief written discussion on "spiritual gifts" he wished them to take. He asked each to read individually the written material the next morning after breakfast and all come to the first session at 10:00 a.m. with the materials and their Spiritual Gifts Inventories. He then gave each person a half sheet of paper on which he requested each to write an honest prayer to God about the evening and return to him without any name attached. Then it was games and rest until the next day. The written material follows.

Spiritual Gifts and Spiritual Practice

By Joseph Santiago, D.Min.
Minister of Intercessory Prayer, Celebration Cathedral

Understanding one's spiritual gift(s) is essential for effective ministry in today's congregation. It is important for ministry leaders to understand their own gifts, appreciate and affirm the gifts of their ministry team, and seek to enlarge the awareness of the gifts of those in the congregation with whom they work. Such an understanding begins with the biblical teachings on spiritual gifts and claiming one's own talents as Spirit-endowed abilities for functioning to build the body of Christ.

I am asking you to participate in an ancient practice of the Church called *Lectio Divina* that integrates the practices of reading (*lectio*), reflection (*meditatio*), prayer (*oratio*), and meditation (*contemplatio*).[16] Read the following passages in both translations.

Lectio: Read the passages with your imagination. Imagine the setting in Rome or Corinth to which the apostle Paul addressed these words. Do you

1 Corinthians 12:4–11 (NRSV)

Now there are varieties of gifts, but the same Spirit; and there are varieties of services, but the same Lord; and there are varieties of activities, but it is the same God who activates them in everyone. To each is given the manifestation of the Spirit for the common good. To one is given through the Spirit the utterance of wisdom, and to another the utterance of knowledge according to the same Spirit, to another faith by the same Spirit, to another gifts of healing by the one Spirit, to another the working of miracles, to another prophecy, to another the discernment of spirits, to another various kinds of tongues, to another the interpretation of tongues. All these are activated by one and the same Spirit, who allots to each one individually just as the Spirit chooses.

1 Corinthians 12:4–11 (*The Message*)

God's various gifts are handed out everywhere; but they all originate in God's Spirit. God's various ministries are carried out everywhere; but they all originate in God's Spirit. God's various ministries are carried out everywhere; but they all originate in God's Spirit. God's various expressions of power are in action everywhere; but God himself is behind it all. Each person is given something to do that shows who God is: Everyone gets in on it, everyone benefits. All kinds of things are handed out by the Spirit, and to all kinds of people! The variety is wonderful:

- wise counsel
- clear understanding
- simple trust
- healing the sick
- miraculous acts
- proclamation
- distinguishing between spirits
- tongues
- interpretation of tongues

All these gifts have a common origin, but are handed out one by one by the one Spirit of God. He decides who gets what, and when.

Romans 12:4–8 (NRSV)

For as in one body we have many members, and not all the members have the same function, so we, who are many, are one body in Christ, and individually we are members one of another. We have gifts that differ according to the grace given to us: prophecy, in proportion to faith; ministry, in ministering; the teacher, in teaching; the exhorter, in exhortation; the giver, in generosity; the leader, in diligence; the compassionate, in cheerfulness.

Romans 12:4–8 (*The Message*)

So since we find ourselves fashioned into all these excellently formed and marvelously functioning parts in Christ's body, let's just go ahead and be what we were made to be, without enviously or pridefully comparing ourselves with each other or trying to be something we aren't.

If you preach, just preach God's Message, nothing else; if you help, just help, don't take over; if you teach, stick to your teaching; if you give encouraging guidance, be careful that you don't get bossy; if you're put in charge, don't manipulate; if you're called to give aid to people in distress, keep your eyes open and be quick to respond; if you work with the disadvantaged, don't let yourself get irritated with them or depressed by them. Keep a smile on your face.

have a sense that some in the church were claiming their gifts were better than others? Did some wonder if they had any gifts? What conversations might have taken place when the people read these words?

Meditatio: Read the passages again. What seems different to you about this discussion from conversations in your congregation? Look at the results from your Spiritual Gifts Inventory and ask how you might have fit in these early congregations. How do you see your gifts being lived out differently from the way they might have been in Rome or Corinth?

Oratio: What feelings rise up within you as you reflect on these words? Do some of the gifts seem strange to you? How do you feel about gifts of healing? Miraculous acts? Tongues and their interpretation? Enter into prayer with God about the grace you have experienced, expressing gratitude for your gifts.

Contemplatio: Seek to be as still and relaxed as you can be. Breathe deeply and, with your eyes closed, listen to your heart. Be open to the presence of the Spirit. Focus on remaining open, and let your feelings and thoughts flow. What is the conclusion you will draw from this exercise?

The group gathered at 10:00 a.m. in their meeting space. Each individual was serious and quiet. "I have one more task for you," Joseph said. "We have looked at two primary passages of scripture about spiritual gifts. How might we apply them? I have prepared a complete list of all of the gifts measured by the Spiritual Gifts Inventory you have completed, with a brief description of each. Please circle the top three according to your score on the inventory."

Administration	Apostleship	Compassion	Discernment
Evangelism	Exhortation	Faith	Giving
Healing	Helping	Interpretation of Tongues	Knowledge
Leadership	Miracles	Prophecy	Servanthood
Shepherding	Teaching	Tongues	

A large marker board was before them. Each person wrote the three highest scores on the Spiritual Gifts Inventory he or she had completed.

Richard	Cynthia	Skip	Monique	Gretchen
Prophecy	Faith	Knowledge	Teaching	Helping
Exhortation	Evangelism	Compassion	Administration	Servanthood
Leadership	Tongues	Teaching	Discernment	Giving

Quiet music was playing in the background, helping create a mood of seriousness. Joseph asked the group to participate in a centering prayer by engaging in silence with eyes closed and body relaxed. He spoke the words, "Holy Spirit come," asking each person to focus on feelings in the moment.

After a few minutes of silence, he asked quietly for the group to open their eyes as each participant shared a brief summary of her or his experiences of the morning. It was quiet for a moment. Skip spoke first, an unusual event. "I feel there is a good balance that reflects the identity profiles we completed earlier in our staff meetings. I am surprised to see Cynthia has the gift of tongues." For once Cynthia was hesitant. "I know our congregation is not charismatic in the sense of speaking in tongues, but I have had occasional experiences of God in my private prayers in which I seemed in another world. I have had the experience of 'speaking in tongues' twice in my life. But what this really means to me is my facility in languages. I speak Spanish fluently and have a passion for including music in our worship from other languages and traditions. You remember the course I took last year on cross-cultural music?" A new awareness of Cynthia's contributions to the group was evident. "I want to comment on Gretchen's gifts," responded Pastor Richard. "You make unusual contributions to our fellowship with your caring and hospitable ministry with children. You have the best 'feel' for the heart of the congregation of any of us and can be a great help to the rest of us in connecting with people who need our attention. Also, I wonder if you might ever have an interest in some course work in the seminary across town. You would be a wonderful ordained minister in our congregation."

Gretchen responded, "Thank you so much Richard for your affirmation. As a matter of fact, I have thought about seminary, but just did not sense there was that much of a future for me in the church given my part-time status. I would love to talk about this more."

Each member of the group confirmed his or her sense of the accuracy of the inventory, and the conversation moved to discussing how the experience might be enlarged for the lay leadership.

"We need to do a Spiritual Gifts Inventory with our teachers," Monique suggested.

"I can see real value in helping our church grow in discipleship." Skip responded, "I am going to plan a spiritual retreat with our youth and our youth leaders. We have several of our young people seeking God's guidance in their vocational choices, and a retreat with a focus such as this one could be wonderful for us."

The time for lunch had passed. Joseph brought the discussion to a conclusion by handing out a written copy of a summary of the New Testament Spiritual Gifts he had developed from the online resource for the Spiritual Gifts Inventory. "After lunch," he instructed, "I would like each of you to take two of the books from the table, go walking in the woods, and find a place to sit on one of the benches located on the various trails we have developed. Look through each of them to get some idea of their usefulness to you as a staff in the coming months. Then I will invite you to walk our labyrinth, praying about whatever is in your heart. Then let's return for our final session at 3:00 p.m."

The group returned at the appointed time to find the room ablaze with candles and Taize music playing in the background. The communion table was prepared. "You asked that there be an opportunity to evaluate this experience," voiced Joseph. "What would you like to say?" There was a long period of silence.

Richard was the first to speak. "I feel I have been rejuvenated by this experience. It is so easy for us to get caught up in the routines as a staff that we lose touch with each other. I feel so much closer to this staff and have a deeper appreciation of what each brings to our common work. I also think my third spiritual gift has not been expressed adequately. After reading the description of leadership as visionary and motivating, I need to give more attention as pastor to our future dreams as a congregation. I thank you Joseph for introducing us to such a variety of ways we can grow in our life together as a staff and to how we can help our congregation grow as well."

Positive insights were offered from each person. Then the discussion shifted to the selection of a book the group would read together. Each gave an evaluation of the two books examined individually. They agreed on *Connecting to God* by Corrine Ware as a useful guide for enlarging their personal experiences together as a staff. They committed themselves to seeking ways to include what they had experienced in their future planning for ministry teams in their respective areas of leadership.

Joseph had prepared a brief litany for their celebration together of the Lord's Supper. With soft music in the background, the group gathered around the communion table, shared the liturgy, served each other the elements of the supper, and concluded with a circle of prayer for each other.

4

Leading—Integrating Being, Knowing, and Doing

Organizations are heliotropic: like plants seeking the sun, they bend toward energy.
MARK BRANSON[1]

Leading the locally autonomous congregation is unlike leading any other form of organism. There are similarities to leading other nonprofit entities, and even some similarities to the principles of business leadership. However, leading a local church is unique in the reality that employee leaders of a local church must relate in intimate and caring ways with the very people who evaluate their performance, determine their compensation, and shape the success of their efforts. Leading the congregation is an organic process full of pitfalls and opportunities for caring at a deep level of relationship with people.

The Uniqueness of the Church

This chapter focuses on understanding this uniqueness. It is a uniqueness the best pastors and staff team members understand and relish. When one does not understand and relish the uniqueness, ministry in the local church can be both frustrating and debilitating for those employed to lead and those lay leaders who are the employers in the congregation.

Leading is the essence of the work of the church. If that is so, one would imagine that a clear understanding of the nature of leading for contemporary congregations would be obvious. Nothing could be further from truth.

Leading and Identity

Leading is rooted in identity: "who I am" is infinitely more important than "what I do." If that is true, every follower of Jesus Christ has inherent leading opportunities, abilities, and tasks to perform. All that a congregation does fulfilling God's mission in the world is engaging in leading in some form or fashion. Leading is who we are and what we do!

The uniqueness of congregational leadership does not require the rejection of helpful insights and skills that can be learned from the extensive research and study of business leadership. Likewise, many of the relational qualities of church-based leadership can be applied to business settings.

Max Dupree was a bridge person in developing this understanding. A devoted Christian and CEO of Herman Miller, Inc., he stresses in his books on leadership that human quality of caring for people so essential for effective leadership in any environment. His approach centers on three qualities of leadership congregational leaders would do well to practice: "The first responsibility of a leader is to define reality. The last is to say thank you. In between the two, the leader must become a servant and a debtor. That sums up the progress of an artful leader."[2]

The Church and the Business World

Most larger congregations of the past sixty years were formed around a dominant corporate ethos. Their most important outcomes are objective and measurable. They can be achieved with structured, rational processes of planning and organization.

Denominations employ executives, and congregations employ pastors with the same agenda as the corporate chief executive officer—improve the bottom line. That expected outcome for the religious world is *growth*—in baptisms, bodies, budgets, and buildings. Most often the core leaders of congregations are executives and middle management employees in corporations. They have transferred the core values of successful business into their churches, where they have become a tradition. Once established, such a congregational culture is difficult to change.

This model is increasingly difficult to sustain. The time demands of these institutional outcomes and their complexity for the average congregation mean they no longer work. The pace of change and the shifting sands of culture no longer support such an approach.[3] Even the corporate experts are developing more flexible understandings that such approaches are less effective than in the past, and they certainly do not fit nonprofit and religiously based entities.[4]

Responding to a Business Culture

What then shall we do? If this reality is accurate, how can it be changed? Congregational leadership that wants to make a difference will highlight the uniqueness of the church. The response, according to Alan Roxburgh and Fred Romanuk, is missional leadership or "cultivating an environment that releases the missional imagination of the people of God."[5] Cultivating that environment begins with a reclaiming of the biblical understand of leading.

Leading by Following Jesus Christ

Hopeful congregations are first and foremost centered in Jesus Christ as their supreme Leader. The local church is a human institution possessing all of the characteristics of any other human entity. At the heart of its identity is the reality that the human vessel of the church is not its central reality. The church is a human community of feeble, fallible, and failing persons. Any meaning it has must be experienced from beyond its human characteristics.

Until the core leaders of the congregation understand the affirmations of the apostle Paul, hopeful leading will be limited:

> For we do not proclaim ourselves; we proclaim Jesus Christ as Lord and ourselves as your slaves for Jesus' sake. For it is the God who said, "Let light shine out of darkness," who has shone in our hearts to give the light of the knowledge of the glory of God in the face of Jesus Christ.
>
> But we have this treasure in clay jars, so that it may be made clear that this extraordinary power belongs to God and does not come from us. (2 Cor. 4:5–7)

Kingdom-Based Values

Until the New Testament understanding of the church has infiltrated the being of the people of the congregation, the values we use to judge our work will be those imported from the businesses in which we work, the families in which we live, and/or the culture in which we are immersed. Those measures are more likely to resemble a shareholder's report from the chief executive officer of a corporation than a kingdom-based understanding of the work of God in our midst.

Being the People of God

The first of these understandings is the accountability for all to participate in the ministry of the church. All of God's people are called to follow Jesus Christ. The first epistle of Peter summarizes the identity of Jesus' followers as "a chosen race, a royal priesthood, a holy nation, God's own people..." (1 Pet. 2:9).

These people are infused with the Spirit of Christ (Rom. 8:9–11; 1 Cor.

1:9, 30–31), have the "mind of Christ" (1 Cor. 2:16), and can "do all things through him" (Phil. 4:13). All church people are called to live as followers of the Christ first and foremost (Mt. 6:33). Until one is first an obedient follower, leading others is an elusive possibility.

Equality of Followers and Responsibilities of Leaders

The second insight of Scripture is the relative lack of hierarchy in the church. The New Testament is replete with visual images or metaphors of the church. The universal understanding of the Church includes all of the people of God. The many metaphors picturing the church are addressed not to the Church universal but to local gatherings of followers—the *ecclesia*—God's called out ones gathered to fulfill the purposes of God. It is the "one body in Christ" (Rom. 12:5), "God's building" (1 Cor. 3:9), "the temple of the living God" (2 Cor. 6:16b), and "the bride, the wife of the Lamb" (Rev. 21:9).[6]

All are members of the body. However, all do not perform the same functions in the church. The apostle Paul summarizes well:

> For just as the body is one and has many members, and all the members of the body, though many, are one body, so it is with Christ…
>
> Now you are the body of Christ and individually members of it. And God has appointed in the church first apostles, second prophets, third teachers; then deeds of power, then gifts of healing, forms of assistance, forms of leadership, various kinds of tongues. (1 Cor. 12:12, 27–28)

Leaders Require Followers

Robert Kelley is a researcher, teacher, and management consultant. He describes how he discovered a different understanding of leadership by reading the gospel accounts from a hotel room Bible. The followership of Jesus' disciples changed the world in which Jesus ministered. Kelley's insights are compatible with the Pauline understanding of the church. Some "forms of leadership" require followers for the leader to lead. Kelley's definition of leadership is among the simplest I have read: "When you cut through all the platitudes defining leadership, doesn't it boil down to this: that the leader is someone who can attract and retain followers? Without followers, leadership is meaningless, and leaders don't exist."[7]

Congregational leading is a partnership in which leaders engage in multiple forms of working with followers to accomplish the work of the church. Kelley suggests the ratio between the two is demonstrated by his research on organizations. Leaders accomplish 10–20 percent of the work that results in organizational success. Followers make the real difference in all entities. He says, *"Followership is the real 'people' factor in the other 80 to 90 percent that makes for great success.* Without followers, little gets done; with them mountains get moved. By sheer numbers alone, followers represent the bulk and substance of any enterprise."[8]

Empowering the Gifted

The third insight of the New Testament is the importance of the gifting of the Holy Spirit for the multiple roles of leading in the church. Ephesians 4 is the paradigmatic passage of the spiritual nature of the leading process for the church:

> But each of us was given grace according to the measure of Christ's gift...The gifts he gave were that some would be apostles, some prophets, some evangelists, some pastors and teachers, to equip the saints for the work of ministry, for building up the body of Christ, until all of us come to the unity of the faith and of the knowledge of the Son of God, to maturity, to the measure of the full stature of Christ. (Eph. 4:7, 11–13)

> But speaking the truth in love, we must grow up in every way into him who is the head, into Christ, from whom the whole body, joined and knit together by every ligament with which it is equipped, as each part is working properly, promotes the body's growth in building itself up in love. (Eph. 4:15–16)

What a description of the contemporary congregation that is fulfilling its Spirit-led purposes! In such a congregation leaders and followers work in a synergy of partnership that honors the respective roles of each. The leaders of the church are not masters of the life and ministry of the church. Neither does the laity function with the expectation that their leaders are accountable for the full success of the church's ministry. A partnership of common purpose allows leaders to lead while followers look to leaders to embrace followers as partners or co-creators in the work of the church. Leaders do so by demonstrating inspiration and encouragement for followers to fulfill their God-given gifts in what they do.[9]

The Tasks of the Pastoral Leader

One of the greatest challenges of the contemporary congregation is the relative lack of meaning of church membership. Realistically, most congregations exhibit multiple levels of commitment on the part of their members. George Bullard visualizes the seven types of congregational participants in Figure 4.1.[10] A description of each type follows:

Figure 4.1: Concentric Circles of People Groups in a Congregation

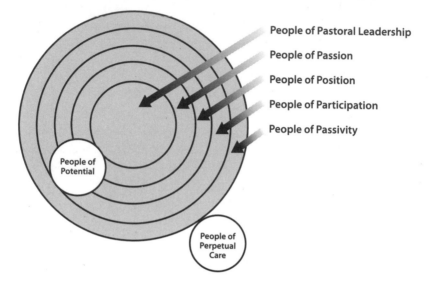

- People of pastoral leadership constitute the pastor and other primary program staff, whether ordained clergy or employed laity.
- People of passion have an obvious and contagious positive, spiritual passion about the future of the congregation.
- People of position have roles of leadership in the life of the congregation, whether informal or formal, whether effective or ineffective.

These three groups, often overlapping, comprise the leadership core or the "enduring visionary leadership community." Bullard estimates that no more than 21 percent of the people of a congregation will be a part of this group. This core must convince the majority of the church's people to engage the congregation with meaningful commitment to attendance, study, and work in the ministries of the church. This majority includes:

- People of participation who will follow trusted leaders, attend, and engage in tasks of managing the church's vision.
- People of passivity whose level of involvement is marginal, at best. They attend and contribute time, energy, and resources at lower

levels of involvement than the previous four groups. Pastoral leaders are especially frustrated by these Advent and Easter Christians who expect from them the same responsiveness in ministry as do the most committed.

- People of perpetual care are dependent on others—usually the pastoral staff—for care and attention. They may have been past leaders, but are now largely inactive by virtue of health, resources, or interest. They place high expectations on others for caring for them even when they do not request it.
- People of potential tend to "swarm" around the "enduring visionary leadership community" and can be cultivated and enlisted into greater involvement and leadership.[11]

A part of the reality of leadership is living with the recognition that congregations are voluntary organizations. Only parents have the ability to coerce involvement, and then only of their children for a limited time in their lives. Attending the congregation today are multiple "clay pots" who have never been "fired" in the crucible of experiences, rooted in deep faith, occupied with profound biblical understandings, or experienced a sense of the presence of the Holy Spirit. The descriptions of communities of faith that resemble the above biblical descriptions are too rare in that they lack the levels of partnership with each other and the Spirit of God to accomplish their missions. For some, there is hardly an awareness of their true mission.

Congregations that are clear in their expectations of membership will be more vital than those who are not. Adam Hamilton demonstrates this in his practice as pastor of Resurrection United Methodist Church in Leawood, Kansas:

> We make clear, up front, that unlike the American Express Card, membership in our church has no privileges, only expectations. We promise to visit them in the hospital, whether they are members or visitors. We will do their weddings and their funerals whether they are members or visitors. They may participate in any of our programs as a visitor. We'll even make up member nametags for visitors if they ask for one.
>
> We tell them that membership comes with only responsibilities and expectations. If they join, they are no longer able to park in the closer "visitor parking"! If they join, they will receive the stewardship mailings in the fall, including a pledge card. If they join, we will call upon them from time to time to ask for their help. We tell them that membership, like marriage, is a sign of commitment.[12]

This is a distinguishing difference from leading employees. An employer has an authority in a paycheck, including the ability to demand a certain amount of work, loyalty, and performance for continued employment. Today's pastor has no such authority except in select traditions in which a theology of divine power is associated with the pastor's calling and role. One follows or leaves in such traditions. The voluntary nature of most churches, however, results in a large portion of people functioning as "people of passivity."

This may be the most difficult burden for the "people of pastoral leadership." Pastors and staff leaders may be competent, visionary, and hard working. If the primary followership is sporadic, undependable, incompetent, overly dependent, or even evil, the burden of leadership can become a weight some are not able to bear. In one sense this burden is rooted in the etymology of "leading." Kelley writes:

> The word "follower" has its etymological roots in Old High German *follaziohan*, which meant to assist, help, succor, or minister to. This parallels the Old High German root of "leader," which meant to undergo, suffer, or endure. In the original meaning, followers helped take care of leaders, though there are few etymological clues as to why leaders suffered or were in need of care. However, the relationship between them appears to be a symbiotic one between equals.[13]

Most of the pastors and church staff I know could describe quite easily "why leaders suffer." Most often they refer to a lack of that symbiotic support so crucial to an effective leader/follower relationship. The leading core has as a primary task of teaching and convincing the congregation of the mission values so essential for a hopeful theology of the church. Kouzes and Posner suggest, "The people who have the greatest clarity about both personal and organizational values have the highest degree of commitment to the organization."[14]

A more complete definition of the leadership task than simply a relationship with followers is needed. Wright comes close to the heart of congregational leadership: "*Leadership is a relationship of influence in which one person seeks to influence the vision, the values, the attitudes, and the behaviors of another.*"[15] The heart of this book defines the kind of influence one has as the congregational leader, namely one committed to the mission of God in the world. A more specific definition of the congregational leader employed here is: *a missional leader is a follower of Jesus Christ with a vision of the mission of*

God living in relationship with other Jesus followers in ways that influence them to embody that mission in how they live, love, and serve.

Adopting a Leading Style

Effective leaders function with awareness of their personal styles of leading. How we lead is a part of our identity. Each of us has leading preferences rooted in personality, spiritual gifts, modeling learned from others, and judgment as to the needs of the situation. The most effective leaders, in my observation, actually utilize each of the styles of leading *depending on an assessment of the needs of the moment.* For some leaders, this is an almost innate ability; for others it is a matter of thoughtful analysis and conscious reflection about the needs of the kind of action needed in a particular circumstance. As mentioned in Chapter 2, Daniel Goleman identifies six styles of leaders: "Authoritative leaders mobilize people toward a vision. Affiliative leaders create emotional bonds and harmony. Democratic leaders build consensus through participation. Pacesetting leaders expect excellence and self-direction. Coaching leaders develop people for the future. And coercive leaders demand immediate compliance."[16] Elements of each of these can be connected to each of the four major styles of congregational leading.

The first congregational leading style is *directing*. The leader functions as a figure of authority—authority that may be claimed by the leader, or granted by those who follow. This style is the most efficient for it requires fewer people to make decisions. The leader can declare his or her actions are "God's will," and followers have only one choice to make—either follow the leader or leave. This style is most like Goleman's coercive leader. The directing leader can more easily succumb to the temptations of dictatorial commands, overconfidence in pronouncements, and abuse of those who disagree. When the leader is correct in his or her judgments, the church can flourish. When the leader is uninformed or demonic, the results for the church can be fatal.

In some situations even the least directive of leaders must act decisively, and often without consultation. A small church in the rural South had a lovely wood-framed sanctuary. A routine termite inspection revealed extensive hidden termite damage in the floor joists of the building. The pastor was a beloved and gentle leader. Consulting engineers informed him that to place the weight of a congregation in worship on the floor could possibly lead to collapse. With minimal discussion, he informed key leaders and moved the next worship service to a fellowship hall. His pastoral abilities were tested when he had to tell a woman in the church whose husband was dying that the funeral could not be conducted in the building. All the decisions were painful for him because they called for skills he did not usually demonstrate. But he acted. He was a wise directive leader in that situation. His actions were coercive in a positive way.

The second leading style is *inspiring*. Other words for this style are charismatic and include Golemans' authoritative and pacesetting styles. Some people have mesmerizing skills that make them attractive to people. Most inspiring leaders are more extroverted than introverted, have excellent verbal communication skills, and are able to exude confidence in even desperate situations. Such individuals are often physically attractive, entertaining, and have a gift of humor. Those inspiring individuals who lead out of the center of their character in relationship with Christ make historic contributions to God's kingdom. The temptation of inspiring leaders is to become so narcissistic in the use of their gifts that the leading becomes more about their personal success than the church's. Their personalities are often somewhat histrionic and may be unpredictable, using the element of surprise in leading the congregation. When the inspiring are also directive, maintaining the boundaries of personal integrity in finances, family priorities, sexual integrity, and honesty may become difficult.

The most effective means of leading for the inspiring style is preaching. Those who inspire are positive in outlook, hopeful about the future, engender confidence in the face of difficulties, and speak directly and clearly. One need not be a Martin Luther King to inspire others, but the optimism of his spirit is essential.[17] Kouzes and Posner suggest, "How can you expect others to get jazzed, if you're not energized and excited?"[18] More attention will be given to the proclaiming ministry of the pastor in Chapter 10.

The third style of those who lead is *collaborating*. It integrates Golemans' affiliative and democratic leader descriptions. It is one in which the pastoral leader interacts with core leaders and the larger congregation in ways that seek input from others, participation in decisions by others, and support for actions taken by all who have participated. The limitations of this style are the slowness with which change occurs. Collaboration is time consuming and people intensive. It requires a fairly high level of education and experience in group process among the people with whom one is collaborating. When the process works, a high level of congregational commitment and exhilaration can be the dominant feeling of the group. Energy is the byproduct of good collaboration. If the process drags on too long, a sense of the "paralysis of analysis" overcomes the group, and the pastoral leader is often accused of poor leadership.

The final style is that of *passive* leading. In effect, the passive leader follows and seldom, if ever, leads. Coaching other leaders can be such a style or can be collaborative. The coach does not bring her or his personal perspective to the situation but guides the coachee to discover within responses that can be embraced. Such a style is altogether necessary at times and in some circumstances. The passive leader waits and watches as others give leadership, an appropriate response when one has too little information or an unformed opinion on what needs to be done in a given situation.

My research with local pastors and a review of the U. S. Congregational Life Survey (USCLS) data of lay responses in their congregations indicate that each of the four leadership styles is employed by effective leaders. Table 4.1 documents the leader profiles of nine of the ten congregations I studied in 2010 that completed the USCLS survey as a part of my research. The table presents the perceptions of the laity of how each pastor leads. The African American pastors in the study employed a more directive style of leading than the Caucasian ones. The dominant style of each of the nine churches surveyed, with one exception of a lay-led congregation, was the inspiring approach. Yet, with few exceptions, each of the four styles was evident in the congregations.

Table 4.1: Pastoral Leadership Perceptions of Congregants in Percentages

Leader Style	African-American Congregations						Caucasian Congregations			
	#1	#2	#3	#4	#5		#6	#7	#8	#9
Leader takes charge	16	22	27	26	30		0	22	7	20
Leader inspires action	71	68	54	62	52		63	57	36	53
Leader acts on cong. goals	5	6	8	8	5		22	22	43	10
People start new actions	3		1	1	3		11	2	14	0
Do not know	5	4	11	3	9		4	7	0	17

Data comparing the self-assessment of pastors with views of laity in their congregations in the USCLS data analyzed by Jackson Carroll indicated considerable contrast between the two groups. Pastors are perceived by the laity they serve as considerably more directive and less likely to be viewed as "inspires and encourages laity to act, but acts alone when necessary" than clergy view themselves.[19]

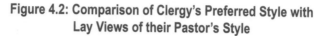

Figure 4.2: Comparison of Clergy's Preferred Style with Lay Views of their Pastor's Style

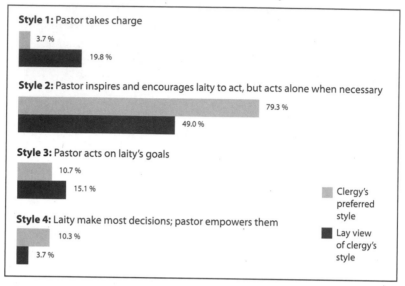

Even more significant than these differences is the correlation between congregational effectiveness and style of leadership. When Carroll analyzed the correlations between eighteen measures of effectiveness with each of the four leadership styles I have identified as directing, inspiring, collaborating, and passive, the most positive correlations were with the inspiring style: "Pastor inspires and encourages laity to act, but acts alone when necessary." Nearly all of the correlations comparing collaborative and passive styles with effectiveness were negative, a powerful finding for the expectations of congregational laity. The highest correlation was between the inspiring style and the percent of the congregation who say there is a good match between pastor and congregation.[20] Pastors who are able to inspire confidence in their visions for the church and encourage the laity in their ministries will make the most significant difference in leading hopeful congregations.

If two words could summarize how pastors actually lead, they would be *flexibility* and *fit*. Congregational needs change from week to week. Pastors respond based on the situation. They also fit well the needs of the congregation at a point in time. The ten pastors studied in depth as a part of this research were asked to select from the following list the best descriptor of their leadership style. None of the ten chose a single descriptor. The variety of the tasks required multiple leadership skills. The choices offered were:

1. Charismatic motivator seeking to impart the energy of the Spirit to the church;
2. Chief Executive Officer of the congregation;
3. Community organizer who mobilizes the congregation for community/social change;
4. Enabler who supports the laity in fulfilling their vision of mission for the church;
5. Family therapist seeking to understand the church as family and promoting healthy relationships within it;
6. Gardener cultivating personal relationships with and among the people of the church;
7. Prophet who declares the word of the Lord without regard for support or understanding from the people;
8. Shepherd serving the needs of persons in the congregation;
9. Strategic visionary seeking to know God's vision for the church;
10. Tribal chief who models wisdom and exercises authority in speaking to the people;
11. Other _____.

I have consolidated the responses of each into a singular description that seems to best describe each pastor. The order of the list is based on the size of the congregation served, with the smallest listed first. Race and gender made little difference in the likelihood of particular descriptions, except for the word *charismatic*. It applied only to Black pastors and was particularly descriptive of three of the pastors.

> Strategic Visionary for the Church's Future
> Equipper of the Believers
> Family Systems Enabler/Gardner
> Shepherd Serving People
> Strategic Charismatic Enabler
> Charismatic Community Organizer
> Chief Executive Shepherd
> Strategic Visionary for the Church's Future
> Charismatic Motivator of the Members
> CEO Servant Leader

Each congregation will shape its leader and vice versa. Stereotypes and "typical" expectations for how leaders should function do not apply to the contemporary congregation.

Building a Leadership Team

The majority of pastors in the United States serve as the single employed leader of their congregations; most churches are too small to afford more. A significant portion of these are bi-vocational. According to Carroll, "… we find that 18 percent of mainline Protestants, 29 percent of conservative Protestants, and 41 percent of clergy in historic black denominations are bi-vocational."[21] Unfortunately, part-time churches and their bi-vocational pastors underestimate the needs for ministry and the opportunities for service in their communities. Leaderless churches are too often the consequence; there is no expectation for doing anything more than gathering weekly or less frequently for a service of worship and possibly a Sunday school. An effective bi-vocational pastor can be an agent of change in these churches, especially in rural regions of the country where church is informal and the family structures of the community shape the congregation.[22] A layperson often functions informally as the pastor of the congregation during the week when a pastor is not available or when the church functions in the interim between pastors. The part-time pastor who can affirm such persons will find her leadership enlarged by a healthy relationship with such a person or persons.

These churches know how to experience fellowship. They still need vibrant worship, inspiring preaching, thoughtful teaching, caring pastoral attention in times of illness and grief, and at least a framework of structure for mission involvement.

Part-time pastors must practice effective time management. A pastor who earns his income at a full-time job will have Sundays and a few other hours available during the week to serve the church. Modern technology compensates for limited time, however. Cell phone access for emergencies, telephone conferences for worship planning, texting or e-mail for consulting on needed decisions, and the use of Skype for critical conversations create pastoral accessibility during the week. A couple of hours in personal follow up on Sundays offer small churches meaningful leadership for utilizing their resources fully. Bi-vocational pastors can lead too.

Along with these churches with limited pastoral leadership time, thousands of Protestant churches employ their pastor as the only full-time employee. They may have a part-time secretary and other part-time staff leading music, playing instruments, or working with youth. Still, the pastor is central and has more power than in nearly any other form of congregational life.

Training laity to embrace caring ministries such as deacon or elder ministry to shut-ins, the hospitalized, or those in crisis situations will enhance the ability of the pastor to give priority to the most important tasks of ministry. Developing a Stephen Ministry within the congregation can be a gift to the congregations of such churches where the pastor is often stretched beyond competence in all of the expectations of the church and the community.

The program church with a multiple staff configuration is one in which much of the tension in the congregation is staff centered. Conversations with both staff and pastors in such settings reveal too little conscious thought and attention to the development of the staff as a working team. This is especially the case when the members of the ministry staff have longer tenures than the pastor and often struggle to "mesh" with new ideas or approaches to ministry.

Building teams, whether teams of employees of the church or the leading core of laity, is a critical task of the pastor in churches. More attention will be given to staff interaction in Chapters 11 and 14. Consider these workable leadership questions for now.

Essential Leadership Questions

Who is in charge?

Accountability and authority go hand-in-hand. I am not suggesting the leader, whether of staff or lay groups, should be a dictator who directs all decisions and actions. What is critical is that leaders and followers agree on accountability for responsibilities. At a minimum, someone must be accountable to any group for calling it together, assuring a consensus on the agenda for meetings, and guiding the process of its work.

When the work group is employed staff, the pastor has this responsibility, except in the largest of congregations with a "second chair" executive pastor. Staff members who resist such leadership will generate dysfunction in the group. Pastors who do those tasks poorly will enlarge resistance to their own leadership.

How do we select our leaders?

Whom you put in charge is critical, whether employees or volunteers. Jim Collins suggests that getting the right people on the bus is the first task of the best leaders.[23] When the role is that of an employee, a job description that includes reasonable expectations for the ministry to be accomplished is essential. A process of selection that includes the involvement of stakeholders for a particular ministry is important. The pastor or other staff member who will be a primary guide or coach for the employee should be convinced there is a "fit" with the prospective person. Clear expectations of salary, benefits, and performance will be included in the negotiations with such a person.

The same principle should apply to the selection of laity for the most critical decision-making roles in the church. Consider the following model developed by one church with whom I worked.

Only three groups are nominated to the church for election for their responsibilities. The deacons are elected and ordained by the congregation for caring ministries with the members and enhancing the spiritual fellowship of the church. The finance committee is elected to emphasize stewardship, recommend an annual budget, and monitor the financial policies and procedures of the church. The personnel committee maintains policies for all employees, selects nonministerial staff, monitors performance of each employee, and addresses conflicts within the staff. All other church functions are performed by ministry teams on which any participant can volunteer for service. Such an approach allows for maximum involvement by the willing. There is an opportunity for service for any who will respond.

Diversity or uniformity?

Churches face a natural tendency to select leaders who are reflective of the dominant groups of the church—educational level, age, tenure, and similarities of ideas in theology, politics, and culture. Those newest, youngest, and most different in the fellowship are often overlooked in developing new leaders. Such an approach is comfortable for people with a tradition that stresses stability over change, control over energy. But these traditional leaders and members whose dominant goal is uniformity should not complain when the church seems so moribund. Look for personalities, skills, and interests that complement those presently in place. Variety is the spice of life and of vitality in congregational life. There is maturity in diversity, though the movement in that direction takes time and stresses evolutionary over revolutionary changes.

Supervision or coaching?

The traditional corporate model of relating to followers was one of supervision. The leader of a unit was accountable for the performance of a group of employees, managed them by negotiating goals for production, and evaluated performance at regular intervals. This kind of top-down approach has been largely abandoned in the competitive environment of the twenty-first century. Self-managing teams and coaching relationships with upper-level executives are more effective than the old supervisory models. Yet, many congregations, especially of retirees whose work embodied that supervisory model, employ supervision as their best practices for improving performance.

Coaching is a more effective model in that the initiative for accomplishment resides with the worker rather than a supervisor. Coaching is a process for drawing out the best in insights, processes, and relationships for those in the learning process. Chapter 11 offers additional information on a coaching process, especially for staff accountability.

Balancing Leading and Managing

I was asked to preach at a congregation several years ago whose pastor had accepted the call to another congregation. Church leaders were beginning a process of seeking an interim to help in healing conflict that had occurred during the departing pastor's tenure. When I asked about his strengths and weaknesses, the consistent response was, "He was a fine preacher and a great visionary. But every Sunday it was vision, vision, vision. He never led us to fulfill any of those visions."

What they were identifying were too few managing skills. By managing, I am referring to those routine tasks that must be accomplished week by week and month by month for a congregation to implement its visions. They are often the bane of visionary pastors.

The ten pastors in the case studies that formed much of the content of this study exemplify disdain for the mundane. Only one pastor admitted to enjoying the administrative roles of pastoral leadership. While most of the pastors rank preaching, pastoral relationships, and strategic leading as gifts and interests, they listed administrative meetings and routine ministry tasks among the lowest of their priorities. However, each of them worked, on average, one day of each week on the managing responsibilities of the church. These tasks are what Louis Weeks calls "scutwork," the routine maintenance necessary for accomplishing good work.[24]

Leading without managing will exhaust the best of laity. Routines left unattended often become the source of major frustration and criticism of the pastor and staff. It is not the responsibility of leaders to do all of the routines of managing. Effective leading, however, is dependent on assuring that either employees or competent laity accept the responsibilities of the routines that serve the key values of the organization.[25]

On the other hand, too much focus on managing without leading will bore all but the most boring of church participants. Much of the apathy observable in congregations is that the congregation is in a managing "rut." Every activity, every meeting, the calendar of every year is as predictable as living in a prison cell. Such churches wonder why no one new ever shows up!

Good leaders work to assure that processes and procedures are in place to assure good management. Time spent on organizing these well will allow the leaders to focus on the strategic paths that will move the congregation into the future. Thus, the chapters in Part 3 address the multiple dimensions of administration or management of visionary initiatives. Some of the materials described will not generate excitement for the youthful, the innovative, or the energetic. But attention to the details of the managing process is one of the ways leaders develop and maintain the kinds of relationships with followers that give them credibility. In the nitty-gritty routines one discovers the leader whose word is fulfilled by actions. Trust grows with every promise kept. Relationships grow as we work together on needed tasks. Respect enlarges when we become aware of competence and character as leaders do what they say we should do. A Chinese proverb summarizes the balance of leading and managing: "Tell me, I may listen. Teach me, I may remember. Involve me, I will do it."[26]

PART 2: Knowing
The Content of the Leader's Repertoire

Leading is an action of the head. It requires knowing along with being and doing. A repertoire of knowledge is necessary for effective pastoral leadership.

The pastor is first and foremost a theologian of the mission of God. If congregations are to fulfill the intentions of God for the church, the pastor preaches and teaches in ways that inspire a commitment to the work of God in the world. A missional church is essentially a congregation that lives out of the *missio Dei*—the mission of God. An exploration of the meaning of that mission in the primary source for understanding it, Scripture, forms the content of Chapter 5.

Effective pastoral leaders are also sociologists of the culture in which the work of congregations is done. One need not be an expert in understanding culture, but awareness of the social forces in our world that bring cultural change will enhance the realism with which congregations understand many of their challenges. Leading is a finely honed balance of the idealism of the gospel with the realism of the culture in which it takes root. Chapter 6 will explore dimensions of the major cultural realities of global change.

Recognizing the variety of congregations is a skill not developed by some leaders. Congregations have identities that differ significantly. Clarity about the variety of congregations is important for leaders in being intentional about their uniqueness. Congregational identity is essential for planning and executing ministry that is rooted in passion for God's mission. Leaders are analysts of congregational ecology, the content of Chapter 7.

5

Theologians of God's Vision for the World

The church today is a recipient of mission before it ever is an agent of mission.
God's mission is open to all who desire to participate with God. Today churches
do not need to discover their particular mission; rather, they must find God's
mission, get behind it, and run with it.

RYAN BOLGER[1]

Every effective pastoral leader lives out of a particular theological
understanding of his or her role in influencing the identity of a congregation.
Some of these theologies are little more than informal "folk theologies"
without roots in the classical traditions of the Christian faith. They are what
Stone and Duke call "embedded theologies" that are inherited from family,
community, and culture. Yet other theologies are coherent and formally
constructed: what they call "deliberative theologies."[2] If congregations are
to embrace the fullness of their calling to become the church God wishes,
they must be led in understanding a deliberative theology of the mission
of God in the world.

The pastor proclaims through preaching and teaching theological
perspectives. They may be carefully articulated and scholarly expositions
of a theological tradition such as Orthodox, Roman Catholic, Reformed,
Wesleyan, Anabaptist, or Pentecostal. Or, they may be personally held feelings
that lack specific content. Every pastoral leader has a theological perspective.
In this book we have no intention to analyze or critique the variety of
theological perspectives one can find in the contemporary church. Rather,
I wish to make the argument that vital pastoral leadership will function out
of a biblical theology that reflects the congregation as a participant in God's
mission. I call these congregations "hopeful congregations."

The Mission of God: A New Cosmic Order

The heart of any dream for the congregational leader is a vision of the purpose of the church. That dream must be rooted in more than an organizational statement of mission that focuses on the building of an institution. It must be an all-encompassing understanding that the story of the contemporary congregation is connected to the historical story of the mission of God in human history.

One must begin with an understanding of the biblical story of the identity of Israel's God as creator of the cosmos. Creator God is working actively in human history to create a covenant community of people who are invited to participate in a universal realm, reign, and rule that ultimately establishes a new world order of peace (*shalom*) in both the present and the future. Christian faith understands clearly that Jesus is central to this story. He bears its vision and its embodiment in his life, death, resurrection, and empowering of a community of disciples whose mandate is to model that vision.

This vision is a challenge to the modern mind, with its focus on the "here and now," the factuality of all information, and the rationality of understanding all reality. This vision is above and beyond such a modern focus. The biblical vision understands the Church as a collection of congregations led by the Holy Spirit to fulfill the mission of God. In this sense, the purpose of the Church is to be a community of faith that transcends human ways of being and doing.

I offer here a summary of this theological perspective of the mission of God, or what contemporary missiologists call the *missio Dei*. This is not to suggest that all effective congregational leaders will resonate with this particular theological perspective. One might choose different language to express these understandings, but unless the leader possesses a vision greater than simply investing in the daily tasks of administering an organization, that minister will see little effectiveness in creating a new community of God's people.

Several definitions may be helpful for reflection on this narrative summary. Who is this God who is the subject of the narrative? I have chosen to use the unpronounceable, indescribable name the Hebrew people used, YHWH, for the One who created all that is and who called them into being. YHWH called Israel to a universal mission of becoming a blessing to the nations. It is the name revealed to Moses (I AM) in the ineffable experience of calling to become a liberator to Egyptian slaves before a bush that was "blazing, yet it was not consumed" (Ex. 3:2). This God is the Holy One who demands obedience. This holy YHWH stands above all human constructions of divinity who might be in competition with such holiness and otherness (Ex. 20:1–7). It may seem awkward to the contemporary reader to use this technical term of four letters for the name of God; but hopefully it will communicate a challenge to our over-familiarity with popular conceptions of God.

A second word important to the mission of YHWH is *kingdom*. It is a word fraught with difficulty in our contemporary understandings. The idea of a kingdom (*basileia* in Greek) communicates a geographical/political entity in our understanding that implies that the "kingdom of Christ and of God" (Eph. 5:5) denotes some earthly domain. That idea limits its true meaning.[3] I considered simply transliterating the Greek word and using "the *basileia* of YHWH" to indicate the New Testament meaning. Whatever word is used, it is a realm, a rule, and a reign that transcends time and space. The power and authority of the one ruling and reigning is what is primary.

The second problem with kingdom language is the masculinity of a kingdom with a king. This distorts the inclusion of the sovereign who is YHWH of all in the human family.[4] Brian McLaren identifies the consensus of much of contemporary biblical scholarship that Jesus was addressing the contrast between YHWH's realm, rule, and reign and Rome's imperial economic and political power represented by a "divine" emperor. He writes, "The term *kingdom of God*, which is at the heart and center of Jesus' message in word and deed, becomes positively incandescent in this kind of framing. As a member of a little colonized nation with a framing story that refuses to be tamed by the Roman imperial narrative, Jesus bursts on the scene with this scandalous message: *The time has come! Rethink everything! A radically new kind of empire is available—the empire of God has arrived.*"[5] Empire language associated with the *basileia* of God suffers the historical failures of the church to distinguish the rule, reign, and realm of God from an earthly economic and political power.

The idea that best conveys the meaning of this concept can be found in Clarence Jordan's amazing translation from the Greek NT into southern gospel. His rendition that best captures what is intended is, "From then on, (following the arrest of John the Baptizer) Jesus began spreading his ideas. 'Reshape your lives, for God's new order of the Spirit is confronting you'" (Mt. 4:17, *Cotton Patch Gospel*). Does that not capture it? "God's new order of the Spirit!"

The Realm of God's New Order of the Spirit

The realm of the mission of YHWH is quite simply the universe. If YHWH is the Creator of all that was, is, and shall be, as the tradition of

Hebrew/Christian faith asserts, then the *missio Dei* includes all of creation. John's declaration, "For God so loved the world [Gr. *kosmos*] that he gave his only Son" (Jn. 3:16a), places no limit on the love of the Creator.

This means the mission of YHWH is ecological.[6] The Genesis story declares the goodness of all creation with a call from God to humankind to participate in "dominion" with YHWH to maintain the goodness of that creation in harmonic balance (Gen. 1:26–31). The interaction between humans and nature is beyond our complete comprehension, yet there is an intricate connection. The power of nature is evident with the catastrophes of major earthquakes, tsunamis, and hurricanes in human experience. To what degree human behavior influences such natural phenomena is an ongoing debate, but surely there is a relationship when the quantum physicists suggest minute changes in air current, even so tiny as the fluttering of butterfly wings, have some small effect on weather half-a-globe away.

Such an understanding also requires a mission that is universal. If the new order of the Spirit of YHWH is cosmic, it embraces all persons, all human relationships, all governments, and all powers that manifest themselves in human experience. The ancient narrative of the creation of humans (Gen. 1:26—2:25) emphasizes the oneness of humanity. If the biblical story means anything, it means that all humans are ultimately connected in spite of apparent differences in race, tribe, geography, language, religion, or culture. We belong to each other, and everything that YHWH intends for the Church is intended for all who will respond to that intention.

YHWH reigns beyond the limits of contemporary time. The community of Christian faith has struggled throughout its history with understanding the limits of current reality on ultimate reality. We wonder, for instance, where the new order of the Spirit may be amid the crises of war, suffering, and pain. Yet, the biblical story proclaims, with little ambiguity, a reign that is historical and beyond the events of contemporary history, is present but also future, and possesses the limits of finitude while hoping in ultimate infinity.

The Reign of God's New Order of the Spirit

Some may wonder, "What are the evidences of the reign of YHWH in a world like ours?" Simplistic responses will not do when the broad sweep of human history has told the story of uncontrolled violence; constant warfare; economic exploitation; and subjugation of nations and individuals in slavery, oppression, and sin.

There can be no denial of the "dark" side of human behavior with its violence and oppression. Yet, woven within the interstices of the horrific is another story of the activity of YHWH/Jesus Christ/Holy Spirit to transform the human situation into hopeful anticipation of a new reality. Space will allow only an outline of that story of the ongoing work of YHWH within and through the people of God to bring forth a different reality than the historically "normal." That story is the biblical narrative that encompasses in summary each of the following.

Promise

The heart of the biblical story is the God who promises blessing to all of the people of God through a covenant of holy relationship. That promise began with the choice of Abraham and Sarah as the parents of a new people who are called to live in covenant with YHWH to become a blessing to the nations of the world (Gen. 12:1–3; 15–18). The Lord God reigns in relationship with an elect people who are chosen, not for privilege so much as for blessing to the people of the earth. Christopher Wright suggests, "Arguably God's covenant with Abraham [and with Sarah] is the single most important biblical tradition within a biblical theology of mission and a missional hermeneutic of the Bible."[7] Lesslie Newbigin adds, "Israel's election means that it is called to be servant and witness of the Lord for all the nations, not to be ruler of the nations. To be the elect is a fearful responsibility."[8] Mission connects the grand narrative of Scripture from this call to the consummation of the story in the book of Revelation.[9] Israel, and then the Church, are elected to bless the nations with the salvific and ethical work of God in their midst.

Jesus embodies that promise in the proclamation and demonstration of the new order of the Spirit: "And after John was arrested, Jesus came to Galilee, proclaiming the good news of God, and saying, 'The time is fulfilled, and the new order of the Spirit [basileia] of God is continually arriving; change the commitments of your life, and believe in the good news'" (Mk. 1:14, author's translation).

The One who had called the long line of Israel's leaders would be at the center of the message and work of Jesus. David Bosch suggests, "Something totally new is happening: the irruption of a new era, of a new order of life. The hope of deliverance is not a distant song about a far-away future. The future has invaded the present."[10] For Christians, the promise of YHWH's covenant is fulfilled in this one who teaches God's new order in parable and sermon. He demonstrates it in healings, exorcisms, miracles, suffering, death, and resurrection. Johannes Verkuhl summarizes:

> The heart of the message of the Old and New Testament is that God, the Creator of the universe and all earthly life, is actively engaged in the reestablishment of [God's] liberating dominion

over the cosmos and all humankind. In seeking out Israel, [God] sought all us and our entire world, and in Jesus Christ [God] laid the foundation of the Kingdom. Jesus Christ, the Messiah "promised to the fathers," is the *auto basileia*: in Him the Kingdom has both come and is coming. In the person, the words and deeds of Jesus, in His life, His death, and His resurrection, the Kingdom of God has come, is present, and is coming in an absolutely unique way and with exceptional clarity. In His preaching Jesus divulges the riches, the *thesaurus* of that Kingdom: reconciliation, the forgiveness of sins, victory over demonic powers. Standing within the tradition of Mosaic law, He expounds the core message of the *Thora* and the prophets; He accomplishes the reconciliation of the world to God; He opens the way to the present and future Kingdom which demands decisions of us in all aspects of life.[11]

Liberation

The reign of YHWH includes sovereignty over all forms of oppression, whether economic, political, or spiritual. The exodus is the central story of YHWH's intention to free the Israelites from their bondage, a prototype of the message of liberation for all persons in all situations of bondage. To Moses came the call, "The cry of the Israelites has now come to me; I have also seen how the Egyptians oppress them. So come, I will send you to Pharaoh to bring my people, the Israelites, out of Egypt" (Ex. 3:9–10). Moses responded in fear and trembling. Still, for a generation he and Zipporah worked tirelessly to fulfill the destiny of their liberation into a new land of promise as they developed new leaders such as Joshua, Caleb, and Miriam.

The exodus is the story of memory for every future generation as they face challenges of famine, moral failure, and captivity. Israel also found the need for her own commitment to liberation from her tendencies to become oppressive to the poor. The concept of "jubilee" was developed to ensure protections from permanent disenfranchisement from the land of promise, ensnarement in oppressive debt, and imprisonment without release (Lev. 25:8–55). While it is debatable whether Israel ever lived by the vision of jubilee, Ezra established it in a new covenant for a rebuilt Jerusalem (Neh. 10:30–31). Isaiah envisioned its restoration (Isa. 61), and Jesus placed it at the center of his own proclamation of mission as he read from Isaiah in the synagogue at Nazareth:

"The Spirit of the Lord is upon me,
     because he has anointed me
          to bring good news to the poor.

> He has sent me to proclaim release to the captives
> and recovery of sight to the blind,
>   to let the oppressed go free,
> to proclaim the year of the Lord's favor."
>   (Lk. 4:18–19)

This fourfold imperative of spirituality is clear: where the Spirit inspires, the poor experience the good news of sustenance, all who are captive to human oppression are freed, the eyes of the blind are opened to see God's reality, and God's blessings are experienced. Wright summarizes, "To apply the jubilee model, then, requires that people obey the *sovereignty* of God, trust the *providence* of God, know the story of the *redeeming action* of God, experience personally the sacrificial *atonement* provided by God, practice God's *justice* and put their hope in God's *promise* for the future."[12]

Cross/Resurrection

The cross/resurrection is the central reality of Christian faith, hence, of God's mission. To separate the meaning of Holy Week in the biblical narrative into two discrete events as cross on Good Friday and resurrection on Easter Sunday is to overlook the holism of the meaning of all that happened as one reality. The history of theology has separated the cross as an event in which the fullness of salvation has somehow been accomplished in a sacrificial event, spawning endless debates about its meaning. Yet the Pauline understanding summarized in the earliest historical words on the meaning of Jesus' death unites both in one reality. First Corinthians 15:3–10 reviews the heart of the gospel—death, burial, resurrection, and appearances of the risen Lord. Then the essential connection: "If there is no resurrection of the dead, then Christ has not been raised; and if Christ has not been raised, then our proclamation has been in vain and your faith has been in vain" (1 Cor. 15:13–14).

What is this cross/resurrection reality? *It is that the being of God in the wholeness of God's self was incarnate in Jesus on the cross as presence with all humanity.* God was crucified as an act of identifying love with the pain, suffering, humiliation, oppression, and alienation of the human family. In the words of Douglas John Hall, "The divine love that is ready to suffer birth in human form 'must' follow through, if it is really love for creatures, for *us*. It 'must' suffer life, not only birth; it 'must' suffer death, too."[13]

God who cannot be destroyed entered into death in that cosmic event. God who cannot be captive to death redeems the universe for new life. In cross/resurrection the love of YWHW/Jesus/Holy Spirit brings to completion the *missio Dei*—the creation is restored, humanity is reconciled, the Church has a mission. It participates in the suffering of humanity with the crucified, as Newbigin states: "Yet, paradoxically, his calling is to the way of suffering, rejection, and death—to the way of the cross. He bears witness to the presence of the reign of God not by overpowering the forces of evil, but by taking their full weight upon himself. Yet it is in that seeming defeat the victory is won."[14]

The gospel of John is the only account of crucifixion in which the last words of the crucified were, "It is finished!" What was finished, completed, fulfilled? For Christians, everything! All of the promises of God; all of the hope for a world of justice, peace and mercy embraced by Israel; all of the longed-for visions of a messianic future in which the creation will be redeemed; all of the quest for meaning in life; and an understanding of death as the "last enemy" are fulfilled in cross/resurrection.

And what is the church on mission to do with this central message? The answer is clear: proclaim it and live it. To follow Christ is to enter into suffering love with humanity in all of its disjointed reality in demonstration of the hope that Jesus saves for a life of abundance that can be experienced in spite of suffering. Hall says, "*Discipleship of the crucified Christ is characterized by a faith that drives its adherents into the world with relentlessness and a daring they could not manage on the basis of human volition alone.*"[15]

Consummation

Any understanding of a God who reigns requires an apocalyptic understanding of faith. The biblical notion of time rejects a sequential, developmental view of history that is so characteristic of our modern, rational approach to the calendar. The mission of God as consummation was rooted in the consciousness of an exiled community whose experience was one of suffering. In the midst of the tragic, the human spirit looks beyond the present to a hopeful future. The Church always lives as an exilic community struggling with the questions of "Why?" and "When?" The Hebrew prophetic literature was mostly a description of the failures and disobedience of Israel, with pronouncements of judgment and the offering of a future hope.

The mission of God is teleological; it has an end, a final dénouement. In spite of the secular skepticism of our world about a church that emphasizes "otherworldly" faith, there is a reality beyond the present that is integral to biblical faith. The church lives in between the past and the future. The present is but a hope for a "new heaven and a new earth" that awaits the people of God. Faith is more than what is seen. "Now faith is the assurance of things hoped for, the conviction of things not seen" (Heb. 11:1). To live as a church in God's mission is to live in the expectation that the future that breaks into the present to transform the past is a future that will fulfill all of the meaning of the reign and rule of God in a new realm of reality. The only language that can describe such a reality is ephemeral, mystical, and majestic. This language can only be spoken of in symbolic ways. Barry Harvey suggests, "The purpose of apocalyptic language is not to 'picture' the world, but to position the church-community in right relation to the things, people, events, and institutions that presently constitute it, a relation determined by the course history will take and the consummation that awaits all creation in the messianic kingdom."[16]

It is impossible to live with the discouragement of the struggle for justice and peace, to observe the failures of one's feeble attempts to share the message of the gospel, to accept the disappointments of a congregation that stagnates in apathy and conflict, and experience the judgments on one's leadership as a failure without an abiding hope in a coming new order of the Spirit. The language of Revelation is finally the language of mission:

> Then I saw a new heaven and a new earth; for the first heaven and the first earth had passed away, and the sea was no more. And I saw the holy city, the new Jerusalem, coming down out of heaven from God, prepared as a bride adorned for her husband. And I heard a loud voice from the throne saying,

> "See, the home of God is among mortals.
> He will dwell with them;
> they will be his peoples,
> and God himself will be with them;
> he will wipe every tear from their eyes.
> Death will be no more;
> mourning and crying and pain will be no more,
> for the first things have passed away."
>   (Rev. 21:1–4)

It is this hope of consummation, according to Newbigin, that ties together the promise of covenant with life in human community. He writes,

> In contrast to those forms of spirituality that seek the "real" self by looking within, the Bible invites us to see real human life as a life of shared relationships in a world of living creatures and created things, a life of mutual personal responsibility for the created world, its animal and vegetable life and its resources of soil and water and

air. This, and no other, is the real human life, which is the object of God's primal blessing and of his saving purpose. Consequently, the vision with which the Bible closes is not the vision of a purely "spiritual" existence, but the vision of a city. The city is the symbol of humankind's supreme achievements in "subduing the earth," as it is also the scene of the most horrible perversions of that divine commission. The city of the Apocalypse is a gift of God, not a product of human wisdom. But it is a city, and the city is the place where the human calling to mutual relatedness and the human commission to subdue the earth have their sharpest focus.[17]

The Rule of God's New Order of the Spirit

If the new order of the Spirit is a realm over which YHWH reigns, there must be some standard of guidance for the content of that reality. Whether one calls such guidance laws, principles, or rules of conduct, there is an ethical reality within which residents of the new order must live. The Great Commission to the Church is a three-fold imperative: make disciples, baptize them, and continually teach them "to obey everything that I have commanded you" (Mt. 28:20). A summary of key elements is important to identify for this discussion.

Centering

There is exclusivity in the sovereignty of God. Where God's rule is present, there is expectation of a centering of self, community, and all of reality in the very being of that rule. The progression of the story is one in which time and place change, but the heart of the story does not change. YHWH is and all reality exists in relationship to the creating One. The first word of the Ten Words given Moses is the centering word of faith, "I am the LORD your God" (Ex. 20:2a). The heart of Israel's faith, the *shema* (Deut. 6:4–5), and the heart of Jesus' faith, the great commandment (Mt. 22:34–40), derive from YHWH's identity. To live in the presence of God's new order is to live one's whole being—heart, soul, mind—as an expression of the priority of one's life. Jesus taught the first rule of life was to seek the new order of God (Mt. 6:33); all other human concerns and issues will find a proper relation to that centering rule.

Connecting

Living in the new order of the Spirit is living in loving relationship with the neighbor. If one's life is truly centered in love for God, the consequence is connecting outside the self to the neighbor. The Great Commandment connects love for God with love for neighbor. Like the lawyer who engaged Jesus, we must ask, "And who is my neighbor?" (Lk. 10:29–37). The response of the parable of the compassionate outsider is, "Whoever is in need of mercy."

The Church of every generation has struggled with defining the meaning of salvation as a polarity between one's personal relationship with God and the larger issue of the needs of the people of the world. A vision of the new order of the Spirit has no such polarity, for whatever human need is present in the world is the agenda of neighbor love. Thus, connecting to God's rule is engaging in caring, compassionate support for whatever human need exists; it is confronting injustice in whatever form such might take to bring fairness and rightness to humans and the created order; it is challenging the violence of oppressive systems to bring the peace of God to human experience.[18]

Commitment

One must decide how to respond to the new order of the Spirit of God. At this level the new order inaugurated by Jesus is individual. Each of us has a choice about responding to the invitation of Jesus, "Whoever serves me must follow me" (Jn. 12:26a). A resident of this new order is one who lives in commitment to its sovereign by following the way of Christ in all dimensions of life. This commitment proceeds by way of humble seeking and graceful dependence on the One who calls us to follow. In ourselves, we do not have the means of being the new order or bringing the Spirit's new order to another in our world. We follow Jesus Christ who announced it, is bringing it into human reality, and will gather all of creation to a messianic banquet where justice, mercy, and love rule because none will be hungry and all will be invited.

The Church as a Community of Mission

The most audacious claim of the biblical story is that the new order of God resides in the community of those who respond. The Church is that community of faith that seeks to embody doing the work of God in its very being. Thus, each congregation of the Church has as its primary identity the active work of God in the world. Each is called to become a *missional* congregation. Bosch is correct in his assertion, "God is a missionary God... Mission is thereby seen as a movement to the world; the church is viewed as an instrument for that mission. There is church because there is mission, not vice versa. To participate in mission is to participate in the movement of God's love toward people, since God is a fountain of sending love."[19]

The difficulty of this perspective is that vision is always embraced in a community of struggling, inadequately informed, and unfaithful followers. There is no perfect missional community because every congregation is a collection of humans who live in the grace of a forgiving God. Newbigin summarizes this understanding of church well:

It is, during most of its history, a weak, divided, and unsuccessful community. But because it is the community that lives by and bears witness to the risen life of the crucified Lord, it is the place where the reign of God is actually present and at work in the midst of history, and where the mission of Jesus is being accomplished... And I believe that the reign of God is present in the midst of this sinful, weak, and divided community, not through any power of goodness of its own, but because God has called and chosen this company of people to be the bearers of his gift on behalf of all people.[20]

One of the cautions one must offer in response to the plethora of missional church literature these days is the tendency to offer a description of one kind of church as missional. Unfortunately, the characteristics one often reads is of church that is contemporary in worship style, new in terms of its formation, growing in terms of size, and innovative in everything it does. Rather, the challenge of contemporary pastoral leadership is to plant the vision of a new order of the Spirit mentality within the fabric and framework of every congregation, regardless of its size, age, organization, or theological perspective. Craig Van Gelder stresses the essence of the missional church rather than its form when he writes:

The genetic code of the missional church means it is missionary in its very nature or essence... In being true to their missional identity they can never function primarily as an end within themselves— the tendency of the self-understanding of the established church. In being true to their missional identity, missional congregations can never be satisfied with maintaining primarily a functional relationship to their contexts and communities—the tendency of the self-understanding of the corporate church. The missional church has a different genetic code.[21]

Every gathering of Jesus followers has within it the capacity to grow in learning and applying a missional vision in its midst. This is to suggest that in every dimension of its life—worship, fellowship, education, and outreach to the world—there is a missional perspective. No two congregations will ever look identical. The pressure for conformity is a temptation to be avoided so that each faith group may prayerfully seek of God's Spirit how it is to be effective in growing in God's mission. Thus, the mission strategist affirms the variety of congregational forms, the differences in practice, and even plurality in how each defines its perceptions of God's work in its midst. Congregational leadership, therefore, must seek to clarify a uniqueness of identity that is consistent with its context and human life rather than some ideal proposed by the "missional expert." Bosch, following the thinking of Newbigin, "suggests that the only hermeneutic of the gospel is a congregation of men and women who believe it and live by it."[22]

6

Flat World and Fluid Neighborhoods

The rapid pace of cultural change, the new fluidity in which we live, and the emergence of new strains and endless variations of human understanding make the distinction between the church and the culture difficult to ignore.

ERWIN MCMANUS[1]

Hopeful congregations understand that factors outside their common life have an impact on accomplishing congregational mission. One of the deadliest temptations for the average congregation is the assumption that attention to the internal life of the community alone is adequate for effective leading. Change is endemic within our culture and failure to understand the dynamics of change and their impact in a given setting will often lead to misunderstanding the challenges of contemporary ministry.

Understanding Macro Change: The "Big Picture"

A new word was introduced into the vocabulary of those born after 1980 on December 26, 2004; it was the word *tsunami*. An estimated 245,000 people died as the result of a 9.0 earthquake and subsequent tidal wave in Southeast Asia that affected fourteen nations in the region.

Tsunami is a Japanese word introduced to the English world in 1897, meaning "harbor wave."[2] The massive earthquake and tsunami that devastated Japan in 1896 killed 30,000 people and brought new awareness to the modern world of the impact of earthquakes under the sea. It was in the following year that *National Geographic* printed the word and it gradually entered the English language as a familiar word.

Earthquakes and tsunamis are a natural part of the geological world, existing for centuries; but only in the twentieth century has media technology created the reality of observing the suffering and the devastation from them as they happen. The news of the Japanese earthquake and tsunami of March 15, 2011, traveled faster around the world than the jetliner speed of the ocean wave rolling across the Pacific. Residents of the U.S. West Coast knew of the patterns of waves moving toward their coastline before they arrived from the quake near Japan.

It is relatively easy to recognize the impact of natural catastrophes and storms. Some, such as thunderstorms, are short-lived and effect relatively small areas of geography or numbers of people. Hurricanes enlarge both the geography of impact and the shattering of human lives, especially when intense like Katrina on the Gulf Coast of the U.S. in September 2005, or Sandy in the Northeast in November 2012. Whenever the earth shakes with high Richter scale intensity, especially when nuclear power plants are damaged, the consequences may be catastrophic and last for generations.

Cultural change reshapes the social landscape and, though not as dramatically as disasters, alters communities and congregations. Understanding this reality is a part of the leading of healthy congregations if one is to make sense of the environment in which people are impacted in how they think about faith. The apostle Paul was a model of flexibility when he sought to impart the power of the gospel in a variety of both Hebraic and Hellenistic cultures in which he travelled, lived, and worked. His principle, "I have become all things to all people, that I might by all means save some" (1 Cor. 9:22), is a call to understand the context in which one seeks to do the mission of God in the world.

Few pastoral leaders have the time or skill to be specialists in cultural anthropology or sociology. Yet, some understanding of what is happening in the world will impact the strategies of ministry at the congregational level. In my recent research with pastors in metropolitan Atlanta I asked each of them, "Think with me about the changes that have taken place in the context in which you serve. What challenges do churches face today that are different from ten years ago? Twenty years ago? Thirty years ago?" While each of them was clear that change was underway that made their work more challenging, none of them articulated the drama of change that is apparent in our global world. They could state such insights as: "People are less willing to commit to the church than in the past," or, "Our people live in a consumerist society with a consumerist mentality that says, 'What can your church do for me?'" Contemporary leading needs a framework for understanding the radical change that is underway and how it impacts the work of the congregation.

Cultural Change: A Subtle Reality

Unlike the immediate consciousness of the impact of a natural disaster, the effects of cultural change are subtle and often understandable only in looking in hindsight at the alterations of the social fabric. Cultural changes occur at varying levels of intensity and speed, but over time make significant adjustments in the values, perspectives, and lifestyles of the people affected by them. I have drawn from the categories of change developed by Tobin Smith to monitor the adoption of new technologies in the marketplace as a basis for recommending specific stocks. The following concepts are his, but the definitions are my own as rubrics for understanding the varieties of cultural change:

- ChangeQuake: The eruption of new, potentially transformational technological, political, economic, or religious events that alter the values, perspectives, or lifestyles of a population or global region. The impact of clearing virgin rain forests in a region of aboriginal tribes is a changequake within their culture. The uprisings against long-term dictator regimes in the Middle East in 2011 had the potential of such a radical change. A changequake is change with the highest potential for significant and lasting change.
- ChangeWave: The impact of a changequake within specific organizations or institutions that alters their identity, effectiveness, or methods of functioning. The impact of the Internet (a changequake) on global communication alters the way all businesses function and changes missionary methods for the church in transformational ways (a changewave). The changewave is a trend established by a changequake. Monitoring the changewaves that ripple through the social order is a critical skill for mission strategists.
- Monster ChangeQuake: An unanticipated dramatic global economic, political, military or technological event that reverberates throughout the social order with immediate and significant consequences. The meltdown of the global financial system in 2008 is an example of a monster changequake with consequences (changewaves) for congregations that continue five years after the primary events.
- ChangeStorm. The cyclical events in the culture that spread more slowly through networks of people and organizations with less dramatic impact, but that affect selected populations and institutions. Religious revivals or cycles of secularity are changestorms that are observable throughout Church history.

Postmodernism: Crumbling of the Foundations

The fundamental changequake that most affects the context for religious entities is a century-long realignment of the foundational cultural ethos, primarily of the West, but increasingly across the globe. The philosophers of culture call it *postmodernism* to describe what has come after the centuries-long era of modernity.

If the question were posed to the contemporary scholar of culture or a current seminarian, "What is happening in the culture that is having the greatest impact on the Church?" the likely response would be, "We are living in a new postmodern culture, and churches have not begun to understand its impact!" So, a brief summary of this cultural transformation that is clearly underway is an important part of the "knowing intelligence" of the contemporary leader.

Culture evolves through a variety of forms as a part of the development of human history and knowing where we are is important. Sociologist Robert Bellah described the impact of cultural change in an insightful description of five principal eras of culture: primal, archaic, historic, early modern, and modern.[3] Cultures evolve from primal through to modern; they become increasingly complex and pluralistic. The tribe is central in primal cultures and the individual has little identity apart from it. In modern cultures, the individual is central and personal identity is often unconnected from the community. The roles in politics, faith, economics, tribe, and family multiply and become more sharply defined with historical developments. Forms of communication must become more sophisticated to cross the differences in culture, and values become identified with groups within the culture rather than with the cultural as a whole. Philosophically, monism is replaced by heterogeneity, and theological orthodoxy is replaced by theological diversity or heterodoxy.

A different structure of economic, political, and religious life emerged to reflect the shape of each of the cultural realities Bellah described. Many thinkers are now grappling with a current era of change that is increasingly viewed as a major shift to postmodernism. It is a changequake!

What is this new reality? Phyllis Tickle has provided the most accessible description I know in her thesis that every five hundred years or so a major transformation has impacted the culture and subsequently the Church. The first was what she called "the Great Schism," the separation of Eastern Orthodoxy from the Western Roman Catholic hierarchy. The second was the Protestant Reformation, with formation of multiple new religious families in reaction to the authority of Rome. And the third current transformation in which we are living she calls "The Great Emergence."[4]

In each of these eras of dislocation of the familiar, the authority structure foundational to Christianity of the respective era was questioned. The Church then had to shed those structures and practices that no longer fit the new realities of questioned authority; she describes such as the Church having a "rummage sale."[5] The third stage in the transformation of the culture setting for the church was the development of a new understanding of the foundations or the authority structure on which the Church could be built. The authority of the Early Church before the "Great Schism" was the creedal structure of early councils that defined orthodoxy for a united Christendom. The authority of the medieval culture following the schism of the East and West was the Roman Catholic Church itself, with powerful popes and bishops. The Reformation shifted authority to the Bible and away from the Church, a foundation that proved durable for the last five hundred years. With the crumbling of the foundation of a grand story such as the one provided by the Bible, postmodernism is in a process of shedding its commitment to one story and moving toward multiple ones; moving from one understanding of faith to many, from Church to communities of faith defined by followers, and from the Bible to the Spirit. The new era of the "Great Emergence" is one in which the individual is central, the Bible can be interpreted according to the values of those communities interpreting it, and experience replaces sets of common belief such as creeds and confessions of faith. Such intensity of change is a significant challenge to the Western Church as an institution.

This changequake in the culture has become a philosophical approach to reality that describes the culture as postmodern. Depending on the philosophy of choice, the dominant theme may be that of tearing down the culture (destroy the remaining elements of modernity) or developing a new cultural understanding of reality (constructing new understandings of reality in postmodernism). Stanley Grenz offers helpful summaries of the reality:

> But postmodernism did not gain wide attention until the 1970s. First it denoted a new style of architecture. Then it invaded academic circles, originally as a label for theories expounded in university English and philosophy departments. Eventually it surfaced as the description for a broader cultural phenomenon.
>
> Whatever else it might be, as the name suggests, postmodernism signifies the quest to move beyond modernism. Specifically, it involves a rejection of the modern mind-set, but launched under the conditions of modernity. Therefore, to understand postmodern thinking, we must view it in the context of the modern world that gave it birth and against which it is reacting.[6]

Grenz suggested three consequences of this new reality: (1) there is no sense that knowledge is inherently good; (2) the idea of truth as inherently certain and rational is rejected; and (3) there is no reality of objective truth. The last of these consequences is the most devastating for traditional expressions of Christian faith rooted in an authoritative statement of faith as universal. All forms of truth, including scientific truth, are relative, so that truth "is historically and culturally conditioned and that our knowledge is always incomplete."[7]

This reality creates a major challenge for the gospel. If there is no absolute truth, how does the contemporary Christian speak of a biblical story, a metanarrative that has meaning for all persons in all settings, regardless of their culture? Those who interpret our new context best, it seems to me, emphasize an understanding of church that moves from the highly individualistic perspective of the modern congregation to one that emphasizes the communitarian impact of faith in Jesus Christ. Thus, the call of a postmodern culture is a call to the church to live as communities of vibrant faith focused on being the presence of Jesus Christ in the world—missional churches. Insight is offered by Grenz in his conclusion as to the church's response to postmodernity:

> In the postmodern world, we can no longer follow the lead of modernity and position the individual at center stage. Instead, we must remind ourselves that our faith is highly social. The fact that God is the social Trinity—Father, Son and Spirit—gives us some indication that the divine purpose for creation is directed toward the individual-in-relationship. Our gospel must address the human person within the context of the communities in which people are embedded.[8]

The Impact of Globalization: The Kingdom of the Consumer

The second major changequake transforming the context for contemporary congregational leadership is the consequence of major technological innovations in the twentieth century. First came the radio with its capacity to broadcast beyond local settings to increasingly larger territories. Then, television, with the advent of satellites in space, could provide instantaneous communication to any place of human habitation on the globe where people could afford it.[9] Add the Internet, and such communication became individualized—persons could now communicate with each other with few borders. Thomas Friedman suggests the expansion of broadband communication that resulted in high-speed cable across the oceans and innovations in software opened the world to the sharing of any form of information. Instant virtual communication makes the decentralization of work possible and the exchange of goods and services global: the Flat World.[10] The consequence is the employment of cheaper labor markets for the production of the world's goods and services so those with the resources can consume nearly any product that can be grown or made for shipping to any market in the world. Affluent Americans can now consume any product in the world economy. We can purchase produce from the most distant farms, or goods from the supply chain of manufacturing. We have choices in ways unparalleled in the past! The culture is now centered in consumerism, and where there are consumers, any resource can be available. The latest soft drink dispensers allow one to choose from 120 options of the drink to be consumed!

A culture of consumerism in economics has impact on the choices people make in their religious lives. If individuals have nearly unlimited choices in the goods and services they can purchase, the exercise of choice extends beyond what they buy, to all choices. It is what Friedman calls "multiple identity disorder,"[11] which forces all elements of the society to define for themselves their choices. When we have unlimited choices, limited only by income, we can shop in the "big box" store or the neighborhood boutique, the automotive superstore or the Craigslist classified, the massive bookstore or download our books from the Internet, or eat in a chain restaurant or the "mom and pop" diner.

Such choice is easily translated into how people respond to the options for faith. Thumma and Travis capture well how the new consumerism enhances the appeal of the megachurch:

> It is absolutely clear that Americans have become more comfortable with large institutional forms. Since the 1950s, hospitals, schools, stores, factories, and entertainment centers have all grown to mega proportions; therefore, why shouldn't churches? Americans have not only grown accustomed to large organizations, but they have even had their character and tastes shaped by them. From the moment of birth, large hospitals, schools, theaters, malls, and amusement parks have been teaching us how to read signs, how to find our path through a maze of hallways, how to wait in lines, how to recall where we parked in a vast lot, how to cope with cavernous indoor spaces, how to watch large video screens, and how to assert ourselves in a crowd if we have a question or need something. The megachurch assumes all of these skills of its members. The megachurch takes

for granted that those coming to church also work, shop, and play in similar institutional forms.[12]

Such a choice is just one of many options, however. The reality is a multiplicity of congregational forms from small to large, informal to liturgical, traditional to contemporary, conservative to liberal, and denominational to independent. Individuals have the choice of whether they will participate in any of them. If they so choose, which ones? No wonder many congregational leaders are mystified by what their identity should be in a world of choice—multiple identity disorder.

Demography: People Matter Most

The third major changequake is the impact of demographic change around the world. Population growth is the first evidence of such change. The world population has grown from approximately 2.5 billion people in 1950 to more than 7 billion people in the world today. The population has grown consistently over the past century, though the rate of growth slowed toward the end of the twentieth century as a result of declining birth rates. Even so, the most recent estimates by the United Nations of world population project a total population of more than 9 billion people by 2043.[13] What is most significant is the leveling of growth in developed regions of the world while growth remains unabated in the undeveloped regions, especially in Africa.

With this growth of population, a process of mobility is quickly transforming the global population into urban centers to which people from the rural hinterlands flow for employment and improved economic life, especially in societies where rural poverty remains high. In 1950, 600 million people lived in global urban places. Presently, half of the global population lives in urban places. The rise of megacities around the world is reshaping the social networks and redefining centers of economic and cultural power. If one looks at size alone as the measure of influence, best estimates of global city population in 2010 indicate that of the twenty largest cities, only three are in the West of the Northern Hemisphere.[14]

When other measures than population size are included in assessing the influence of a city, the geography of importance changes significantly. The 2010 Global Cities Index, a collaboration between Foreign Policy, management consulting firm A.T. Kearney, and The Chicago Council on Global Affairs, ranks the world's largest cities on twenty-five metrics across five dimensions of urban life: business activity, human capital, information exchange, cultural experience, and political engagement.[15] An examination of the top twenty-five cities of "global influence" shows the continuing influence

Table 6.1: 2010 Estimates of Population of Twenty Largest Urban Places

Rank	City, Nation	Estimated Population
1	Tokyo, Japan	32,450,000
2	Seóul, South Korea	20,550,000
3	Mexico City, Mexico	20,450,000
4	New York City, USA	19,750,000
5	Mumbai, India	19,200,000
6	Jakarta, Indonesia	18,900,000
7	Sáo Paulo, Brazil	18,850,000
8	Delhi, India	18,680,000
9	Ōsaka/Kobe, Japan	17,350,000
10	Shanghai, China	16,650,000
11	Manila, Philippines	16,300,000
12	Los Angeles, USA	15,250,000
13	Calcutta, India	15,100,000
14	Moscow, Russian Fed.	15,000,000
15	Cairo, Egypt	14,450,000
16	Lagos, Nigeria	13,488,000
17	Buenos Aires, Argentina	13,170,000
18	London, United Kingdom	12,875,000
19	Beijing, China	12,500,000
20	Karachi, Pakistan	11,800,000

of the traditional urban places of Europe and the United States. However, the trends are clearly shifting, as the editors of Foreign Policy summarize their findings on the index:

We are at a global inflection point. Half the world's population is now urban—and half the world's most global cities are Asian... In 2010, five of the world's 10 most global cities are in Asia and the Pacific: Tokyo, Hong Kong, Singapore, Sydney, and Seoul.

Three—New York, Chicago, and Los Angeles—are American cities. Only two—London and Paris—are European. And there's no question which way the momentum is headed; just as more people will continue to migrate from farms to cities, more global clout will move from West to East.[16]

If population growth is a major change factor, so also is the pluralism of that growth. Nowhere is this more evident than the United States. Diversity is ingrained into U.S. history as a result of the growth of the Black population from the unfortunate history of slavery, and settlement of the nation by waves of immigration in the nineteenth and early twentieth centuries. More recently, the change in immigration policy created by the Immigration and Naturalization Act of 1965 opened the United States to immigrants from Asia, Africa, and Latin America. When one adds the impact of illegal immigration the past four decades, the Church in the U.S. ministers in a context of unprecedented diversity.

In 1950, the population of the United States was slightly more than 152 million people, with 89.5 percent Caucasian. By 2010, the population had more than doubled to 308.7 million persons, with 63.7 percent Caucasian, 16.3 percent Hispanic/Latino, 12.2 percent Black, 4.7 percent Asian, and 1.9 percent more than one race.[17] The same study identifies 91.7 percent of all growth in the past decade as growth of the minority populations of the country. Consequently, Diana Eck labels the U.S. "the most religiously diverse nation on earth" with the growth of Buddhist, Hindu, Muslim and other world religion groups."[18]

Understanding Congregational Context: The Local Environment

The global changequakes described above develop into changewaves within more local contexts. Postmodernism, consumerism, and demographic shifts make their way across the boundaries of nations and settle in our towns and cities to bring new trends in the social structures of our local environments.

The Flow of Change

Change affects communities at differing rates and in differing ways. The flow of change is multidimensional. There are centers of change and recipients of that change as it trickles from the centers of change to the hinterland where their adoption may take years to have an impact. The consequences are that some communities are early adopters of new realities, while others are subcultures of stability and resistance to change.

Change flows in multiple directions. The first direction is the flow from the seacoasts to inland communities. Seacoast cities are the ports-of-entry for new global products, ideas, and immigrants from overseas locations. Those products, ideas, and people over time make their way to the inland towns and cities that soon become recipients of the trends of change.

Large cities, wherever they are located, are a second source of change. The flow of change is from the major cities to smaller cities, then towns, and eventually the rural hinterland. These different directions of change explain the stability and seeming resistance to cultural change in isolated and small communities. The values of a highly urbanized population are quite different from a small community because of the time change takes. Stephen Johnson's creative work on the flow of ideas suggests, "When you share a common civic culture with thousands of other people, good ideas have a tendency to flow from mind to mind, even when their creators try to keep them secret. 'Spillover' is the right word; it captures the essential liquidity of information in dense settlements."[19]

The third source of change is major research centers, usually associated with a major university. Places like Silicon Valley; Austin, Texas; Boston; and the Research Triangle in North Carolina are important regions for emerging technologies and new industries.

Major media centers are the source of major changes in values. The music, television, and movie centers of Southern California, Orlando, Detroit, New York, London, Paris, and Mumbai are the sources of changing values that reshape ideas and social values. Even the residents of subcultural communities who may seem quite isolated from many changes adopt the values communicated through the media, values that are often at variance with the values of the gospel.

Generations: We Cannot All Be Young!

A significant changewave to which churches must adapt is the differing understandings of one's generation in how faith is defined and practiced. Social theorists suggest that each generation develops a worldview and lifestyle based on the events in the culture during late adolescence and early adulthood.[20] Change occurs from generation to generation, with older generations maintaining the traditional values of their youthful life experience while younger groups embrace new values and perspectives. Much of the change identified above is most evident among those born since 1980, a generation the Pew Research Center calls "millennials." Competing currents of understanding reality flow within generational groupings. Since older persons are more involved in churches, the congregation often becomes a bastion of traditionalism based on experiences of faith when the older leaders were young. Church becomes defined by what was relevant when today's leaders were young adults.

The Pew Research Center conducted a survey of millennials in January, 2010, that should inform every congregational leader committed to missional relevance in the second decade of the twenty-first century. Pew researchers identified five generational groupings:

- The Millennial generation refers to those born after 1980—the first generation to come of age in the new millennium.
- Generation X describes people born from 1965 through 1980. The label long ago overtook the first name affixed to this generation: the Baby Busters. Xers are often depicted as savvy, entrepreneurial loners.
- The Baby Boomer label is drawn from the spike in birth rates that began in 1946, right after the end of World War II, and ended almost as abruptly in 1964, around the time the birth control pill went on the market. It's a classic example of a demography-driven name.
- The Silent generation describes adults born from 1928 through 1945. Children of the Great Depression and World War II, their "Silent" label refers to their conformist and civic instincts. It also makes for a nice contrast with the noisy ways of the anti-establishment Boomers.
- The Greatest Generation (those born before 1928) "saved the world" when it was young, in the memorable phrase of Ronald Reagan. It's the generation that fought and won World War II.[21]

While the Pew study documents a full range of attitudes on values, politics, and work, the focus for our work is on the religious differences within these generational groupings. Generally speaking, the millennials are increasingly unaffiliated with any religious tradition, while older generations remain relatively committed to traditional expressions of faith. Robert D. Putnam and David E. Campbell describe this trend as a new form of polarization within American society. The strong social bonds within families and the growing social networks prevent the emerging differences from destroying the unity of the society.[22]

To be sure, the polarization is real. Millennials are more likely to express liberal views on the family, acceptance of homosexuality, and civil liberties than older ones. They are more accepting of government solutions to social problems, are more liberal on political issues, but are less likely to be regular voters.[23] Religiously, when compared to older cohorts, they are slightly less likely to be affiliated with a religious tradition, less likely to pray daily, more likely to "drop out" of previous religious affiliations or attend less if they do not, less likely to consider religion as "very important" in all religious traditions, less certain in their belief in God, less certain in the authority of the Bible, more open to the legality of abortion, more tolerant of making pornography legal, and more accepting of homosexuality. However, they are more likely than older groups to affirm their belief in an afterlife, heaven, hell, and angels and demons. They just are not as certain of only one way of obtaining eternal life.[24]

While he identifies different understandings of change than those proposed here, Anthony Robinson has proposed an excellent summary of the many ways the ministry of the church is challenged by our changing culture. He states, "In summary the key factors in the religious sea of change have been: (1) the gradual disestablishment of Protestant Christianity and the emergence of an officially secular society; (2) the growth in North America of other religions and the emergence of a religiously and culturally pluralistic society; and (3) the infusion of a consumer ethos—and with it choice—into the area of religion and spirituality, resulting in the emergence of a large and ever-changing menu of spiritual choices. All in all, we're not in Kansas anymore!"[25] I would suggest even Kansas is not in Kansas anymore!

Implications for the Church

Some congregational leaders will read this description of the contextual realities of change with anxiety or even despair. Clearly the challenges for the local congregation are quite different from the challenges of previous generations. Yet, Christian leaders have been called to provide creative responses in every generation. The changes described above have affected different faith communities with various levels of challenge. The most vulnerable to this description have been traditional mainline Protestant denominations and congregations. Conservative-evangelical groups and churches in the historical Black traditions have been affected less, as have more insulated groups such as the Church of Jesus Christ of Latter Day Saints and small sect-like groups that resist the larger culture in their theology and practice. The greatest impact for Roman Catholic parishes has come from the rapid growth of the Latino population, forcing major changes in their demography and approaches to ministry.

Yet, the hopeful response to these data is for congregations to understand their settings for ministry and innovate new forms of connection to a growing population outside the church. The healthy congregation of the future must find ways to connect with and incorporate worship, spiritual practices, and organizational structures that will appeal to a technologically savvy youth culture. The real question is: How do we do this without alienating those whose commitments remain strong to the traditions that have brought us to this place, and which are being increasingly rejected by the young? The answer calls for new ways of "doing" church, and to this challenge we turn.

7

Congregational Ecology

The congregation remains the bedrock of the American religious system. It is in congregations that religious commitment is nurtured and through them that most voluntary religious activity is nurtured.

STEPHEN WARNER[1]

Every congregation, no matter its size or effectiveness, has a structure. It is a system and includes all of the essential elements of any human system. These include:

- A boundary that separates the congregation from its environment;
- A collection of people that gathers for specific purposes;
- A set of core values, whether stated or assumed, that define why it exists and what it hopes to accomplish;
- A way of relating to persons and entities external to it; and
- visible results, either positive or negative, from its multiple activities.

This structure may be formal, clearly understood, and easily articulated. Or, it may be "fuzzy," undefined, or informally understood as a kind of hidden reality.[2] Whichever the case may be, persons leading the congregation must understand the congregation if they are to be effective.

The following description is a summary of varieties of congregational life. Multiple systems have been developed in congregational studies to describe this variety, and most have an organizing principle upon which their descriptions are based. These include the variables of size,[3] organizational structure,[4] classical mythological designations,[5] empirical designations[6] models for understanding conflict,[7] and interactions between them and their communities.[8] Most of these descriptions are logical, rational, and coherent, providing typologies that can be descriptive, but are never exhaustive.

For instance, the sociological categories of sect/denomination/church or numerical designations of micro, small, medium, large, and mega have been used widely, but when one begins ascribing a specific designation to an individual congregation, they are usually of limited usefulness.

A verbal understanding of ministry calls for a more organic, even ethereal view of the congregation that often defies logic or comprehensive description. Rather than descriptions that emphasize, "small churches need leaders who _____," organic descriptions are fluid and mysterious. The best one can do is to offer a metaphor such as, "Our church is like a garden full of weeds in which an occasional brilliant flower breaks forth in splendid bloom," or, "It is difficult to describe what our folks believe about the Trinity because most of them are like freshly planted seeds, having been baptized fewer than three years." Even the most organized of congregations often prove difficult for those leading them because the bylaws are ignored, committees compete for each other's responsibilities, or fallible humans rehash the same issues over and over.

The summaries that follow are based on efforts to understand the way congregations work without becoming mechanistic in describing them.

Organic Congregations

Cell Systems

The foundational structure of the universe is a cell. Cells in the biological world are the building blocks of the growth of an organism. While there is no effort here to make a biological model the basis for understanding human groups, there are certainly analogies between the elements of a cell in nature and a cell congregation. Much of the congregational life of the New Testament is descriptive of what are cell congregations. Most were house churches that included an extended family of a central believer, and were seldom larger than sixty to seventy people.[9] Jesus concluded one of only two uses of the word for "church" with a summary of the power of the few in shaping the community of faith: "Again, truly I tell you, if two of you agree on earth about anything you ask, it will be done for you by my Father in heaven. For where two or three are gathered in my name, I am there among them" (Mt. 18:19–20).

Structures of Cell Congregations

There is no normative description of a cell church. Every cell has a unique identity based on the foundations of its origin and the way it which it develops over time. But there are some common characteristics of the cell church.

First, every cell has a *nucleus*—the center of the cell from which the cell's energy is generated. For congregational cells, the nucleus is two people who share a vision of what the cell can become as the presence of Christ. In most cell churches that nucleus is a couple called by God to form a small group of people who intend to become an outpost of God's mission. The health of any cell is dependent on the vitality and health of the nucleus out of which it is formed.

The second element of the cell church is a set of *core values* that shape the identity of the cell as church. Core values are inherent theological convictions that define what some have called the "DNA" of the church. These foundational values testify to what the cell members believe, the meaning of faith, and the practices that will shape the relationships within the cell. Often these values remain unspoken until the cell grows into an organism of people who become a community of trust and love.

Collective relationships form the third element of the cell. Cells are high touch organisms where intimacy is an inherent value. The quality of the relationships that emerge in the cell determine the growth of any cell group.

Finally, every cell must have a *cell membrane*, a boundary that defines who belongs and who does not belong in the cell. In reality, most cells in their origin are quite homogeneous in terms of some specific boundaries that define who they are. Most often these become human identifiers of age, ethnicity, race, family, education level, or other human characteristics. Such homogeneity can be expanded only by a central theological identity that serves as the unifying element of the cell. A cell whose chosen boundary is to become a more diverse unit must have a larger vision of Jesus Christ as the unifier across the cell's human differences.

How Cells Grow

Multiple processes lead to the growth of cell congregations. In nature, cells grow into organisms by the process of division. As the cell reaches a certain size, the nucleus divides into two similar nuclei to form two cells that grow and then divide again.

Congregational cells that develop into larger groups apply this concept well and intentionally in their growth. This principle recognizes an ideal size for a cell. Most group theorists suggest that a cell usually stagnates or fragments if it does not divide when it grows to a size of 12–15 people. Intentional cell growth will focus on the development of new nuclei from within the cell group. These people must be committed to launching a new cell that then requires more complexity as multiple cells interact with each other. This process can be visualized as follows:

Figure 7.1: Cell Congregation Division

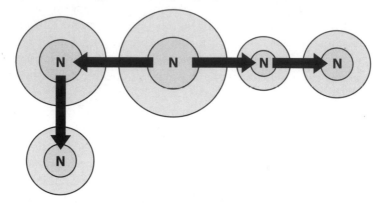

Implementing such a process of growth can result in a vibrant congregation of multiple cells with a high degree of similarity. When the number of cells reaches four to six, a change in the organism is necessary to provide the connective resources for the cells to function together as one congregational unit. Usually this change involves a common experience of collective worship in which the multiple cells gather monthly or weekly to unite in praise, study, giving, and development of collective mission outreach.

My thesis states that when as many as ten cells are formed, a different form of congregational life must be developed. If the congregation does not develop such a new life, the cell structures will tend to stabilize into a small congregation in which people begin leaving the cells. Intimacy becomes more difficult to maintain as individual cells separate to form their own congregations, or as individuals leave the cell group. Thus, the energy of the body becomes focused on replacement of departing participants rather than the development of new participants.

The reality of cell church growth is as likely to be a process of grafting as it is cell division. Multiple cells composed of quite different groupings of people are formed as individual cells without previous connection graft into an original cell. This is especially characteristic of multiethnic congregations formed around individual cells of distinct groups with their own identity. In these cases, the integration of the congregation must occur almost exclusively in worship. As individual cells grow, they tend to move away from the multi-cell congregation to form their own congregation as an identifiable, homogenous group.

This is the pattern of a highly innovative congregation in Clarkston, Georgia, called Cellebration Fellowship. The fellowship has been the dream

Figure 7.2: The Multi-Cell Congregation

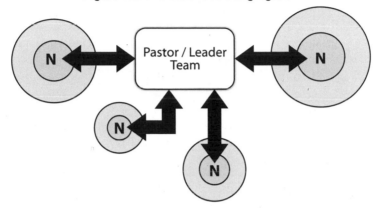

of the pastor Dave Lambert and his wife Marg for the past sixteen years. They live in the center of a major international community of refugees. They connect newcomers in their community at the local World Relief refugee center and use their home as the center of hospitality. House churches of ethnic congregations are formed. An elder for each language/ethnic group leads weekly Bible study and prayer. Each month the house churches worship together. The international worship times include multiple languages and worship traditions in a highly diverse congregational experience. Over time, the pattern has been for the individual house churches to grow into ethnic congregations, leaving the larger group. This creates the challenge of reaching new groups of people for the church.

Challenges of Cell Congregations

Given the informality and fluidity of cell churches, a leader faces a basic challenge—a lack of thorough research on culture of the nuclei. One of the major limitations of the research that decries the decline of Christianity in the West and America in particular is the ignorance of the vitality and extent of these informal communities of faith. Globally, there are thousands of Christian cell groups, from Latin American base groups to small African tribal groups to European, Chinese, and American house churches.

No one knows the true extent or size of this organic church movement that is often more akin to the New Testament pattern of church than more programmatic, denominational congregations that are the focus of most research. Lisa Miller reported the findings of the Pew Forum on Religion and Public Life, that "seven percent of Americans say they 'attend services in someone's home.'"[10] Such statistics makes the "decline of church" narrative of popular news less potent! Based on the limited case studies and research of such groups, some challenges can be clearly identified.

First, there is the issue of intimacy boundaries. Given the intimacy of these groups, stories abound of small groups in which relational boundaries are crossed sexually, emotionally, or theologically. There is little control possible in such informal groups, and leading such congregations requires the highest degree of personal honesty, integrity, and theological fidelity if God is to be honored within them.

Toxic members can have a profound effect in small groups. If the nucleus or participants of a group are made up of controlling personalities, persons with dysfunctional emotional illnesses, or unskilled group leaders, significant harm can be done to participants in such groups. Cell groups will be only as healthy as the leaders around which they are formed.

A third challenge is the tendency for cell congregations to become reflective of the family agendas of their participants. Many of the small congregations of all kinds are family churches in which one or several family units control the practices of the congregation. Too many established rural congregations in America are cell churches that function as microcosms of the patriarchal or matriarchal families that control them. Few of these congregations are able to fulfill the potential of God's mission in their settings unless there is mature pastoral leadership able to relate to the family systems of the church.

For all of the challenges of the cell congregation, this organic understanding of congregation is one in which multiple opportunities for the development of innovative and emergent congregations are possible. These are churches that can function with fewer maintenance costs because they seldom own property or facilities. The tradeoff is finding space in which to meet, and there are always tasks required for any gathering. Ministers who are committed to leading missional congregations will find the cell model a useful one in planting new congregations with the potential of growing into significant outposts of God's presence in the world. They can be especially attractive to the postmodern seminary graduates who long for opportunities to follow Jesus into creating a new wineskin of God's new order.

Pastor-centered Micro Churches

The predominant form of congregation in the American context is the micro church with fewer than 100 weekly participants. According to the findings of the U.S. Congregational Life survey of more than 500,000 persons in more than 2,000 congregations, the median size of all congregations, including both Protestant and Catholic congregations, was 277 people associated with the congregation with 130 participating on a regular basis and 95 in average worship attendance.[11] If one looks only at Protestant churches, the size factor ranges from one-half to more than two-thirds of congregations with fewer than 100 weekly worshipers.[12] When one considers that medium-sized and larger churches are most likely to participate in such surveys, and nondenominational and independent congregations tend not to participate, it is fair to say 70 percent of Protestant churches are smaller than 100 people gathering in weekly worship.

While many of these smaller churches desire trained pastoral leaders, a significant portion do not have them. Lay persons, part-time student pastors, or bi-vocational pastors lead many of these small congregations. As mentioned earlier, Carroll found, "18 percent of mainline Protestants, 29 percent of conservative Protestants, and 41 percent of clergy in historic black denominations are bi-vocational."[13] Many small rural and more independent groups such as Southern Baptists have nearly 40 percent of their clergy as bi-vocational, with as much as half being so in some locales.[14]

Size is less determinative of the leading process for these smaller churches than other factors. The context in which such churches are located is crucial, with many of them in formerly vibrant rural communities that are now depressed in population and opportunities for creative ministry. The most likely role of the pastor in these settings is to provide a chaplaincy function of caring for an aging and declining membership. Such is a valid ministry; few younger, seminary-trained leaders demonstrate interest in such settings. Retired, bi-vocational, or lay pastors serve most of them.

Another factor that limits leading opportunities in the micro church is the openness of the leadership to change. The older the congregation since it's founding and the older the membership that comprises it, the greater the resistance to new initiatives even in contexts that offer opportunities for growth. There is perhaps no more difficult small church to lead than one located for decades in a rural setting that has been enveloped by the expansion of urban areas. One can find decades-old church buildings in which twenty to thirty long-time members gather for worship as it has always been—surrounded by new subdivisions of young and professional families to whom there is little capacity to appeal.

Family systems theory as it is applied to the congregation has been one of the most helpful resources to develop in the past three decades. Analyses of the church as family often reveals small congregations "stuck" in patterns of rigidity that prevent much potential for change. Ronald Richardson's analysis of congregational systems that function "enmeshed" or "isolated" is especially helpful in understanding these small congregations. Only wise and long-term leading by a well-trained pastor with enormous patience will change these kinds of patterns.[15]

Family systems theory is also useful in understanding the power structure of older small congregations. Often their potential is limited by the presence of a powerful patriarch or matriarch who can and will control the decisions of the congregation. When one adds the influence of individuals who are toxic in their personalities, perpetual conflicts tend to debilitate the congregation from any significant change.

For all of the stagnant and difficult small congregations, there are thousands of smaller churches that offer opportunities for leading in innovative applications of God's mission in their settings. Most pastors of denominational churches and many others of more independent ones will develop their pastoral skills in just such a church; some remain there throughout their careers. Carroll summarized the importance of size:

> The distribution of Protestant churches by size is like a pyramid, with the number of congregations narrowing dramatically as size increases. As a result, *a large majority of Protestant clergy will almost inevitably spend their entire ministry in small or medium-sized congregations.* While there is nothing intrinsically wrong with this, what makes it an issue is the penchant among clergy, denominational officials, and laity for equating career success with climbing ever higher up the pyramid, serving ever-larger congregations. This is quite simply a goal that most clergy will not reach, if for no other reason than that there are, proportionally, so few large Protestant congregations. Furthermore, bigger is not always better.[16] (*emphasis added*)

In reality, the smaller congregation provides one of the primary opportunities for pastoral leading. Most pastors, especially female pastors, have their first taste of the challenges of ministering in a small church that proves to be a testing ground for applying what has been learned in seminary or other career experiences. The key challenge for the new leader is honing the skills of understanding people and how congregations work. Research from the 1960s pointed to the first five years of full-time ministry in micro churches as the most stressful for a ministry career.[17] It is during the initial service in one's first leading responsibility that many pastors decide the seriousness of their calling. If one can survive this transition, during which the idealism of the student years involving study, thinking, and research is replaced by connecting, caring, and dealing with daily interruptions in one's work plan, a lifetime of pastoral leading can be the outcome of these early experiences.

Patience may be the most important quality for leading the micro church. Based on my personal experience in serving two micro churches as pastor, as well as observations of dozens of others, there is a five-to-eight-year process before one fully becomes the pastor of even small churches. There are three stages in this process.

The first is the connecting stage in which the primary agenda is to learn the people of the congregation, the family relationships within it and the community, the story of the church's history, and its formal and informal ways of functioning. During the first six to nine months, it is typical to expect a testing conflict—an issue arises that is seemingly insignificant to the outsider. But to the insider, there is a kind of innate testing of the new pastor to measure how he or she will respond. If there is a nonanxious response that demonstrates trust toward the people, a reservoir of confidence for the next conflict accumulates. On the other hand, a mishandled response sets the agenda for a lose-lose reaction for the second stage of testing.

The second stage in connecting leading skills with a new congregation occurs at the 18–24 month interval. If the first stage was handled poorly, the intensity of reaction at this second testing event often results in a resignation or termination. The relatively short tenure of many pastors in smaller congregations can be explained by this cycle of congregational testing. On the other hand, a confident response that demonstrates reciprocal trust between pastor and people will enlarge the reservoir of trust. When this happens, the period between each conflict is longer as the pastor establishes tenure and effectiveness.

A third challenge will often emerge sometime during years 5–8, which, if managed successfully, extends the trust level into a series of years with relative success and smooth sailing. A long-term pastor in Carroll's focus group for research referred to this process as "longevity capital."[18] Someone in the congregation is constantly "banking" trust and good will that become the deciding factors in who will be followed in times of congregational stress.

A final stress point occurs for the long-time pastor as the normal years of retirement are approached. I have observed numerous congregations with beloved pastors who, when the pastor reached early sixties in age, suddenly demonstrate unexplained anxiety about the future. Pressure is exerted to force a "date certain" for retirement, and usually before the pastor is ready for it. The anxiety is often demonstrated in a loss of energy and drifting away of younger families who want to see a quicker change in leadership than longer-term members desire.

Seedbed Micro Churches

One of the overlooked dimensions of the small church for young and ambitious leaders is the opportunity of growing one's dream from infancy. Most congregations begin as cell groups who connect effectively with an ever-larger number of persons until, over time, the congregation transitions into another kind of congregation. Two of the pastors in the case study group I studied were pastors of megachurches who were the only pastors in their churches' histories. The Ray of Hope Christian Church is the second largest congregation affiliated with the Disciples of Christ. But it began as a Bible study in the apartment of the founding and current pastor, Rev. Dr. Cynthia Hale. That Bible study was a seedbed for what is now a remarkable congregation with a nationally recognized pastor.

Johnson Ferry Baptist Church was formed as a mission congregation in the emerging suburbs of east Cobb County in suburban Atlanta in 1982 with fifty to sixty people. They called G. Bryant Wright as their pastor and that group now worships in six different worship venues each weekend, as 4,300 people gather for celebration and fellowship. The pastor with a vision and the skills of leading in congregational effectiveness can plant, cultivate, and harvest the results of those skills—if committed to the long term and willing to adjust with the changing demands of an enlarging organization.

Catalysts for Change

Most small congregations have limited potential for numerical growth. Either their context of stable or declining populations, or their dysfunctions, keep them plateaued or declining. Yet, even the small congregation with limited potential for numerical growth has choices. It can choose the *status quo*, or repeating what it has always done in the past. A kind of stale repetition of the same folk theology, the same hymns sung Sunday after Sunday, the same clichés in prayers, and an unchanging calendar of events keep it boringly predictable. Or, the smallest of congregations can launch innovations in learning, worship, relating to its community context, or investing in personal mission efforts—either locally or in distance places. Such innovation can prepare the congregation for proactive responses to unexpected changes in its community context, such as a new manufacturing plant or influx of immigrant families with whom it can minister. The choice is often shaped by the attitudes and courage of the pastor. Sadly, Carroll's study showed that the smaller the congregation, the more likely it is to focus on maintaining tradition than leading in innovative directions.[19]

Pastor-centered Large Churches

The last form of the organic congregation is the number of larger congregations who have a nonprogrammatic, fluid organizational style that flows from the charismatic gifts of the pastor. Much of the congregational literature has tended to connect the charismatic pastor with a strong authoritarian leader who functions as a CEO of a well-organized and skillfully managed organization. The large organic congregation is different from this popular image.

This is a congregational form that is new for me, given my background in a traditional denominational approach that emphasized organization and programs. Yet, hundreds of independent, Pentecostal, neo-Pentecostal, and African American congregations function more like a fluid mosaic than a mechanistic flow chart. At the core of these congregations is the bigger-than-life personality of the pastoral leader who functions with authority that is more granted by the congregation than forced upon it

These pastors are highly energetic, capable of strong emotional connections with people, have enormous capacities to remember the names of participants, and are strong auditory learners. They remember stories with ease, tell them with a fluidity that resembles a jazz musician improvising from a vast repertoire of chords and melodies, and are able to connect to the emotions of an audience with intuitive awareness of their needs in the moment.

The organizations they lead are equally fluid. The laity of these congregations grant enormous authority to their pastors based on the personal relationships their pastors maintain and the ability of the preacher to connect as the person with God's word for the day. Rhetorical abilities are often honed to maximize their effectiveness. So, the pastor's vision is often affirmed with a minimum of committee processes or organizational review. I have observed such pastors announce a new program for the church without prior review by any lay group with an almost immediate acceptance by the people—because it came from the pastor.

These churches have small paid staffs with a minimum of bureaucracy. They can often be a frustration for pastors of more organized churches who do not understand why a message left with a secretary is never answered by the pastor. A direct, personal connection is often required to get a pastoral response, and staff members are trained to "take care" of member needs without bothering the overburdened pastor.

These pastoral leaders are unique in American Christianity, though they are often the most recognized in developing world Christianity where a more authoritarian and Pentecostal style is the norm. Consequently, it is difficult to find leadership descriptions of them. Biblical characters are often identified to mirror their leadership styles. "He is a new Moses among us," or, "She has the vision of a Mary with the communication skills of a Priscilla," may be descriptive.

An adequate leadership description of this kind of leading is fleeting. Something akin to "tribal royalty" or "Father" or "Mother" of the church are partial but inadequate. Perhaps analogies are the best descriptors. These pastors are like symphonic conductors who are clearly in charge, know the depth of the traditions behind the score being played, but guide the orchestra in an interpretive presentation of the score that moves an audience with its creativity and power. They also know each player in the orchestra is capable of creating dissonance; hence there is enough individual attention and instruction given to assure a skillful performance by all.

Consequently, worship and preaching are the dominant expressions of church in these congregations. Every service is a mixture of the expected and surprise. One never knows for certain what might happen, for the Holy Spirit may descend and transform. Thus, there is an excitement and energy in these churches that is quite unique in comparison with the broad sweep of American congregations.

Emergent Congregations

Emergent congregations defy easy description. They are among the most organic of the congregations described in this chapter. The word can be used either as an adjective meaning "rising out of or as if out of a fluid" or as a noun that largely refers to a plant growing.[20] No wonder there are so many different expressions of such congregations, and the attitudes toward them vary so much. One will search in vain for a directory of emergent congregations. At best, one should call "emergent" a conversation or movement.

Emergent Village provides most of the connections for conversations among those interested in connections with truly postmodern persons. It was begun as a result of the support of Leadership Network of a young pastor's group in 2001. From that effort have come multiple gatherings, the spawning of blogs and websites, and the development of innovative congregations. Scott McKnight, an evangelical who identifies himself as emergent, suggests much of the language about emergent congregations is more rooted in urban legend than actual realities. His focus is on the practices of emerging congregations. He describes them as prophetic in the sense of being theologically provocative; postmodern in their focus on relating to those self-consciously postmodern; praxis-oriented with focus on worship, right living, and mission; and post-evangelical in that they stress theological dialogue, inclusiveness, and centrist political involvements.[21]

While much of the attention on the emergent movement is addressed to its provocative attempts to reshape the theological language of the church to appeal to a changing culture,[22] it is the practice of emerging congregations that is important in this discussion. Emergent congregations differ most clearly from others in their efforts to embrace creative forms of worship. McKnight concedes worship in the movement is creative, experiential, and sensory. Such approaches range from reclaiming ancient musical forms and liturgies to embodying the most "funky" of artistic genres.

The real question for most congregations is whether emergent practices can be grafted onto or included in traditional Protestant congregations as strategies of appealing to postmoderns. My own observations indicate that congregations who have tried these changes have been largely unsuccessful. Emergent strategies work best in the form of new congregational efforts; yet the resources for such efforts are often difficult to develop. A better strategy would be to offer support by more traditional congregations as mission efforts to new organic and fluid methods of planting new congregational expressions for the emerging culture. "For the Christian faith to remain viable," suggests Barry Taylor, "we're going to have to let go of the attractional model— inviting people to come to us—and instead go to where they live, and there live out our faith."[23]

Organizational Congregations

Most denominationally-connected congregations are organized formally. Whether mainline in their connections or conservative-evangelical in their theology or approach, structure is important. These congregations usually have constitutions and bylaws that describe clearly the processes of making decisions. Respected lay leaders lead most with strong traditions in the congregation and the trust of the people of the church. Thus, they are nominated and elected to their roles of leadership. The pastor is expected to work through these structures, and the wise leader understands the slower and more definite conclusions to policies and procedures essential in these structures.

Committees, Committees, Committees

The formally organized church is one in which lay committees are charged with the work of the congregation. Central to them are two kinds of committees.

Management Committee

One group is charged with policies, management of conflict, and recommendations to a central decision-making group. Depending on the tradition of the church they may be called deacons, elders, synod, vestry, or church council. Some highly organized small congregations may function as a "committee of the whole" with all management the business of every member.

Finance Committee

The most important of these committee structures include a finance committee charged with the development of an annual budget and financial processes of the church, including raising and managing the funds needed for the church's programs.

Personnel Committee

A second key committee is usually a personnel committee charged with establishing policies for employment, compensation, and ensuring healthy staff relationships. Most of these kinds of churches have multiple staff, and the role of the pastor is one of connecting with these groups as a team participant in their work.

Ministry Committees

A variety of task groups are charged with the programmatic work of the church. They focus on functions of worship, education, fellowship, and mission outreach. Most of these committees have budgeted funds for which they are accountable to the finance committee. Committee handbooks describing the purposes of each committee of the church, procedures for decisions, and financial guidelines round out the structure of the organizational church.

Pastoral leaders of these congregations complain most about the demands of administration. Such pastors regularly invest 20 percent or more of their time in church administration, even when they view it as a burden.[24] Some pastors over-invest in the outcome of these committees as a result of their personal anxiety that their wishes might somehow not be included in their decisions. The result can be the authoritarian image that some congregations attribute to their leaders.

Some pastors tend to find the resources for their leadership style from the literature developed for corporate organizations that focus more on efficiency of operation than effectiveness in fulfilling the mission of God in the world.

Few of these leaders have developed a theology of administration that leads the congregation to focus its organizational structure more on mission than the routines of weekly tasks that can consume the energy of the church.

Staff and More Staff

One of the consequences for the contemporary organized church is the tendency to employ staff to manage the multiple programs that require increasingly large numbers of volunteers to serve. The larger the congregation, the larger grows the staff of both professional ministers and the support staff they need for effective work.

While this trend is understandable, it creates a new challenge for the busy pastor. More staff means more time and attention to support, coordinate, and assure effectiveness of staff. In the face of these challenges, hierarchical staff structures often emerge that place the pastor in authority over the staff, with a CEO mentality at the top and middle managers employed to implement the programs chosen for the church laity the pastor does not wish or does not have the time to engage him- or herself.

It is unlikely many of these congregations will be changed into more organic structures. Better processes of staff leading are possible, however, if staff can be organized as teams of cooperative and committed leaders in their own areas of responsibility. Chapter 11 will develop team ministry approaches more fully.

Megachurches

Any contemporary understanding of church ecology cannot be complete without a discussion of the newest congregational style in the global context. The megachurch is the latest phenomenon of church life, and is both praised and reviled by those who observe the successes.

By definition in this study, megachurches are those congregations that average two thousand or more participants in weekly worship. The megachurch is a unique congregational structure that is the subject of a growing body of research and attention. According to Scott Thumma and Dave Travis, in 2007 there were some 1,250 megachurches in the U.S., with a growth of fifty new ones annually.[25]

While large congregations have been important in the history of the Church, most notably the form of the cathedral model of the church, contemporary megachurches bring a new dimension to American Protestantism. This trend of the past half century finds its origin in the founding of the Yoido Full Gospel Church in Seoul, Korea, by pastor David

Yongii Cho in 1958. Large gatherings for worship in this church now number over a million people, supplemented with weekly meetings of small groups led by church pastors.

Multiple groups around the world, including a significant number in the U.S., have replicated this model. However, the pattern of megachurches in the U.S. is even more complex. Thumma and Travis differentiate four basic styles of megachurches:

1. Old line/program-based churches. These older large churches tend to be established as First Churches of central core urban regions. They are more traditional in style and include 30 percent of churches they studied.
2. Seeker congregations. These newer, suburban churches embrace contemporary worship forms. Their evangelistic preachers/teachers create environments of easy entrance into the church for the unchurched. Small groups function for assimilation. These seeker congregations comprise about 30 percent of mega congregations.
3. Charismatic/pastor-focused congregations. Spirit-focused worship with appeal to multiracial and multiethnic groups that congregate in varied urban settings. These churches comprise approximately 25 percent of megachurches and are exuberant in worship style with more authoritarian styles of leadership.
4. New wave/re-envisioned congregations. Composed of predominantly younger participants in varied urban settings, these churches are often associated with the emergent movement. They are about 15 percent of the studied churches.[26]

Whatever may be the view of megachurches on the part of leaders of smaller congregations, they are clearly effective in attracting participation in a largely consumerist culture. They have become so successful that "45 percent of the persons attending worship did so in churches in the top 10 percent in size."[27] The largest 20 percent of the churches have around 65 percent of the resources.[28] They are a part of the large institutional participation of the consumer in mega-malls, large-scale sporting and cultural events, and the choices of the American public. They are not diminishing in their influence.[29]

Implications for Leadership

Understanding the ecology of the congregation you lead is important for effectiveness. Each of the above descriptions of congregations can be missional in their context. Wise leaders will consider the following implications for their given setting for hopeful ministry.

1. No singular approach to leadership will fit all congregational settings. The personality and spiritual giftedness of pastoral, staff, and lay leadership that fits some styles of congregations would be a significant failure in other congregations. Thus, fit in leadership abilities must match the needs of the congregation one leads.

2. Discerning the being and skills of each individual pastor or staff leader is an essential part of the calling of the congregation.[30] It is unfortunate when decisions are made to extend or continue the call that are not consistent with the style of the congregation served.

3. Clarity in the organizational qualities of the congregation limits the levels of frustration and discouragement of those who lead. Nothing can be more difficult than the expectations that an organic congregation should be more organized and structured when informality and flow are critical to effective service.

4. Leading the congregation in self-understanding of its setting and the appropriateness of its ecology in that setting are helpful for implementing God's mission through that congregation.

An Exercise in Analysis

Gather the core leadership group of your congregation. Create a brief written summary of each type of congregation in this chapter. Discuss together the ecology of your congregation. Ask, "Are there aspects of the congregation that are organic? What aspects are more organizational? How could we simplify our internal tasks to free time and energy for connecting to people outside our congregation?"

Likewise, ask: "What other kinds of congregations are located in our immediate geographical area? Is there anything we could learn from them about ministry in our kind of community?"

PART 3: Doing
The Actions of Leading

You have read the foundations of congregational leading. Identity is crucial for one's effectiveness. So is knowledge of the theology of God's mission, an awareness of change in the world in which you serve, and the organism/organization of your congregation.

Leading accomplishes ministry. Until all one is and all one knows is translated into the constant tasks of doing the work of God's new order in a specific place and time, there is no leading. Ministry is the work of head, heart, hands, and feet in accomplishing the Spirit's leading.

Dreaming is a critical leadership function. Leaders think more about the future than the past. A hopeful leader imagines visionary potential of the group of people being led. Hopeful leaders dream the challenges and opportunities of the congregation three to five years into the future. Vision energizes and motivates. "Where there is no prophecy, / the people cast off restraint" (Prov. 29.18).

Equally important is managing. The manager's view narrows the scope of the future. The manager translates long-term vision into short-term accomplishments. If the time frame for leading is three to five years, the manager's outlook is annual. "What must we accomplish this week, this month, this year to embody our vision?" asks the manager. Chapter 8 explores the processes that generate strategic thinking for the future that include dreaming and managing.

Caring for the people of the congregation is a managing function. Compassion is the essential quality of caring, but proactive caring will assure congregational health and well-being. Caring requires work; caring is a doing function, the subject of Chapter 9.

Missional congregations proclaim the gospel. The pulpit is the primary medium of the proclaiming work of a congregation. Proclaiming includes other practical means of communication. Chapter 10 addresses this aspect of the practical work of the church.

Organizing how we make decisions, the nitty-gritty work of developing policies, documents, and evaluations of our work, is a primary managing function. Whether organized informally in the small congregation or massively with complex forms in a large corporate structure, work does not get accomplished without organization. Numerous resources for thinking about organizational structures may be found in Chapter 11.

The mantra of leaders is: no resources, no ministry. Resources address financial stewardship, but so much more. Hopeful congregations learn how to view all of their assets as important resources in missional work. We will look at resource management in Chapter 12.

"Mending" in Chapter 13 describes the important work of assuring hopeful outcomes when conflict emerges in congregational life. All healthy congregations have conflict. The real question is, "What processes will we follow when it occurs?" Conflict ministry is as essential an aspect of leading as doing.

Evaluating and celebrating are often overlooked dimensions of the church. How many congregations of which you are aware ever ask of themselves, "How well are we accomplishing the challenges God has placed before us?" Processes for evaluation provide the content of Chapter 14.

Practicing the celebration of leaders who achieve the mission of the congregation fulfills the final dimension of a verbal, organic approach to leading. Chapter 15 summarizes ways of affirming the accomplishments of the church and its people.

8

Dreaming

When faith communities want change, leaders usually can't stop it. When faith communities don't want change, leaders usually can't force it.

ROBERT D. DALE[1]

Imagining new possibilities, with awareness of congregational reality, is at the heart of hopeful leadership. All of us live with the blaring news accounts of political dysfunctions, economic dislocations, and social conflicts. We face a cacophony of personal disasters and disappointments within our families, our communities, and our churches. These challenge even faint efforts to be optimistic about the future. Yet, rooting the decisions of the church in the difficulties of the present or even the challenges of the past is inadequate for effective leading.

The Christian leader lives in hope because the promises of God's realm, reign, and rule offer a new future of peace, reconciliation, and joy in the presence of the Creator, Son, and Spirit.

The challenge of leading is to imagine beyond the traditions of the past or the pressures of the present to what is possible for the future. Leaders of hopeful congregations have what Diana Butler Bass calls "pastoral imagination," a spiritual gift that grows out of the partnership of pastoral leaders and people. She writes, "The pastoral imagination and a congregational imagination are two different angles of vocational calling and vision, one from the pulpit and the other from the pew, of a common spiritual gift of seeing God at work and embodying faith, hope, and love in the world."[2]

The Christian faith is a future faith. It lives out of the power of the Spirit of God to participate in change of the realities of a fallen world. The apostle Paul's description of the transformed life is living in Christ as a new creation where the past is passing away and the new is coming (2 Cor. 5:17).

It is consistent with the preaching of Jesus: "the kingdom of God *has come.*" ("*angican,*" Gk. meaning "is coming and will come") (Mk. 1:15, *emphasis added*)

Understanding Innovation

A myth in the minds of many claims that innovation is the consequence of an amazing idea of a singular genius. The stories we tell our children about Benjamin Franklin discovering electricity by flying a kite with a key amid a thunderstorm or Thomas Edison inventing the light bulb as a lonely scientist slaving away in the solitary confinement of his laboratory are false myths. All new inventions and innovations tend to flow out of a community of conversation with many from which a new insight emerges for an individual or team of discoverers. The burden of change does not rest on the solitary leader; it grows out of communities of change.

Cities are one of those community environments for change. According to Steven Johnson, innovation arises out of networks of interaction in which individual's ideas are enlarged. He writes, "On a basic level, it is true that ideas happen *inside* minds, but those minds are invariably connected to external networks that shape the flow of information and inspiration out of which great ideas are fashioned."[3]

Cities are the context of networks. The larger the city, the greater the potential there is for new ideas. A city ten times larger than another will have seventeen times the number of innovations, and a metropolitan area fifty times larger than a town has 130 times the number of innovations.[4]

Not all churches have the advantage of participating in networks where new ideas may emerge. But even the most isolated of congregations can interact with people outside the church. Learning experiences that help the leadership of the church engage its context—such as walking tours of the neighborhood, conversations with community residents about their hopes and dreams, and connections with people-serving organizations—can be "eye-opening" experiences.[5] Dale summarizes well, "Invest in lots of ideas and initiatives. Harvest the ones that flourish. Plant your best seeds in your best seedbeds, and trust God for the increase."[6]

Medium-sized and larger congregations can enhance their capacities to dream by connecting to congregations engaged in vital ministries in another community setting. Be clear that the methods in another congregation fit your setting, as not all approaches are transferable.

One of the most destructive conflicts in a congregation with which I have consulted resulted from the pastor's efforts to transform the worship in the church after participating in a national conference on contemporary churches. His vision was not transferable.

Isolation is a major limitation for the pastor and leaders of autonomous congregations, as they may function without any denominational or other networks for new perspectives and ideas. In such cases, a budget for the pastor to participate in regional or national continuing education or conference events can be the avenue of renewal and new dreams for the congregation. The wise pastoral leader will know how to translate such new perspectives into the particular realities of the church.

In my case studies in Atlanta, one African American pastor led his deacons to visit another large megachurch, also in our research group, to learn how they organized for more effective ministry in their setting. The new ideas engendered by the visit allowed for changes in how the deacons did their work.

If external connections are essential to innovation, so is practice. Change requires time, and effective leading builds on experience after experience to move into a new future one step at a time. The wise pastoral leader knows that change is cumulative. Big changes are the product of a series of small changes.

Sometimes that practice is lived out in the same congregation for a lifetime of ministry; for others the experience in one church becomes the platform for effective leading in a different setting. One pastor in Carroll's study called it "longevity capital" when one recognizes the trust factor inherent in leadership.[7] From it one has the capacity to act with wisdom to effect change. The leadership challenge is to lead in such a way the congregation wants to change.

The importance of practice in ministry is reinforced by the studies of Malcolm Gladwell. Citing neurologist Daniel Levitin's studies of "world class" experts in a host of fields from athletes and artists to criminals, he suggests that 10,000 hours of practice are required for success in any field of endeavor.[8] When one achieves such a standing, there is present the quality of "practical intelligence" so essential in all meaningful human interactions. It is "knowing what to say to whom, knowing when to say it, and knowing how to say it for maximum effect."[9] Experienced pastors understand practical intelligence.

The resources available for congregations to engage in the dreaming process are extensive. The issue for most congregations is not whether they will think about the future, but how. Thinking about the future is too often more wishful thinking than realistic thinking. The choice of how one engages in creative and productive future thinking that generates results will depend on the size, previous experiences, age of the membership, available resources, and openness of the congregation. My purpose here is to identify some of the primary resources that can serve as a process guide for congregational visioning. Each congregation will need to make the choice that best fits its situation.

Most congregations will profit from employing an external coach or consultant to assist in clarifying the process and providing assistance in the event the process gets bogged down. However, the primary leadership for change must come from within the congregation and someone, either the pastor or a capable lay team, must guide the process if it is to impact how the church moves forward into the future.[10] Consulting and coaching resources can be located at:

- The Hartford Institute for Religious Research has an extensive list of consulting organizations for congregations with links to each at http://hirr.hartsem.edu/leadership/consultants.html.
- The Center for Congregational Health provides professional training for congregational consultants and maintains a network of consultants to work with congregations in revisioning/strategic planning at http://www.healthychurch.org.
- The Columbia Partnership has a team of congregational coaches with varied denominational and congregational experience at http://www.thecolumbiapartnership.org.
- Pinnacle Leadership Associates provides training, consulting, and coaching with resources that address any congregation's needs for visioning at http://pinnaclelead.com.

I am convinced, based on consulting experience, the more complex the strategic process and the longer the time it takes to complete, the less likely meaningful results will be the outcome. A simple framework in which clear outcomes can be chosen is to be preferred over a lengthy document that gets produced but never implemented. Core leaders will need to choose from several options those that would best fit the congregation.

Congregational Life Cycle

Every congregation, like all organizations, follows a predictable cycle of growth, maturity, stability, and decline. Where the congregation is in its life cycle development is a product of its age, adaptability to change, and the environment in which it is located. Leading the congregation through a process of understanding its life cycle can be a foundational step in preparation for a dreaming process.

Congregational life cycles usually follow, by a number of years, the life cycle of the community setting in which they are located. Figure 8.1 visualizes the relationship between these two. Communities go through processes of growth, maturity, decline, and renewal. Community change may be socio-economic, racial-ethnic, or structural in the form of physical structures located within them. Churches follow the trends in communities. Planning that is unconnected to community change will result in strategies that lag behind where the context is. When plans for future growth are implemented too slowly, the context that was growing and energetic may be in a decline cycle. The church soon follows that trend. Communities emerging from their decline cycle into renewal may provide opportunities for change for the declining church that are missed through inattention to new realities.

Figure 8.1: Community Life Cycle and Church Life Cycle

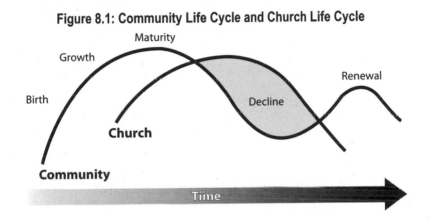

Good planning begins with an awareness of where the congregation is in its natural life cycle. The issue is addressed by several congregational strategists. Table 8.1 summarizes the three most helpful ones for autonomous congregations in the work of Robert Dale,[11] George Bullard,[12] and Israel Galindo.[13] Any one of these resources will provide guidance to leaders.

Each of these approaches pictures an arc of development as a visual representation of congregational change over time. There is a growth side of the arc and a decline side, with a period of stability that can last for months or years in the middle.

There is a planning agenda for each of these primary stages. The growth agendas are to clarify identity, establish goals and ministries, decide about facilities, and assure pastoral leadership capable of adjusting to the transitions toward maturity. The decline agendas are to assess the congruence of the congregation with its context, seek to simplify and energize organizing processes and decisions, seek alternative uses of facilities, and determine the capacity for change. Sometimes the decline has so weakened the congregation

Table 8.1: Three Models of Life Cycle Descriptions

Robert Dale	George Bullard	Israel Galindo
Birth — rooted in dream	Growth Phase 1— birth, infancy	Establishing Stage — exciting and hopeful
Growth — develop goals and structures	Growth Phase 2 — childhood, adolescence	Formation and Formatting Stage — identity formed
Maturity — height of size and influence	Prime/Plateau Phase 3 — adulthood, stability	Adolescent Stage — energy with turbulence
Decline — nostalgia, questioning, and polarization	Redevelopment — maturity, decline	Prime Stage — culture fully formed
		Maturity Stage — stability valued over energy
Dropout — moves to survival mode	Aging Phase 4 —empty nest, retirement	Aristocracy Stage — exclusivity forms
Death — change or die	Aging Phase 5 — old age, death	Bureaucracy Stage — chronic anxiety
		Dissolution Stage — survival mode

a serious discussion of redevelopment through sale of the facilities, merging with another congregation, closing of the congregation, or initiating a re-churching process of a new congregation to replace the old one is needed. Churches on the plateau will explore new efforts at outreach and evangelism, alternatives to enhance the attractiveness of the congregation in its setting, and more fluid means of engaging in ministry. The growth cycle emphasizes channeling of energy, the plateau cycle the renewal of energy, and the decline cycle changing the control mechanisms that prohibit energy.[14]

Dreaming Models

A framework for dreaming can be helpful for congregations motivated to explore new future possibilities. All planning models share similar features. They differ in the level of their complexity. It is important for the congregation to identify its primary needs in choosing a dream path that will enliven a new future in its midst.

Strategic Planning

A first planning model is strategic planning. This is a discipline churches have incorporated from corporate practice, but which corporations are abandoning in the face of the fast-paced changing of their markets. The process often takes too long for strategic planning to keep up with the swirl of environmental change.

Many churches still function within environments stable enough that strategic planning can be a useful tool. Models of strategic planning are similar in terms of the processes they follow. They differ in the language used to describe their processes or the complexity of detail they utilize. They are most helpful in providing a "road map" to the process that can be learned and applied by thoughtful leaders. A brief summary of four strategic planning models will provide congregational leaders a framework for selecting an approach that best fits their setting.

Congregations in Transition

Carl Dudley and Nancy Ammerman designed a most useful guide for congregations committed to a detailed process of exploration and analysis of both their context and congregation. Metaphors of the children of Israel in their journey from Egypt to the promised land shape the outline of their process: journey, exploration of the land, assessing your tabernacle, looking for signs of God's presence (pillars of fire), and settling into new realities (promised land). A complete journey in this process will require considerable collection of useful data, frequent meetings, and participation in multiple creative exercises. Even if the entire process is not employed, the practical learning exercises and descriptions of congregational timelines will be useful for congregational learning.[15]

Leading Congregational Change

Jim Herrington, Mike Bonem, and James H. Furr have developed one of the most detailed and thoroughly organized processes for congregational change.[16] This strategic planning model integrates case studies of applications of the plan in groups of churches in the Union Baptist Association in Houston, Texas, including organizational theories and processes. It is a useful process for program churches that are willing to engage in an in-depth analysis of their setting with detailed development of documents that include a clear statement of mission, vision, visionpaths (specific objectives), and integration into the fabric of the church's organizations. The advantage of this resource is its detailed description of a step-by-step process with practical applications of the outcome. It will be most useful in larger congregations with reasonably well-educated laity.

Take the Next Step

Lovett Weems offers a clear and inspiring emphasis on the importance of vision in the planning process with a five-step process: create trust, define reality, discern a vision, take the next step, and persevere.[17] This is a simple process that can be utilized in most congregations. It is practical, readable, and motivating for both clergy and laity.

Pursuing the Full Kingdom Potential of Your Congregation

George Bullard offers similar approaches to each of the above with three major differences.[18] First, he suggests kingdom language as the key motif of the planning process. Second, his preparation for the kingdom journey includes a well-developed prayer ministry of 100 days of prayer by triplets of members gathered weekly to pray for the congregation and the planning process. Third, the outcome of this process is a written future story of what the congregation would look like if it implemented what it learned in the planning process. The final outcome is a more creative narrative of the congregation's future than the typical planning documents of detailed goals and objectives to be accomplished.

Holy Conversations

Gil Rendle and Alice Mann connect processes similar to those described above with a helpful parallel exploration of biblical stories. This book is a solid handbook for the coach or consultant who wishes to draw exercises and processes from it.[19]

Effective strategic planning will invest time defining not only the church's identity, but also the setting in which it is located. The Internet makes such a process much easier than in the past when community research required poring over paper census documents and community planning studies. By accessing Factfinder at http://factfinder2.census.gov/faces/nav/jsf/pages/index.xhtml, the latest census materials can be assembled by census tracts, ZIP codes, or counties.

PRIZM can be a helpful tool in understanding the primary lifestyles of a given community. It identifies fourteen lifestyle groups that may or may not be compatible with membership of the church: http://www.tetrad.com/demographics/usa/claritas/prizmne.html. It can be expensive for the smaller congregations, but denominational research offices may offer it free to congregations.

Another helpful research tool is the location of current church participants in relation to their location. Identifying by ZIP codes the residences of members is a good indicator of commute times to the facilities and the density of members living in the neighborhoods of the church's primary location.

Finally, exploring the structures of an area by viewing Google maps via computer can be a learning experience for a planning team. Satellite images of the housing, office areas, or industrial areas near the church can be a clue for thinking about strategic outreach to the community.

Master Planning

Few congregations need to engage in master planning. It is appropriate, however, for those congregations in a growth cycle that must make important decisions about property and facilities that will shape their identity and effectiveness for years to come. Master planning is a long-range process of assessing the church's human and financial resources to fulfill a set of long-range goals, including:

- What is the current size of the congregation, its growth trajectory, and the costs and availability of property for its future? The most important decision within this triad of factors is the amount of land it owns or can purchase. Most congregations purchase too little land for their first effort at developing facilities. I recommend that congregations purchase twice the amount of property they anticipate needing to allow for greater growth than they can imagine. If growth does not occur, unneeded portions can be sold in the future with appreciation on the investment (an assumption that might not hold true between 2007–2012).

- What is a realistic appraisal of the financial capacities of the congregation? Given the current economic realities of the second decade of the twenty-first century, restraints on church debt will be more severe than in the past. A hopeful church must not build beyond the commitments of its people. A realistic rule of thumb in this economy is to invest in each building project an amount equal to the dollars the congregation commits in one three-year capital campaign as one half of the total cost. Financing over ten years for the remaining half of the costs is realistic as long as total annual debt payments do not exceed 10 percent of the annual budget. This formula will mean a church with a $500,000 budget, and able to secure $300,000 in pledge commitments over three years, can borrow $378,000 at 6.00 percent interest for a total project of $678,000. It will budget $50,000 in annual debt payments for ten years. To do a second capital project would require either waiting ten years or experiencing numerical and financial growth that would allow additional capital campaigns.

- Are we willing to employ professionals outside the congregation to develop an early master facilities' plan that provides a set of fluid options of how the congregation might develop its facilities? Consideration of a professional planner or architect may be a wise decision at some stage in the process. A successful relationship with such a professional will require the church to know what it wants and have a clear vision of what it intends. An architect is dependent on the clarity of the congregation in what it needs and wants. Experienced *church* architects are preferred as well.

Too many churches make decisions about facilities based on dreams of an idealistic pastor or unrealistic suggestions from a powerful layperson about such matters. Most congregations build too much space rather than too little space in their facilities planning process. They also build space with such permanence that new configurations are costly, or they erect additions that create traffic flow problems through the entire church campus.

Hopeful churches plan for sizes and configurations that can accommodate multiple worship and learning experiences as the church grows. Visionary twenty-first–century congregations will worship three times in a space each week with attendance at 80 percent of capacity before adding additional worship space. Consequently, space that can be easily and quickly converted into alternative forms of use are essential.

Seek to incorporate into the core values of the congregation resistance to the idolization of its space. This is difficult because the places in which we worship and learn, participate in the baptisms and weddings of our children, and eulogize our loved ones become sacred. One of the most difficult leadership agendas of all congregations is the natural resistance to changing facilities, whether it means reconfiguring space, relocating to a new setting, or selling to another congregation.

These kinds of decision are more difficult when the spaces, the stained-glass windows, or buildings are named as memorials to a former pastor or church leader. A congregation will likely face each of these decisions. When such decisions reflect the measure of their hopefulness, the congregation must ask, "Is willingness to make the change based on what will allow us best to engage in God's mission?"

A master plan is effective for about ten years in most congregations located in rapidly changing community environments. After that, major changes will be needed.

Appreciative Inquiry

Sue Annis Hammond has suggested a different approach: "If an organization keeps hearing how ill it is and how much it has to fix itself, members will behave as if the organization were ill."[20]

This approach envisions new realities for congregations by applying the process of appreciative inquiry (AI). This process was begun in the 1980s as a management process to assist business managers to move from a problem-solving approach to identifying positive actions that would change the culture of management teams.[21] According to Hammond, "[O]rganizations are viewed as organic, which means that all parts are defined by the whole."[22]

The AI approach can be applied to almost any group setting in the church, from committee or task force meetings to congregation-wide explorations of the positive values of the church and its ministries. The basic AI design is a series of assumptions that emphasize the best of what is possible in a group. Multiple applications of the process have been made, including one described for congregations below. The foundational assumption identified by Hammond is, "[A]n organization is a mystery to be embraced."[23] Such language is consistent with religious entities. Discovering that mystery is a part of the four-fold process of AI:

- The Phase of Discovery, "The best of what is"—the search for an emergent positive core in which as many of the strengths, accomplishments, inspirations, innovations, and every other positive experience can be identified by a group in a systematic way.
- From Discovery to Dream, "What could be"—group conversations that identify the emergent positive core of our experiences that could develop into potential directions for a new future.
- Design, "What should be"—moving from the vision of a new future to the creation of an organism that can involve all in working toward the accomplishing of the dream. It asks the question, "What would our organization look like if it were designed in every way possible to maximize the qualities of the positive core and enable the accelerated realization of our dreams?"
- Destiny, "Action plan and execute"—the outcome of the process as the design of the dream is "set free" to be embraced by all who will participate in the possibilities of a new future through new relationships, networks, and connections that enlarge the participation of the several into an inspiring experience of the many.[24]

The AI process is similar to the asset-based approach to planning. Arising from the field of community development, asset-based thinking emphasizes the resources available to a group with an effort to link those resources to specific actions for change.[25]

The pace of change and the busyness of the typical congregation make the kinds of efforts required for detailed, drawn-out planning process nonproductive. Yet, every congregation needs cycles of planning in which they pay attention to the future, and they make an effort to infuse into the mindset of the congregation a sense of its future priorities. Strategic thinking for congregations is a broadly shared understanding of who we are (our discovered identity), what we are about as partners with God (our mission), a vision of who we want to become (our dream for the future), and a set of specific priorities we intend to accomplish in the next five years (our destiny). Strategic thinking is more about the process in which congregations engage than a specific outcome; the interaction of the process builds community, enlarges understandings of the church, and builds the confidence we can work together to do what would otherwise be left undone. When those connections happen, ministry gets initiated, leaders emerge who were previously submerged, and the church grows seeds of faith and confidence.

"Okay," you say. "I am convinced we need to become a strategic thinking community of faith. How do we do that in this place?"

My response is, "You do that by designing a process that fits your community of faith, its community setting, and builds on your congregational strengths." Cooperrider and Whitney express the goal well: "Put most simply, it has been our experience that building and sustaining momentum for change requires large amounts of positive affect and social bonding—things like hope, excitement, inspiration, caring, camaraderie, sense of urgent purpose, and sheer joy in creating something meaningful together."[26] That takes time, but the rewards are life-giving.

Every congregation will do strategic thinking differently. The framework in Figure 8.2 illustrates the process of appreciative inquiry.

Preparation

Congregations need to be prepared for strategic thinking. Most congregations are rooted in a routine that includes annual repetition of the tasks essential to maintaining stability: develop a calendar of program events, plan weekly worship, conduct an annual stewardship emphasis and budget, and organize fellowship meals on a regular basis. There may be an annual cycle of mission events.

Strategic thinking is a process that will raise questions, stimulate change, and possibly create resistance even to the suggestion of exploration. Change always foments risk. Often the outcome is conflict. Risk is also present with no change; it is just not as obvious.

Pastoral Leadership

The pastor must be onboard with the process. At a minimum, the pastor will need to prepare the congregation for what lies ahead. The pulpit is the most important platform she or he has. Unless the pastor is willing and

Figure 8.2: A Framework for Strategic Thinking

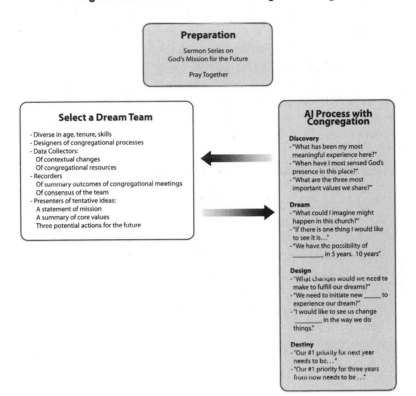

Preparation

Sermon Series on
God's Mission for the Future

Pray Together

Select a Dream Team

- Diverse in age, tenure, skills
- Designers of congregational processes
- Data Collectors:
  Of contextual changes
  Of congregational resources
- Recorders
  Of summary outcomes of congregational meetings
  Of consensus of the team
- Presenters of tentative ideas:
  A statement of mission
  A summary of core values
  Three potential actions for the future

AI Process with Congregation

Discovery
- "What has been my most meaningful experience here?"
- "When have I most sensed God's presence in this place?"
- "What are the three most important values we share?"

Dream
- "What could I imagine might happen in this church?"
- "If there is one thing I would like to see it is..."
- "We have the possibility of _____ in 5 years. 10 years"

Design
- "What changes would we need to make to fulfill our dreams?"
- "We need to initiate new _____ to experience our dream?"
- "I would like to see us change _____ in the way we do things."

Destiny
- "Our #1 priority for next year needs to be..."
- "Our #1 priority for three years from now needs to be..."

committed to proclaim the hopefulness of the gospel for the congregation's future, the pastor will assure the church's "stuckness." A sermon series on the mission of God for the church can inspire openness in the same way Peter's sermon on Joel 2:28–29 was a catalyst for the coming of the Spirit at Pentecost. Pastor, it is worth the risk!

Likewise, a new emphasis on praying together will help prepare people for God's blessings on a dreaming process. Be creative in providing such opportunities. Bullard's approach to organizing triplets of people who will pray daily and meet together weekly for one hour of prayer for the church for 100 days is one way. What if you organized groups of four to six persons—each including teenagers, median adults, and senior adults committed to pray daily for each other and the church? They could utilize tweets or Facebook interaction around their prayer concerns. Be creative! Design your own prayer connections! Let new, younger leaders organize some of the groups.

Dream Team

Effective strategic thinking needs a balance between a core group of persons focused on the process and the larger congregation engaged in exercises that generate ideas and fresh insights. Someone has to guide a strategic thinking process. Selecting a core group of forward-thinking persons to comprise a "dream team" proves workable. Pastoral leadership is essential, but a truly creative process will assure the pastor neither dominates nor controls the process. Input, yes. Guidance, yes. Control, no!

The Dream Team's Tasks

- Design the congregational AI inquiry. The creativity of the team should be allowed to flow in organizing meetings that assure maximum participation, stimulate people to talk together across their differences, generate information from each individual in ways it can be displayed for all to see, and collect the key ideas summarized from each meeting.
- Collect only essential data for understanding where the congregation is. This includes a summary description of the geography of its location for worship. Ask, "Who are the people in our context? How have they changed in recent years? What new trends are evident in our setting?"

Collect census data described above. Local planning organizations can be helpful. Organizing face-to-face conversations with local residents, conversations with business owners, and questions for the local coffee barista will surprise even long-time residents with new insights.

Congregational information should be collected, including the strengths of its resources in people, finances, programs, and facilities. An asset-mapping process with existing groups such as Sunday school classes can be useful.

Most congregations collect too much information. Focus on a few essential benchmarks for identifying who inhabits this congregation and its setting.

- Record essential summaries of the entire process. Detailed minutes of meetings are useless for this process, but a dated, written summary of what was decided, circulated to all, will keep the process on track. Include meetings and information from the dream team and from the congregation meetings.
- Write initial statements of mission, core values, and proposed strategic priorities for presentation to the congregation for affirmation, modification, or rejection. Strategic thinking that is not embraced by the

most active congregants will fail to change anything. The dream team shapes that thinking as it collects information from the congregational processes, summarizes and fashions it into tentative documents, and presents it in a way that allows for collaborative discussion. Thus, three documents should be presented to the congregation for decision making:

1. A one-sentence statement of congregational mission.
2. A summary of the core values of the congregation, including those needing change. For instance, it may be a core value of the congregation to allow only those with demonstrated commitment to participate in crucial roles of leadership. Another core value may be inclusion of all into the community of the congregation. There is inherent tension between these two. Strategic thinking will seek a way to transform the value of inclusion into opening paths of leadership for newcomers.
3. A set of proposed priorities for the future: three-year and five-year priorities with some means of communicating the long-term impact of achieving them.

At this point, the Dream Team must be flexible in allowing conversational interaction between the team and the congregation. Large groups need time to understand and assimilate the more concentrated work of small groups. Listening, adjusting, revising, and proposing again may be needed to achieve the change.

The Team

Who then should be on the Dream Team? This is a crucial opportunity for developing new leadership resources, as such participation will be a learning experience. One cannot engage in such a process without becoming aware of dynamics few in the congregation will know. Depending on the size of the church, a Dream Team of three to fifteen persons should be selected.

I recommend one-third be younger and future-thinking (include a teenager); one third have special internal church knowledge; and one third be trusted leaders who can help the congregation with change. No power broker who uses power to project a personal agenda on a group should be on the team. The team should include select persons with special skills:

- a "geek" who is great at collecting and disseminating information through technology;
- a scribe who can record information succinctly and accurately; and
- a facilitator who can enable the team to stay connected and productive.

The balance of the team should be listeners and thinkers who willingly invest their energy in hearing and suggesting new futures rooted in God's mission for the church.

The Congregation

Remember, this book is written to the leaders of those congregations who say they practice local autonomy in their decisions. What this sometimes means is the congregation gets "off track" and functions like a secular organization that "not even God can tell what to do." Congregations unwilling to explore alternative futures are wasting time engaging in this kind of strategic thinking. Not all congregations are hopeful. Pastors of such churches will have to live with God's call to serve as chaplains to the comfortable with no anxiety about the need for change.

To make such a choice is also to choose to travel the long road to decline in vitality and insignificance in the work of Jesus Christ. It is a worthy calling to care for the dying, including dying congregations. It is more exhilarating to seek to follow the One who proclaimed, "I am the vine, you are the branches; those who abide in Me, and I in them, bear much fruit; for apart from me you can do nothing" (Jn.15:5, *author's translation*).

The congregation's responsibility is to connect its dream process to the annual activities of its routine functions. The calendar process will need to include new initiatives that grow out of the strategic thinking process. If the congregation allots no consideration in budget planning to the priorities identified by the dream team, the congregation will stagnate. The leadership core must follow through in implementing the decisions of the congregation to move in new directions. If such happens, a look backward in five years will reveal a substantively changed congregation. Amazing results are possible and worthy of celebration.

And so I conclude this section with the words of Robert Dale, "During transitions, systems open up like flowers to the sun during significant turning points, or close up like a turtle retreating into its shell. Encourage the flowers, and comfort the turtles."[27] Learning to celebrate the flowers is to experience the joy of the new order of the Spirit in your community life together.

9

Caring

Care of the soul is a sacred art.

Thomas Moore[1]

Compassion distinguishes congregational leadership from all other forms of leadership. Leading a congregation without the empathetic qualities of caring for the people led is a contradiction of the meaning of being a church. At the heart of the identity of a Christian community is compassion—toward God, for each other, and for the world in which it is engaged.

Pastoral Compassion in a Contemporary World

The images of compassion in Scripture are largely agrarian in their context. Surprisingly, for all of the focus in church history on the role of the pastor in congregations, the word *pastor*, from the Greek *poimēn* (Eph. 4:11), appears only one time in the NT. The Hebrew equivalent *raah* describes a "feeder" or "shepherd." The one who feeds the flock of God's people naturally connects to the role of "teacher" in Ephesians 4:11–13:

> The gifts he gave were that some would be apostles, some prophets, some evangelists, some *pastors and teachers*, to equip the saints for the work of ministry, for building up the body of Christ, until all of us come to the unity of the faith and of the knowledge of the Son of God, to maturity, to the measure of the full stature of Christ. (*emphasis added*)

Chapter 4 discussed the importance of spiritual gifts in the church; they are universal in the sense that the Holy Spirit gifts all who live in Christ. This Ephesian text moves from the universal gifting of God's people in earlier Pauline writing toward some gifts embodied in specific roles of leading for the church: apostles, prophets, evangelists, pastors and teachers. Other Pauline

texts include likely offices of bishops, deacons, deaconesses, and prophets. [2]
The universal has moved to the specific.

The primary congregational leader will be identified by one of these roles, depending on the polity or denominational tradition of which the church is a part. All you have to do to discover which leadership title has been adopted is read the sign in front of the church building or access the church's website.

The dominant title of the primary congregational leader remains that of pastor. Whatever the title, the expectations of the pastoral role in the contemporary church are infused with multiple functions that often change its historic meaning. Emblematic of the shift in meaning is the title "Senior Pastor." What does that mean? Are we speaking of the one who is older than all other pastors within a congregation? The one paid the most? Senior in terms of status, or more important than the other pastors? Senior because the church is large enough to employ staff and everyone needs to know who is in charge?

Charles J. Scalise explored the historical development of two master images of ministry leadership. He suggests the historic image of the minister as shepherd was used "to describe one who cared for the multitude of God's people."[3] The shepherd was modeled after the good shepherd who "lays down his life for the sheep" (Jn. 10:11) and who is the Chief Shepherd of the Church. (1 Pet. 5:4).

Scalise contrasts the imagery of the pastor as business executive or CEO, best represented by megachurch pastor Rick Warren, as largely replacing the shepherd image. The challenge is whether the contemporary minister can integrate historical clergy imagery with the entrepreneurial, corporate-like expectations of many contemporary settings in ministry.[4] Perhaps the use of "Senior Pastor" is descriptive of this synthesis. The senior pastor is the leader responsible for assuring the accomplishing of traditional pastoral responsibilities, though he or she may not do them.

Whatever a pastor is, the biblical imagery of the shepherd describes her or his functions. The shepherd was central to the economy of Israel; survival was dependent on a caring relationship with animals who both followed and wandered. Marvin McMickle says, "A shepherd seeks to meet all the needs of the flock, from feeding and watering to protecting and occasionally having to discipline and correct... [W]e establish the image of the pastor as a shepherd who serves out of a heart for God and God's people."[5]

The caring ministry of the church is essential on two levels. The "needs of people" most clearly demonstrates the humanity of the church. In the act of caring in the midst of such needs, the spirituality of the church is most clearly observed. Care is of the essence of God-likeness, for the God of Israel and Jesus our Chief Shepherd know our needs and demonstrate care for us. "The LORD is my shepherd..." (Ps. 23:1) is more than a meaningful psalm in times of special trouble. It is the nature of God:

> He will feed his flock like a shepherd;
> > he will gather the lambs in his arms,
> and carry them in his bosom,
> > and gently lead the mother sheep.
>
> > > > (Isa. 40:11)

"I am the good shepherd. I know my own and my own know me, just as the Father knows me and I know the Father. And I lay down my life for the sheep" (Jn. 10:14–15).

A critical mark of hope for the congregation is care. A church that cares for those who choose to participate in its community and seeks to bear witness to Jesus Christ by caring for those in its community is a church that has a hopeful future. It engages in following the example of a compassionate Jesus.

Care is a distinguishing mark of the church because care requires compassionate giving. Care is costly. It costs time, energy, emotion, and money. That is the meaning of compassion, "to bear, suffer...sympathetic consciousness of others' distress together with a desire to alleviate it."[6]

Was that not the nature of Jesus' earthly ministry? His was a compassion (literally "to have the bowels yearning") that can be described as pity, love, mercy, and tenderness. He engaged in actions of healings, exorcisms, teaching, feeding, and raising the dead as acts of compassion to bring wholeness to the human person. McMickle includes the array of human needs identified in Matthew 25:35–36 as the focus of his approach to caring: feed the hungry, clothe the naked, visit the sick, embrace the stranger, and engage the incarcerated.[7]

Leading and Caring Ministries

Not every minister called to lead has the gift of compassion. Our personal identities may lend themselves less to compassionate kinds of personal/social connections with others than to a driving passion to accomplish multiple tasks effectively. The pastor who is not naturally caring must lead in such a way as to assure the provision of care by others. The larger the church, the less likely the pastor will be available for engaging in the personal, highly relational acts of caring so needed in serving the needs of congregants. That same pastor had better assure a competent and caring person is available.

The leadership core of the congregation will involve the full range of staff, lay ministers, deacons, and volunteers to do the work of caring.

Pastoral Theology

The classic understanding of the work of the pastor was that of the congregational parson who "envisioned the cure of souls primarily as a remedy for sin."[8] Holifield identified the four theological traditions that shaped the diversity of approaches to remedy sin as: Roman Catholic, Lutheran, Anglican, and Reformed.[9] The dominant tradition of the autonomous congregations of our focus is that of the fourth approach.

The seventeenth-century puritan Richard Baxter (1615–1691) was among the most published and popular authors of his day. His book on pastoral theology, *The Reformed Pastor*, provided guidance for generations of the past in the tasks of the parish minister who was so attuned to the flock that directive teaching was a primary role. The pastor was responsible to God for the quality of soul resident among the faithful of the church. This was accomplished by providing "oversight" to the flock by:

- working for the conversion of the unconverted,
- advising inquirers under conviction of sin,
- building up those who are partakers of grace,
- exercising oversight of families,
- visiting the sick,
- reproving and admonishing offenders, and
- exercising Church discipline.[10]

While the language may be more modern in tone, and the concepts less rigidly stated, a significant number of contemporary pastors in a conservative-evangelical ethos and in independent congregations would define their ministries of care in similar fashion. This fits the environment of the congregation in which the pastor has authority to "name sin" and take initiative to address specific behaviors in the congregation. Whatever the dominant therapeutic interests of those more educated and affluent, thousands of contemporary believers will make their spiritual home where an authoritative word or a movement of the Spirit to comfort and control will be a more likely approach to pastoral caring.

The rise of larger congregational forms and the emergence of "participatory" congregations in the 1950s shifted the work of the ministry in the direction of more specialized forms of ministry.[11] Programs of recreation, child care, community outreach, education, and any identified need called for staff leaders trained to lead them. None of these specializations has been given more attention, especially in theological education, than that of the discipline of pastoral care and counseling.

Pastoral Care

The pastoral care "movement" was in its earliest manifestations largely a focus on applying the emerging therapeutic insights in the 1940s to the work of pastors. Wayne Oates, one of the truly exceptional pioneers of this movement, included in his classic, *The Christian Pastor*, the four traditional "levels of pastoral care": friendship, comfort, confession, and teaching. Then he added a discussion of the "deeper" disciplines of "counseling and psychotherapy."[12] While Oates maintained a strong scriptural framework for his approach, others such as Seward Hiltner shifted the framework of pastoral care to a more dominant therapeutic approach.[13] William Willimon's caustic critique is that this approach added to the consumerist approach to ministry as "helping people." He suggests, "I believe this is one reason many pastors are so fatigued. They are expending their lives, running about in such busyness, attempting to service the needs of essentially selfish, self-centered consumers, without critique or limit of those needs."[14]

The Clinical Pastoral Education experience, which has been so helpful to many in ministry, enlarged the concept of pastoral care as therapeutic in focus. Rather than a dimension of the work of the local church pastor, the specialization has become one of addressing the emotional needs of persons with a level of skill few pastors have the time or training to practice. Holifield traced the shift from a theology that addressed "sin" to one of "self-realization" and "acceptance." Likewise, the context in this understanding of pastoral care moved from the congregation to the hospital and counseling center[15] As an observer of several generations of seminarians, the majority of persons I know whose focus in seminary was pastoral care are serving in roles of chaplaincy and counseling rather than congregational ministry. The exceptions make truly outstanding pastors when the urge to engage in therapy is balanced by the demands of leading the congregation in more generalized ways.

Leading and Caring

McMickle developed a helpful visual of the three concentric circles of care in which hopeful congregations will be engaged. While I have drawn from his three categories of care,[16] I have enlarged on his suggestions of the kinds and ways leaders are engaged in caring for people in need.

Circle One: The Pastor Caring

All pastors have a role of caring for those involved in the life of the congregation whether as observers, participants, or members. Both individuals and families will be the focus of attention in the work of the pastor. No pastor need, indeed should not, do all of the caring internal to the life of the congregation, but each pastor does need to assure the congregation has an organized way to provide attention at specific times of needs for those involved in the church.

Caring Worship

The best opportunity of the minister to express congregational care is in the totality of the experience of worship. The church at worship gathers as a community of need before a holy God to:

- experience new insights into God's Word for the daily challenges of living,
- receive the resources of prayer,
- engage in active prayer for the needs of others in the congregation,
- participate in the Lord's Supper as forgiven, and
- demonstrate mutual support for the hurting.

A pastoral prayer is essential for care in worship. Whatever the theme of worship or the text for the sermon on a given day, the prayers for the people led by a minister who is sensitive to the current needs of the congregation should address known issues of pain within the congregation. To do so, the minister(s) must be in touch with the heartaches of the people. Visiting personally with parishioners, whether in the home or places of employment, is more difficult than in the past, especially in more urban contexts. The requirements of privacy laws protect hospital patients from disclosures of conditions. Ministers must be assured of consent from parishioners before announcing personal needs. This means an atmosphere of openness to receiving communications of need can be created where trust of such information is paramount. A prayer request card in worship, telephone prayer lines, a prayer room with a request book, or e-mail encouragement to communicate requests can personalize the interest of the church in the needs of those willing to share.

Liturgies that lift up the heaviness of life and the struggles with failure can be collective means of voicing cries for deliverance from a congregation. Prayers of confession and congregational or ministerial absolutions are means of grace. Even the offertory prayer as a voice of gratitude for God's graciousness in times of trouble can pronounce words of hope.

Caring worship will include the reading of Scripture whether or not one follows a lectionary tradition in the selection of biblical texts. Psalms that comfort and encourage along with prophetic challenges for more just living bear healing words.

The two dominant sacraments or ordinances, depending on one's theological tradition, are both caring celebrations of the congregation when properly led by a loving pastor. Baptism is that central action of grace on the part of God in response to the confession of the Lordship of Christ in human experience. Baptism led by the sensitive pastor expressing seriousness for the occasion becomes itself an invitation to others: "Here is water. What hinders you from the confession of your faith?"

The Eucharist, Holy Communion, or the Lord's Supper, depending on the theological tradition of the congregation, is the central healing act of worship. What could be more caring than a solemn remembrance of the death of the Lord Jesus, symbolically relived in the eating of consecrated bread as the body of Christ given for us? Or, the blessed cup representative of the sacrifice of Christ on the cross? The salvific act of Jesus Christ—"For as often as you eat this bread and drink the cup, you proclaim the Lord's death until he comes" (1 Cor. 11:26)—is the constant reminder that the grace of the One we worship is the ultimate source of healing for all our needs. Moore suggests, "In church people do not eat bread in order to feed their bodies but to nourish their souls."[17] There is collective pastoral caring in the sharing of bread and cup with God's people, whose power none should underestimate.[18]

Compassionate Preaching

Effective preaching addresses the human pain of the congregation. The pastor will preach and pray with compassion as he or she visualizes the recently unemployed, the recovering addict, the cancer patient, the couple sitting next to each other whose marriage is on the rocks, the single mother struggling to feed her children, the young man just released from prison who needs a job, the lonely widow, the mother struggling with depression, the young man diagnosed with HIV/AIDS, the bereaved, the returning veteran now a paraplegic, and the silent woman whose livelihood is prostitution.

Compassion is more than empathy. Empathy is the ability to feel what others feel, according to Craig Barnes. Empathy, he says, is a "twentieth-century invention that achieved popularity about the same time that we were beginning to make all things center on the self."[19] More than simply identifying with the pain, the compassionate preacher suffers alongside the pain of those who listen. The compassionate brings a voice from God into the pain of human experience. When such occurs, the sermon is an act of weeping at the heartache in the human family. In the face of such, the preacher confesses the sinfulness of the human situation with its sins of violence and injustice, and resists the manifestations of such human evil.[20]

Not all effective pastors are compassionate preachers. Some do not want to be because their own pain is too raw for public revelation. Others fear the creation of a greater demand for personal counseling and attention. All pastors can develop resources of clergy and lay persons to provide individual prayer and counsel or referral to resources of care within the community or church.

Life situation preaching or narrative preaching that connects at the level of feeling will assure addressing human needs in ways that limit the necessity of individual pastoral ministry. Harry Emerson Fosdick, whose preaching ministry spanned much of the first half of the twentieth century, was known for his "life situation" preaching. He described his pilgrimage from the expository and topical approach of his day to what he called his "project method." He wrote:

> People come to church on Sunday with every kind of personal difficulty and problem flesh is heir to. A sermon was meant to meet such needs; *it should be personal counseling on a group scale.* If one had clairvoyance, one would know the sins and shames, the anxieties and doubts, the grief's and disillusionments, that filled the pews, and could by God's grace bring the saving truths of the gospel to bear on them as creatively as though he were speaking to a single person. The place to start was—with the real problems of the people… [N]o sermon which so met a real human difficulty, with light to throw on it and help to win a victory over it, could possibly be futile.[21]

Whatever one may think of their theologies or styles, Joel Osteen, T. D. Jakes, and Joyce Meyers are among the contemporary television preachers with unique gifts in touching the hearts of people from the pulpit.

Caring Preaching Is Confessional

Should the preacher share her or his personal struggles and pain with a congregation? Does that not risk too much weakness for one's effectiveness in leading? Does it shift the focus of the sermon from the word of God embodied in the sermon to the personality of the preacher? My response would be that variety in the content of sermons is essential for holistic congregations. Without an experience of the "word from God" in the sermon at the intersection of major crises, both individual and collective, worship will be empty.

John Claypool made the case for confessional preaching in his Lyman Beecher Lectures on Preaching in 1979. Pathos flowed in his approach to preaching because, for him, the sermon was a confession of life struggle, doubt and pain, suffering and exhilaration. "I" was prominent in his sermons, an approach many preaching specialists decry. For Claypool , the "I" was authentic because the sermon was his public confession of the challenges of his faith pilgrimage. Henri Nouwen's *The Wounded Healer* became a central metaphor of Claypool's approach: "What came together for me in this image was the realization that the secret of ministry consists of two things: first, the faithful tending of one's own woundedness, and second, the willingness to move to the aid of another and make the fruits of one's own woundedness available to others."[22] Claypool recognized not all could manage this interior struggle of the soul, especially when, a month following the death of his ten-year-old daughter, Laura Lue, he preached as much about the darkness of the experience as the light he had experienced.[23]

Grief Ministry

A third primary pastoral responsibility is the ministry with the grieving. The church is still the caring center for Christian believers when the "last enemy" of death makes its visit to the human family. Pastors are among the first to be called when a loved one dies. The care of presence, prayer, acts of sharing food and support, the funeral, and continuing grief ministry are essential internal ministries.[24] Failure to provide sensitive care in such times erodes the capacities of leaders to offer new directions for the church. Staff specialists such as associate pastors or ministers of pastoral care in larger congregations may allow the pastor freedom not to participate in every such experience. The burdens of carrying the pain of too many families in grief can be among the heaviest burdens a pastor bears, especially for the pastor of congregations of older members, where death is a frequent visitor.

Weddings and Family Care

My research with pastors identifies the challenges facing contemporary families as among the most critical issues changing the traditional value systems of the church. Ironically, the church is still the favored place for a wedding, whether the bride and groom have particular faith commitments or not. The more aesthetic and more "sacred" the architecture of the church sanctuary, the greater the number of requests for the use of that space. It is not unusual for churches with a more liturgical tradition to receive requests to host weddings for young couples whose personal worship is in a megachurch that is more architecturally akin to a mall pavilion. They may never have had a conversation with a member of the ministry staff of the church they attend!

The question is whether the congregation's leadership core views such requests as an opportunity for connection, hospitality, and witness or an inconvenience to be discouraged. In the current context of a significant "outsider" young adult population, missional churches will view requests from the inquirer for ministry at a time of wedding as an opportunity *if* the couple and their families are willing to engage in a pilgrimage of exploration for faith in their mutual commitments.

Caring ministries for families require either competent resources or referral to such for premarital counseling, wedding planning, ongoing communication with the new family, and support when the dreams of love fall apart. The experience of divorce is as prevalent for the churched as for the unchurched, a reality that suggests the need for ongoing encouragement of the quality of marriages and available counseling when troubled. A hopeful sign is the less judging attitude within the church than in the past of those whose marriages do not endure. When they do not, divorce recovery resources can be life-giving and grace-filled for members and nonmembers alike.[25]

Circle Two: Members Caring for One Another

The temptation of the pastoral leader is to engage personally in all of the demands of congregational care. To do so is a recipe for long-term exhaustion, or neglect of other needs such as excellence in worship and preaching, effectiveness in administration, and strategic future thinking. McMickle describes the issue accurately:

> An all-too-common "let the pastor do it" mentality exists in far too many churches today. When that mind-set governs, it usually indicates that people are stuck with a traditional sense of pastoral care in which clergy are expected to do all the work of ministry. Indeed, even some pastors feel guilty if they do not accept every assignment offered to them from within the ranks of the congregation. The circles of care model challenges pastors and congregations alike to resist this pastor-centric ministry mind-set. Such a view of ministry creates a fellowship of passive and underutilized members and produces a pastor who is burned out and overworked.[26]

All leaders must learn the importance of sharing the work of ministry with other leaders and caring members who have time and energy to give for the work of God's new order of the Spirit. Moses learned the lesson of shared leadership in Exodus 17:13–18 when he was required to hold up the "staff of God" as a signal to Joshua's army under attack from Amalek that God was present in their battle. Only the assistance of Aaron and Hur allowed him to keep the weight of the staff lifted so the army could prevail.

Likewise, as the Israelites settled into their nomadic life in the desert after fleeing Egypt, Moses became the "chief problem solver." His father-in-law Jethro returned his family to him, observed the weight of the burden Moses was carrying, and encouraged him to organize the people into manageable groups with leaders for each group (Ex. 18:1–27). Thus, he became the final court of appeals as "hard cases they brought to Moses, but any minor case they decided themselves" (Ex. 18:26b).

The apostles of the early church discovered a similar need. As the church grew, widows in the Greek-speaking fellowship of the church felt they were being overlooked in the distribution of food. We call the seven selected by the Hellenists to care for their widows deacons, though that language is not present in the text. Deacons are a critical caring group of servants who enlarge the work of a pastoral team in meeting specialized needs within the congregation. The widespread use of e-mail and social media allow for nearly instantaneous communication of needs for attention to specific individuals and groups within a congregation by deacons and other caregivers identified by the congregation.

When care is a primary leading agenda, the partnership among ministerial staff, deacons, and laity for caregiving can provide resources to serve one of the most challenging groups for pastors: the people of perpetual care. One of the most difficult dilemmas of the pastoral leader is the question of how to balance the needs of inactive individuals within the congregation for time and attention with the competing needs for leading functions for the active and healthy. Leading and chaplaincy are competing roles for time and energy. Yet, it is crucial for the congregation that hospitalized members, long-time participants who are confined to home or care facilities, those limited by debilitating illnesses or injuries, and the emotionally needy receive appropriate attention.

The level of care must be decided by each congregation, but a contact from the pastoral staff on occasion and at least monthly communication by personal visit, telephone, or a written note on the part of deacons and caregivers can transform the healing atmosphere of a fellowship. Thomas Oden's analogy between clergy and laity suggests the value of discerning when the pastor must act and when the laity's work may be more productive. Oden wrote, "There remains a line as thin as a hair, but as hard as a diamond, between ordained ministry and the faithful layperson."[27] Keeping the line thin will enlarge the effectiveness of the missional congregation in communicating the love of Jesus Christ to its own fellowship. Keeping the line appropriately hard will encourage lay ministry and allow clergy focus in ministry.

Circle Three: The Congregation Caring for the Community

The most challenging of McMickle's concentric circles of caring involves the church caring for the people outside its life in the setting of its community. Such is challenging for several reasons. First, in most urban church environments it is difficult to define the geography that constitutes a community a congregation should serve. In rural environments, this is more manageable. Some urban churches are clearly neighborhood churches in terms of their identities and history. This does not limit what they do, but does allow focus in providing help to those most likely to connect with the church as a physical location. When one lives in an urban space and shares a rightful concern for the "welfare of the city" (Jer. 29:7), the needs of people can be overwhelming when the city includes thousands of people.

The second challenge is the strategy one employs to develop ministries. Most churches live out of a "needs assessment" approach to the work in ministry they should do. Such an approach in any community today will identify more needs, heartaches, and human suffering than any single congregation can meet. Thus, the usual response is simply to feel guilty, give up in the effort to do anything, and address no one's needs.

A more effective approach is to begin with a "resource or asset management" approach. Ask, "What are the levels of interest in our congregation for engaging the community? How much time would we be able to commit to a ministry of caring outreach? What financial resources can we provide to make a difference in the lives of our neighbors?"

Once resources are clear, a prioritized approach will assure better effectiveness. A church that provides funds to enlarge the work of a cooperative community ministry may be more effective than one attempting a solo ministry. "Filling the gaps" by providing a ministry no one else is providing also prioritizes action.

The third challenge is to participate with other helping agencies in the community. A cooperative approach that is ecumenical or interfaith in nature concentrates resources for persons in the community.

Robert Franklin has developed a highly attractive understanding of the role of the church in its community environment. He offers five phases of ministry in the community context:

- The ministry of charity serves the basic needs of persons and requires little more than a caring heart and some resources to be effective.

- The ministry of transitional support extends encouragement as persons move from dependency to independency.
- The ministry of social services provides multiple services such as day care, pre-school care, tutoring services, food resources, clothing distribution, and many other services to community residents. A manageable fee may be required to fund them.
- The ministry of justice stresses legal and/or political advocacy around critical community issues.
- The ministry of transformation changes the community as an outcome of all that is done collectively to enhance the quality of life in the community.[28]

Robert Lupton represents the effective change agent of Franklin's level of transformation. A Presbyterian minister, Lufton committed himself to invest his life and family in one particular neighborhood area of southeast Atlanta. He founded FCS/Urban Ministries to develop a comprehensive community renewal effort that involves housing renewal, social services, and arts programs to develop the talents of the young.[29] He emphasizes the development of communities as an indigenous renewal by residents rather than betterment services designed to provide help to residents. He suggests, "Loading a depressed neighborhood with human services, while at first pass may seem curative, may in fact be the very approach that keeps a community from rebounding. Doing for a community what it could do for itself is as damaging to a community life as it is to an individual."[30]

Most churches have not considered another avenue of community ministry that needs attention. Churches, especially larger ones with solid resources of property, connections to community agencies, and funds can be agents of community development. The church has a self-interest in the quality of housing, commerce, jobs, and services in its environment. By participating in development projects, churches can help communities be improved. One of my early forms of ministry was to give leadership to the Neighborhood Development Corporation in Louisville, Kentucky. This nonprofit organization consisted of nine congregations committed to the renewal of the Old Louisville neighborhood area of the city. The ministry developed a long-range renewal plan that included housing rehabilitation efforts, construction of new housing for seniors, working with the city to improve community services, and creating a physical network of parks and living spaces that would attract diverse residents.[31]

Most of the churches in my case study research in Atlanta revealed a rich variety of outreach to community residents that ranged from feeding the hungry, to clothing resources, to a statewide health initiative, to athletic facilities and programs, to construction of government subsidized housing for seniors, to plans for assisted living facilities. With the future anticipation of reductions of government expenditures for lower- and moderate-income families, the burdens of care will fall increasingly on the churches of their communities. It is a burden we dare not shirk as Jesus followers challenged by his teachings and examples to care.

Stephen Ministry as an Integral Part of a Church's Caring Ministry: A Case Study

One of the more effective national organizations that is a resource for congregations in bridging the gap between circle two and circle three forms of caring is the Stephen Ministry. The Dawson Memorial Baptist Church in Birmingham, Alabama, has utilized the resources of the Stephen Ministry and supported a Samaritan Counseling Center with professional therapists for more than twenty years. Neal Schooley and I have been friends since college days. He gave leadership to this program for eighteen years and continues to be involved in its work, locally and nationally. His description of this superb resource and its impact on a local congregation follows with my deep gratitude.

Stephen Ministry was founded in 1975 by Dr. Kenneth Haugk, a Lutheran pastor and clinical psychologist, who realized that as a pastor he could not meet all of the care needs of his congregation. Since that time, 11,000 congregations representing 150 denominations have enrolled in Stephen Ministry and thus began the process of providing a lay-caring ministry in their churches. The name Stephen Ministry comes from the Stephen of Acts chapter 6, one of the first chosen to minister to a congregation loaded down with intense needs. Stephen Ministry is built on the New Testament tradition that establishes a corps of trained laypeople who can provide one-to-one Christian care to people who are going through many different kinds of crises. Stephen ministers are trained laypeople who can assist the pastor in providing care on a regular basis after the onset of the crisis. This allows the pastor not only to continue serving as the care receiver's pastor but also to give attention to the multiple tasks of preaching, teaching, administration, leadership, and caring for the crises that arise in the congregation week after week.

The implementation process for Stephen Ministry in a congregation begins with recognizing that the church's vision for ministry includes an effective caring ministry to the congregation and community and that one pastor cannot meet all of the needs for care in one's congregation or community. Stephen Ministry provides training, accountability, and support.

Churches who utilize Stephen Ministry must first enroll in Stephen Ministry. This is a lifetime enrollment, which grants the church use of the materials of Stephen Ministry, excellent leadership training, consultation as needed, and participation in a proven system of lay-caring ministry. Because the materials are copyrighted, enrollment is a necessity. The website of Stephen Ministries, www.stephenministries.org, provides a wealth of information about the process of Stephen Ministry, enrollment information, and other available resources.

After enrolling in Stephen Ministry, a church will send at least one person, and ideally four or more, to a weeklong Stephen Series Leader's Training Course. These weeklong courses, held six times each year, are professional in quality and prepare the Stephen Leader to recruit, train, and supervise the Stephen Ministers of the congregation. The function of a Stephen Leader is to lead the Stephen Ministry program of the church. It is recommended that one of the church's pastors attend the Leader's Training Course even though he or she will not necessarily be involved in the day-to-day administration or leadership of the Stephen Ministers. By attending one of the Leader's Training Courses, the pastor will gain an appreciation and understanding of Stephen Ministry, lend legitimacy or credibility to the congregation, and be instrumental in referring potential care receivers for assignment to a Stephen Minister.

After attending the Leader's Training Course, the new Stephen Leaders will return to the local church and begin recruiting people who will serve as Stephen Ministers. The Stephen Leader's primary resource will be the *Stephen Series Leader's Manual,* more than 400 documents organized into 67 file folders. The folders include documents on leadership and administration of Stephen Ministry in the church as well as twenty-five folders that include teaching documents with which they can train the new Stephen Ministers. Stephen Leaders can use this material as resources for training and leadership.

Stephen Ministers are lay members of the congregation who generally make a two-year commitment to be trained, serve in the caring ministry, and participate in supervision. We have several Stephen Ministers at Dawson Memorial Baptist Church who have been serving continually for the eighteen years since the church enrolled in Stephen Ministry.

The Stephen Ministers will participate in fifty hours of training. They learn listening skills, the distinctiveness of Christian caregiving, the importance of confidentiality, how to refer care receivers to mental health professionals and other community resources when appropriate, the process of supervision, and how to bring closure to their caregiving relationship. They are equipped to provide one-to-one quality Christian care to their care receivers. After their training, the church will commission them to serve as Stephen Ministers and then assign each Stephen Minister a care receiver. The care receivers to whom they minister may be members of their congregation or people in the community. Stephen Ministers generally meet with their care receiver about one hour per week.

One of the most important aspects of Stephen Ministry is the process of peer-group supervision. Supervision groups made up of five to eight people meet twice a month under the leadership of a Stephen Minister or Stephen Leader who has been trained to serve as a Supervision Group Facilitator. The group will offer support to the Stephen Minister, instill accountability in caregiving contacts, and foster a healthy caregiving process. Generally speaking, the Stephen Minister will attend about five hours of continuing education and supervision per month, and meet with their care receiver about an hour per week. Their time commitment generally includes one or two continuing education sessions per month. Therefore, the Stephen Ministers are continually developing their caring skills. While some Stephen Ministers will choose to take a sabbatical after at least two years of serving, many will choose to serve again as Stephen Ministers or utilize their caring skills in other church ministries. Some Stephen Ministers who move to different cities and churches will serve in the Stephen Ministry program of their new church.

The church where I served as Minister of Pastoral Care has utilized Stephen Ministry as an important part of its caring ministry since enrolling in 1993. In addition to training people who have ministered to care receivers to whom they were assigned, Stephen Ministry has benefited the church in several ways. In an unpublished statement, Senior Pastor Gary Fenton explains three ways that Stephen Ministry has strengthened Dawson Memorial Baptist Church:

1. The recruiting and training process has significantly increased the number of people who have confidence and competence to do individual ministry. Prior to Stephen Ministry, we had many with willing hearts and who wanted to help, but they lacked confidence because they were not trained in caring ministry.

2. Stephen Ministry has helped our church understand the responsibility side of the historic truth of "priesthood of believers." The gift side is that God has given to each of us direct access and that has been the dimension most emphasized in Priesthood of Believers congregations. But being a priest carries with it the responsibility to minister. Stephen Ministry has influenced even those in our church who are not Stephen Ministers that ministry is not optional.

3. The entire process of Stephen Ministry, which includes recruiting, training, commissioning, and assigning, has influenced the church family to have a larger picture of ministry. Our tradition has often seen ministry as a quick fix, assuming that if church members have the right heart for caring for others, everything else will fit into place. The process of Stephen Ministry has influenced our church to recognize that meeting human need in the name of Jesus is a complex process and that closure in their formal caring relationship really means transition to a new stage of ministry.

A critical element of how Stephen Ministry at Dawson Memorial Baptist Church has contributed to the development of effective pastoral care in the church ultimately comes back to intentionality. Will the church adopt a means of caring for the community that intentionally includes effective recruiting and training laypersons who are gifted for a caring ministry, or does the church simply assume that the members are supporting one another in crises and reaching out to people in the community who are hurting? Stephen Ministry has proven to be an effective means of intentionally developing a caring ministry for the church that trains leaders, recruits "ministers," and trains people to give quality Christian care to those in need. It also puts in place a system of accountability for the caregiver.

10

Proclaiming

There is no one activity that a pastor does that can have a greater influence on the vitality of the congregation than preaching.

ADAM HAMILTON[1]

The very act of proclaiming the good news of life in Christ is an act of leading. Congregations communicate the gospel, either positively or negatively, in all they do in worship, learning, community life, and connections to the larger world. Leaders seek to assure all modes of communication in congregations are positive messages of the love of God.

Proclaiming as Preaching the Gospel

The pulpit is the most important platform for leading the church. No other comparable role in our society provides a forum for one person to address a weekly gathering of people who incorporate what they hear into changing the world or be changed by it. When congregations are nourished week by week with a word from God that challenges and inspires, hopefulness is the outcome. William Self, a veteran of sixty-plus years of preaching, writes, "The pulpit is the last place in our culture where a person stands before essentially the same group of people each week and opens his heart to them. I know of no other place where this audience is inclusive in age, education, social position, experience (both religious and personal), and who are there because of their free choice."[2]

Such a responsibility is intimidating to any person with the awareness of the holiness of this task. Even the apostle Paul recognized the recipients of his letters evaluated him negatively: "For they say, 'His letters are weighty and strong, but his bodily presence is weak, and his speech contemptible'" (2 Cor. 10:10).

St. Chrysostom, the fourth-century preacher, stressed the need for constant study because "the art of speaking comes, not by nature."[3]

A preacher as recognized as Harry Emerson Fosdick confessed, "Preaching for me has never been easy, and at the start it was often exceedingly painful. In later years I used to envy some of my students at the seminary who from the start seemed to know instinctively how to prepare a sermon and deliver it."[4]

But human anxiety at the task never deterred Paul from understanding the power of the spoken word of grace. He wrote:

> But how are they to call on one in whom they have not believed? And how are they to believe in one of whom they have never heard? And how are they to hear without someone to proclaim him? And how are they to proclaim him unless they are sent? As it is written, "How beautiful are the feet of those who bring good news! (Rom. 10:14–15)

Preaching is an invitation for people to follow Jesus, to participate in the work of God, and to walk in pilgrimage in a transforming process that grows throughout life (Rom. 12:1–2). Preaching is both an evangelizing and sanctifying act, for the gospel "is the power of God for salvation to everyone who has faith" (Rom. 1:16). The most basic challenge of the pastor-preacher is to encourage/challenge/cajole/inspire a deeper commitment on the part of those who listen. That commitment is first to the Christ of the Church. Then it is a commitment to the mission of the church as a reflection of the will of Jesus Christ in its midst.

No single sermon will accomplish such a lofty hope. Rather, the totality of all that is preached—telling the biblical stories of the presence of God in Advent, Christmas, Lent, Easter, and Pentecost, teaching specific texts during the ordinary time of summer lulls and vacation breaks, encouraging generosity during an annual stewardship emphasis, or reflecting on the challenges faced by the congregation in its setting—serves to build up the body and enlarge its vision. William Hull reinforces this emphasis when he writes:

> Even the uncommitted who may be present for worship usually come either to understand what difference Christianity claims to make or to test whether it is actually making such a difference in the lives of believers gathered for worship. Unless the sermon becomes one instrument for implementing those changes mandated by the imperatives of the gospel, then the very nature of the congregation

will subtly shift from being a community of purpose to being an audience of consumers.[5]

The preaching pastor serves as theologian-in-residence for the congregation. The value systems of the congregation are shaped by what the pastor says. If there has been a dreaming process completed recently in the congregation, as described in Chapter 8, the sermon gives theological underpinnings for the major priorities of the congregation. For instance, how would a sermon on hospitality provide theological resources for enlarging the connections between long-time members and newcomers, between the first-time guest and the charter member seated on the same pew, between the great grandmother and a teenager, or between a traditional lifestyle reflected by congregants and less traditional groups in their community? How we practice what we say we believe begins with clarity about what we believe!

The pastor as theologian helps the visionary realities of the gospel take root in the consciousness of the people. The visionary preacher connects the congregation's story with God's story. The rich narratives of Scripture provide the content of vision. The pastor is being a leader whenever there is a "word from God" about the possibilities of God's people for living authentic life and embracing such life in the ministry of the congregation. Perhaps I can illustrate.

Numbers 13 tells of the scouting of the spies in the land of promise. You may remember twelve Hebrew spies were sent to investigate the land they were to occupy. As they reported back, ten of the spies focused on giants in the land, legendary Nephalim who were "sons of Anak." They were so large they were assumed to have descended from the intermarriage of angels with the residents of the land (Num. 6:1–4). Their size made conquest impossible. Yet two of the spies, Caleb and Joshua, countered with a confident assertion, "Let us go up at once and occupy it, for we are well able to overcome it" (Num. 13:30).

This story lends itself to a sermon on the challenges facing a congregation. The pastor can identify the seemingly insurmountable obstacles facing the church. Yet God's story brings the faith and confidence that, with God in our midst, we are capable of overcoming those challenges, even if the congregation relies on a minority viewpoint.

Whenever the pastor preaches, the congregation has multiple understandings of the person who stands before them. The pastor is their theologian, their biblical interpreter, their representative of the presence of God, their priestly confessor, and their leader. If these identities are maintained in trust and esteem, the pastor assumes a reified presence within the congregation that gives to the office authority and power. The pastor as preacher, when trusted, becomes what Landon Whitsitt calls a benevolent dictator. Before you react negatively to such a thought, let me explain. Whitsitt is pastor of an "open source" congregation. It is one that functions like an open computer resource—like Wikipedia—that any can edit or add materials to. It's a very creative, flexible, postmodern congregation that one might think would shun a "benevolent dictator." Nevertheless, does not every congregation have one, whether pastor or trusted layperson? Read his explanation of what he means:

> At first glance, the term seems to combine two mutually exclusive ideas... Although the BD is a person with almost unlimited power to take a unilateral action (a dictator), it is commonly understood that this person can never exercise that power for his or her own self-interest or benefit, or for the interest and benefit of a small group of people. BDs should always exercise their power in a way that benefits the entire community (should be benevolent). The BD functions as the chief protector of the community, sometimes even protecting it from itself. Because of the openness of open source communities, it is understood the BD's power is given at the consent of those being "governed" and can just as easily be taken away.[6]

There are multiple kinds of preachers. A preacher experiences many opportunities to preach in which he or she has only a limited leadership agenda. A guest preacher is not a congregational leader and has a more limited voice in addressing important congregational issues. Simply put, preaching *about* leadership has limited compelling power for the listener of a sermon. What the outsider *can* do is to lift a "word from God" that has the power to motivate and inspire in general ways to greater involvement in the work of God's mission.

One might preach as a leader in a noncongregational context. Surely, Martin Luther King Jr. was exercising great leadership when he preached "I Have a Dream" on the grounds of the Washington Mall. His leadership base was a social one, and he was addressing the nation. The same sermon from an unknown who had not been catapulted into national prominence by his pastoral leadership in Montgomery, his participation as a leader of the civil rights movement, the publicity that accompanied his "Letter from a Birmingham Jail," or his role as the president of the Southern Christian Leadership Conference would have fallen on deaf ears.

Leading is not all the pastor does in proclaiming the gospel. To preach week after week, month after month, year after year and fail to offer words that provide resources for the church to engage God's mission is to fail at the pastoral calling. How then does one lead from the pulpit?

Preaching Shapes Community

The pastor proclaims the gospel as a person to a collection of persons who will never fully embrace the grand vision of God's great story. The pastor-preacher fashions her or his leading like a potter shaping resistant clay into a usable vessel that contains, but never exhausts, the glory of God (Jer. 18: 1–11; 2 Cor. 4:7). In some traditions, that leading is rooted in divine unction or giftedness that protects God's servant from any criticism.

Those traditions experience high levels of the abuse of power among their clergy leaders—whether in the form of ridicule of followers, financial improprieties, or violations of sexual norms. In other traditions, such as the moderate Baptist one of which I am a part, too little authority is granted pastors. The pastor lives with the expectations of accomplishing too much with too few resources and too little authority to meet those expectations. Apathy, boredom, and burnout grow from such settings.

The wise leader enriches theological vision with sociological awareness. Understanding the practical processes of a community is essential for effective leading. Otherwise, the leader lives with a form of faith in which God does everything and humans do nothing. It is as much a heresy as the view that we can be and do church without the leading and blessings of God. James Gustafson's classic work, *Treasure in Earthen Vessels*, is a worthy guide for the contemporary leader. The church is a human community of natural needs, makes its governance decisions by political processes, communicates its message through human language and interpretations of that communication, proclaims truth through the memory of symbols and stories, and seeks to improve the lives of other humans because of its members' faith. The church is an institution. Its faith grows by social processes of construction.[7] The wise preacher will exegete the context of the larger culture, parse the dynamics of the local community, and script an understandable description of the congregation that will help move it to action.

Knowledge of the Congregation

Knowing the history of the church, the families that have shaped its story, and the conflicts that have diverted its focus are essential. The pastor should be the most knowledgeable person in the congregation of the church's past realities. Such knowledge may well avert a blunder in leading in directions that have been previously rejected.

Delivering the Word in a culturally sensitive style is crucial to communication. The recent emphasis on the listeners who hear the sermon is an important movement from a classic exegetical/expository style or a modern rhetorical/thematic style. The development of narrative preaching is an effort to connect the hearer with the story. Any such connection will require knowledge of the culture of the listener. Leonora Tubbs Tisdale recommends exegeting a congregation through analyzing its stories, archives, demographics, architecture, rituals, activities, and people as foundational to the "choreography" of the sermon. She uses the analogy of a "dance" to describe the interaction between pulpit and pew when the preacher has "read" the congregation in a way that creates words to integrate context with gospel.[8] Such a skill requires that the preacher be an "ethnographer" who delves into the subcultures of the congregation to understand the people who hear the word of the Lord Sunday by Sunday. It is akin to Paul's understanding of "missionary anthropology" in, "I have become all things to all people, that I might by all means save some" (1 Cor. 9:22b).

Craig Barnes is a most creative writer describing this ethnographic reality in pastoral ministry. His concern is not just preaching, but also the totality of the pastoral calling. His approach is to function in every dimension of ministry as a "poet" of the divine story amid the ordinary, the conflicted, and the confused. Whether engaging in the small talk at the midweek church dinner or listening to the anger of a parishioner, his role is to seek the spiritual reality under the text of the conversation, what he calls the "minor poetry" of conversation. The same process applies to the challenge of preaching as the pastor struggles to come to terms with the major poetry of the biblical texts to embody the meaning first in the preacher's life. From that deep interaction with the major poets of Scripture, the preacher speaks the message of the gospel to the realities of human experience.[9] Barnes writes, "A minor poet earns his or her salary on the days that the congregation is certain they know everything there is to know about a text. But those in the pews will not be startled by the power of God's Word unless the preacher is. No one should be more surprised on Sunday morning than the person in the pulpit."[10] When such surprise occurs, the person in the pew struggling with the subtext of a week of harried struggle relaxes in the reality of a poetic Word that changes the mundane into a compassionate experience of holiness "that can fill their deep yearning. The name of that Word is Jesus Christ."[11]

Strategic Thinking in Sermon Construction

What difference does it make to include the leadership dimension in thinking about how one preaches? William Hull offers four questions as to what he calls the strategic framework of every sermon:

- Where are we now in terms of the situation that this sermon seeks to influence? In candor rather than criticism, with honesty rather than hostility, what is a realistic assessment of the needs that this message is designed to meet?
- Where do we want God's people to go in the near future in response to the appeal of this message? What realistic vision of new possibilities is needed to encourage the confidence that this goal is attainable?
- What stands in the way of moving forward to realize the hopes awakened by this sermon? Where is resistance or opposition most likely to surface? Do attitudes need changing? Do priorities need reordering? Do social pressures need combating?
- What must be done to overcome those forces that would seek to thwart the claims made by this sermon? What resources of the gospel may Christians utilize in achieving the purpose that it seeks to fulfill?[12]

Not every sermon should address the strategic future of the congregation. Balance is the key. There is a calendar of congregational life that shapes the planning of preaching. Hull disagrees with following the lectionary, because of programmatic emphases and congregational issues that need addressing with coherence that may not fit the liturgical calendar.

However, the lectionary need not be an excuse for avoiding strategic leading. A most creative sermon on hope during Advent by my pastor, James Lamkin, included a powerful illustration of strategic thinking in preaching. The texts of Isaiah 9:2–7 and the Magnificat of Luke 1:46–55 gave opportunity to speak of hope grounded in memory, fueled by imagination, flourishing only when freed from the restrictions of the past. Isaiah's hope for peace was embodied in a baby to be born. The pastor spoke of the costs of war in our time. The prophetic words of Mary presented a hopeful subversion of the status quo, another evidence of hope. Then the application to the church was given as he contrasted participation in a graveside service of a charter member of the church in whose parent's home the church first met and visiting an ill baby on the same day. He reflected:

> If you ever ask me, and by the way no one ever does, "What is the toughest part of being a pastor?" I would say it is being a steward of

hope. The question is, "How do we embrace God's hopeful future that is like the past, but different? What does vitality look like when the pews are not as filled as many of you remember? What does it look like to be robust without large numbers of people?"

After affirming the contributions of the "builder generation" in the church who remembered well the successes of the past and valued measurable outcomes of them, he suggested the sign of future hope was Isaiah's—babies. He then described the growing cadre of babies being born to young parents in the church as our hopeful future:

> It would be nice to have buildings that were full and cheap to maintain, but God has given us babies. It would be nice to have budgets easy to raise and large enough to enjoy, but we got babies. It would be good to have a bulging membership that would make the balcony sag, but we have a row of babies in rockers in the balcony. So every one of you that has wanted the church to grow, I want you to sign up to keep babies in the nursery, to work in the extended session for children during worship, and teach in our Sunday school.[13]

The pastor can lead and preach from the lectionary!

There are several suggestions I would offer for including strategic thinking in the construction and delivery of sermons:

1. Maintain focus on God's mission for the church. If a congregation has not engaged in a process of clarifying its identity, core values, and statement of its purpose, preaching can be a resource for assisting the congregation to begin that journey.

2. Connect the proposals of the pulpit for specific forms of ministry to the mission of God through the congregation.

3. Set forth a calendar of annual program emphases for the congregation and include them in the plan for preaching:

    a. *Mission engagement.* When special projects are underway, encouraging participation in person or financial support is important.

    b. *Age group activities*—youth emphases, children's program emphases. Show pastoral support by attending such events, encouraging the congregation to communicate with the youth and children, and preaching on the importance of youth, ministry to youth, and the youth's ministry within and without the church campus.

c. *Budget planning and underwriting.* Strategic churches must be encouraged to provide adequate resources for undergirding all they will undertake.

d. *Special capital needs.* Any capital campaign for a church must be addressed from the pulpit.[14]

4. Reinforce the emphases being made in particular programs of the church. Most program congregations have some kind of annual emphasis on the importance of education, mission outreach, and stewardship that encourages member participation. Integrate plans for preaching with these emphases. If lectionary texts do not connect when critical words are needed in the church calendar, preachers should deviate from the lectionary. It is a tool to assist, not a chain to bind.

5. Recognize teaching opportunities outside the context of formal worship. Prayer gatherings, devotional moments in a variety of meetings, discussing the agenda of a committee meeting, and group mission projects offer leadership moments for staff and lay leaders who are attuned to the directions of the church.

Adam Hamilton is pastor of Resurrection United Methodist Church in Leawood, Kansas. He began the congregation shortly after completing his seminary education. The church has grown to megachurch status and is the largest United Methodist congregation in the U.S. He has a well-developed philosophy and practice of leadership that encompasses all areas of church life. His preaching is biblical and creative, a major reason for the church's growth. He proposes a planned approach to the preaching task, with time for planning and preparation being crucial to his ability to maintain energy and effectiveness. Five aims in his preaching provide the agenda for his annual planning: "evangelism, discipleship, equipping and sending, pastoral care, and institutional development."[15] Institutional development is the focus of this discussion.

Hamilton suggests that three or four sermons on the mission of the church are adequate for each year's sermon plan. He encourages balance: "These should be preached sparingly. If congregants, especially the nonreligious and nominally religious, feel that the pastor is always preaching sermons about the church and its needs, they will soon recognize the congregation as one that is inwardly focused and primarily concerned about its own survival needs rather than the needs of people."[16]

Remember the "Hidden" Sermons in the Church

The twenty to forty minutes afforded the pastor to address the congregation in worship each week, as important as they are, cannot be the sole source of communicating the leading agendas of the congregation. In a sense all that the congregation does communicates its priorities and values to all who observe it.

Newsletters

Columns by the pastor and staff reinforce pulpit emphases and offer ministry opportunities that may never be addressed formally in worship. A church newsletter can be a source of encouragement to congregants and should include a rich balance of inspiration, personal experiences of the writer, and suggestions for meaningful involvement in the ministries of the church. In an information-laden culture, repetition of the multiple opportunities for study, fellowship, and engagement in mission service is necessary to enlarge involvement. One can be more specific about planning processes, giving, and attendance in this medium than in the sermon itself. Written testimonies from congregational participants of various ages can be excellent sources of inspiration for enlarging the awareness of the congregation.

The newsletter can be a place for educating the congregation about the multiple ethical issues confronting the community of which it is a part. Worship is not the best arena for endless promotion of events and issues of concern to the larger congregation. However, the newsletter can be a place for both promotion of such and creation of a spirit of dialogue around important issues.

Electronic Communication

The Internet is one of the best resources for communication. The church website has become the first connection with non-churched individuals, especially young persons who retrieve almost all their information electronically. An attractive, up-to-date website that is easy to use is a must for effective congregations. The posting of a brief history of the church, a summary of its mission, its unique emphases, a calendar of activities, resources for study, even audio or video presentations of sermons or teaching materials can be important educationally.

As a visitor to many church websites, I often experience difficulty in finding contact information such as address, telephone number, and directions to the church facilities. This information should be among the most visible. I recently conducted a Facebook survey of friends engaged in ministry to ask for resources in constructing a church website. Figure 10.1 summarizes a sampling of resources identified as useful for simple and inexpensive design.

Figure 10.1: Website Resources Recommended by User Friends

http://bridgevision.me
http://www.christianpathway.com
http://e-zekial.com
http://flavors.me
http://www.thefaithlab.com

E-mail is replacing print media. It is faster than "snail mail" and more effective than telephone contact. I am a part of a congregation in which regular e-mails are sent to members noting pastoral care needs and announcing events and programs. E-mail delivery of the newsletter is both cost saving and more likely to be read by the electronically savvy. Members can still request snail mail print media if that is their preference. The key is to balance the number of such communications in a given week.

Some pastors and staff have been able to enhance their ability to address issues beyond the congregation with blogs and regular publications in a host of web-based arenas. The blog is the twenty-first–century equivalent of the syndicated column. With the expense of radio and television broadcasting, only larger congregations are able to afford the use of such media for broadcasting worship or developing forums for communicating the Christian message in the secular arena.

Community Leadership

The church's involvement in its community proclaims who it is. When the congregation is willing for the pastor and other staff to give time and energy to ecumenical and interfaith ventures, the church's identity is enlarged. Any activity that communicates to residents outside the church fellowship is a means of extending God's mission.

Use your creativity. How is your church interacting with your community?

Testimony

A word of personal experience in worship can be a significant resource in the spiritual pilgrimage. Some congregations have strengthened the spiritual life of their participants with Advent or Lenten devotional guides written by the members. Every congregation has persons who have made an impact on others, their places of employment, and their communities as well as the congregation they serve. Creating the opportunity for them to become proclaimers of their faith will encourage others to grow toward the high calling of God in Jesus Christ.

Conclusion

The church proclaims the mission of God in the world. The sermon is crucial in that proclamation of the good news of Jesus Christ. The pastor who makes the sermon an effective instrument will connect his or her heart to the leadership needs of the congregation and stir responsiveness from those who hear. Sermons can create trust for the messenger and enhance the ability to lead in other arenas of congregational life.

The congregation, however, communicates its mission in multiple ways beyond the sermon. Every avenue of communication—from the symbols of worship, the worship folder, announcements in worship, newsletters, website, community activities, to visual representations of identity embodied on publications and in signage—are avenues of proclaiming to the world. The hopeful congregation is committed to excellence in the quality of its multiple means of communication.

11

Organizing

My understanding of institutions is that there is an ever-flowing movement from structure to Spirit and back. Spirit needs structure, and structure needs Spirit... There is some structure in every movement of the Spirit... Structure can *be lethal.*

ROB BELL[1]

Organizing may appear to be the most mundane of the "doing" tasks of ministry. Yet without some workable organization, whether formal or informal, the channels for effective ministry will be missing. Congregations experience two major problems in their organizations.

The first is complexity. Some years ago I was consulting with an historic urban congregation in Washington, D.C. The congregation was a flourishing church of eight hundred worshipers at one time, but at that time I was consulted only ninety people gathered in worship. The church was demoralized. A predominant group of elderly persons and a handful of middle-aged adults constituted the congregation. They had few children. An examination of their documents revealed that it required 250 volunteers to staff their committees and organizations. They had downsized their levels of participation through a series of conflicts, but refused to downsize their organization. Anthony Robinson addresses well this reality:

> While people *are* busy (it is practically un-American not to be), people will find the time for what matters to them and for what energizes them. I suspect that, beyond busy-ness, too often the jobs that we ask people to do are not life-giving precisely because they are about maintaining structures and systems for an era that ended thirty or more years ago. They are not structures that are doing truly engaging and important work in our new time. It is a little like maintaining an antiquated association or club that was very important to our grandparents. We may do it as a yearly task out of a mixture of

164

sentimentality and devotion, but it is not where we live. This takes us back to purpose and to structures that are derived from a clear, compelling, and core purpose. Instead of having the proverbial tail (the structure) wag the dog (the purpose/mission), we must meet the adaptive challenge of making the dog wag the tail again.[2]

The response to the first problem of congregational life is simplicity. Any organization should be the smallest necessary for the church to fulfill its biblical functions described below. A small church can function quite effectively with as few as seven organizational leaders.

The second problem involves developing the church's organizational life on the pattern of another church. A structure imported from another congregation or a denominational pattern may not fit another church's environment or resources for ministry. Imagine an organization as a house. Some houses are new constructions. We think about a design that fits the landscape of its location. We consider size, shape, special features, utility connections, construction costs, and maintenance costs. We experience energy and excitement in building a new house. Frustrations and setbacks accompany the process, too.

Renovating an old house is different. You have to decide what to change and what to keep. Some things are too expensive to change. These include the foundation, basic structure, plumbing, electric system, and configuration of space. It can be easier and less expensive to demolish the old house and replace it with a new one if you want to make too much change.

Ministry organizations work best when they have clear designs and functional purposes. The design of an organization describes its parts and how they interact. Functional purposes describe the essential outcomes of why we are organized. Good design begins with the functional purposes we seek to accomplish.

A new congregation has much more flexibility in its design than an old one. Creativity with out-of-the-box thinking is paramount.

If your church is an existing one, it may be too costly to think about revolutionary changes in organization. Instead, work toward modest changes that will reshape its structures to fulfill more effectively its essential functions.

What functional purposes are at the heart of doing church? My bias finds the New Testament provides the framework for answering that question.

The New Testament Functions of the Church

The New Testament reveals a rich diversity of organizational forms, from small house churches praying and studying in intimate household gatherings, to large worship settings in temples or marketplace environments, to worship and study in a synagogue. Each city in Paul's ministry had its own pattern of organization. Explore the differences between the small group in Philippi and multiple groups of believers in Corinth. They share commonality, however, when one explores the functions performed by early Christian communities.

Common Functions of the Church

The Doxological Function—Worship

The most important function of the Christian community is worship. If there is one unique aspect of being the people of God in a given locale, it is the gathering of saints week by week to pray, read the Scriptures, sing hymns and praises, proclaim the truth of the gospel, give of their financial resources, and celebrate the Lord's Supper together.

Glorify God

Two Greek words describe the character of NT worship. *Doxa* speaks of the celebration of the glory of God in the midst of the worshiping community. The primary purpose of worship is to glorify God. Genuine worship does not concern itself with the preferences or tastes of a people in a given cultural context. God is the chief actor in worship. People participate to demonstrate awareness of God's presence and God's blessings.

Liturgy or Planned Context of Worship

Leiturgia is the second Greek word. It describes the liturgy of worship, the form in which worship celebration occurs. All worship has a liturgy. It may be an informal one with no written order, but the people *know* the elements and flow of the sequence of worship. It may be highly ordered with a finely defined liturgy that becomes familiar to those who are insiders to the worship tradition.

Vibrant worship is the source of hope for the contemporary congregation. One of the tragedies of the past thirty years is the adoption of war language to describe the competing interests around the style of worship rather than collective focus on the meaning of worship.[3] Worship is the most important task of leading for the congregation to experience growth in understandings of faith and the challenge for applying that faith to daily life, as they introduce the outsider to the good news of Jesus Christ.

The first point of entry for newcomers in the church is public worship. If worship is inviting and inspiring, and the congregation welcoming, the potential for connecting to the searching outsider is created.

Planning for worship is a critical managing task for congregational leaders. The pastor is the central figure of worship, for the sermon is the central proclaiming event of worship. A prayerfully planned integration of the elements of the liturgy creates potential for an experience of the presence of God.

The human dimension of worship joins the collaborative efforts of the pastoral team and the laity to prepare for worship. These include the aesthetics of the worship space, the symbols of divine reminder, and the artifacts of memory that create receptivity for the people gathered to experience the Holy. Humans are the choreographers of this drama. If done well, God may well decide to show up.

The Didactic Function—Learning

One of my most cherished friends was Bill Treadwell. He was a pastor of multiple congregations. He served as a gifted educator on several large church staffs and as a seminary adjunct professor. I learned more about church from him in a fishing boat than in any classroom. He had a favorite saying that communicates an insight too few in the church have learned, "Sunday school is the only school in which there is never a graduation." Learning is a lifelong challenge of growing in the understanding of one's faith.

The structure of the learning process is less important than that it occur. Jesus was the master teacher, a Jewish rabbi who was as comfortable teaching on Galilean hillsides and fishing vessels as in synagogues. Not only was teaching the primary means of inspiring and training his disciples, but he also left for his followers the mandate of the Great Commission for those who became disciples of the risen Christ.

The early Christian Church was a learning community. They taught Scripture (biblical knowledge). They learned the story of Jesus' life and ministry and the records of growth of the church (history). They gained understanding of the meaning of Christ's death and resurrection (theology). They sought to practice the teachings of the church in life and society (ethics). They communicated the nature of the church as a community (ecclesiology). By the second century, the Early Church was so concerned about the importance of well-informed followers of Christ that the *Didache* was written as a primer for new Christians. The work of scholars and scribes in assembling accounts, ideas, and understandings was an early Christian development that continues in importance for followers who model their discipleship after Jesus who "increased in wisdom and in years, and in divine and human favor" (Lk. 2:52).

Christian education as a specialization in ministry achieved its apex of influence in the mid-twentieth century. Most Protestant churches had a Sunday school for children at least. Some developed full programs of learning with standard curricula written by denominational publishing houses. Christian education today is being replaced by teaching sessions in worship or small group conversations. Reclaiming the importance of learning demands the attention of our most creative leaders. When worship becomes the only activity of the participant, the depth of faith will usually not be adequately addressed.

Organizing for learning will be critical for future hopeful churches. Most effective learning will occur within families as habits of study, practices of prayer, and rituals of faith take place in homes. Learning communities of faith with creative curricula and use of media form a framework for study, whatever the time and place.

The Koinoniac Function—Hospitality

If you happen to live in the rural South, church fellowship is dinner on the grounds or in the fellowship hall with plenty of fried chicken, potato salad, home-grown vegetables, and home-made desserts of ice cream, pecan or apple pie, and angel food cake. Such a menu can be conducive to Christian fellowship—as well as to obese preachers.

The menu of the church dinner is a rather trivial reflection, however, of the meaning of *koinonia*, the NT Greek word for fellowship. Contemporary understandings have made fellowship into a description of the intimacy of the internal life of the congregation. Such tends to produce ingrown small groups that become cliques of family members or friends whose major purpose becomes keeping outsiders on the outside.

The Acts of the Apostles describes a different understanding of the intimacy of the early believers following Pentecost. They gathered together in prayer, experienced the filling of the Holy Spirit, and became bold in their declarations of faith (Acts 4:31). From that experience emerged a community of such equality that for a time they practiced the mutual sharing of resources to assure a common partnership in their life together (Acts 4:32–37). Jews, Greek-speaking proselytes, and seekers came together as followers of the way of Jesus. When the deception of Ananias and Sapphira threatened the unity of the body, only the unusual event of their deaths brought a harmony that empowered the church to heal the distressed and to give their leaders courage to face persecution (Act 5:1–42).

Hospitality is a better postmodern word than *fellowship* to describe the functional agenda of today's congregation. The quality of hospitality shapes the hopefulness of the congregation. Have you ever attended a congregation for the first time and sensed an aura of warmth, openness, energy, a sense that the congregation was doing well? Or, conversely, has attending a different congregation produced feelings of distance, apathy, even anger? *Koinonia* is that qualitative dimension of relational life that grows out of healthy social interactions among the people. Hospitality creates an atmosphere that welcomes the outsider, gives attention to incorporating the newcomer into the life of the church, and refuses to keep out any who would respond to the inviting word of Christ. It is the most difficult function of the church to practice.

Can *koinonia* be created? Probably not! The congregation's intentional actions can create the vessel that shapes the potential for an inviting, open, community capable of attracting people on the margins of church life and society. Whether the Spirit chooses to fill the vessel so created is beyond our doing. Hospitality can infuse all the church does. *Koinonia* can be experienced in the intimacy of "passing the peace" as a ritual of worship, the bonding of a group of strangers who work together on a mission event, the small group sharing of a Church school class, or tears for a person in crisis at a house church meeting.

Congregations can best be intentional about their relational life by allowing the organic connections that are possible to arise naturally in the church. Joseph Myers suggests that persons choose their connections with others. Participation cannot be coerced or planned; it is chosen.

The most intentional one can be is to invite participation into community. Drawing from Edward Hall's work on proxemics, Myers suggests that the spatial references of relationships shape how we participate.

Levels of Participations and Relationships
Local Level
Public Fan
Social Space with Neighbor
Personal Friend
Intimate Confidant

Some of our gatherings are public, where the level of participation is akin to being a "fan." Think about the exhilaration of attending the national championship of your college sports team the year they won! You buy team clothing and join with thousands of others whom you do not know; it is exciting. The rituals of the crowd build a certain level of community, but it is not intimate. Worship in the largest of the megachurches resembles this spatial level.

Social space is where we interact with others at the level of the neighbor. It is a more direct connection, with potential for friendship and sharing of ourselves with others. Churches connecting to people beyond their congregation practice loving neighbors.

The third spatial level is the personal, where "we share private (not naked) experiences, feelings, and thoughts." Finally, intimate space is where the most private details of our lives can be shared with honesty in an environment of trust.[4]

Being a hospitable community of faith is akin to growing a garden. We prepare the soil for planting the seeds of faith, nurture the plants as they grow, pull the weeds that spring up, and enjoy the bounty when harvest comes. It takes time and patience, and the garden does not always produce. When it does, the bounty of community energizes and motivates the people of faith.

Rather than designing programs of fellowship, the hopeful church nurtures the opportunities for people to relate. Such relationships may begin with people with whom they feel comfortable. The relationships enlarge to the stranger and the newcomer.

Several practical suggestions for enlarging fellowship can be offered:

- Provide opportunities preceding, during, and after worship through singing, praying, and interacting together. Well-established congregations may be threatened by new patterns of interacting. New connections will enlarge the fellowship of the body if the anxiety of connecting can be overcome.
- Develop learning opportunities in a way that enhances open dialogue, offers expressions of difference without judging, and stimulates ownership of the truths being explored.
- Organize small group meetings outside the normal meeting times of the church that will allow connections to emerge.
- Create gatherings of grandparents and children to bridge inter-generational differences.
- Encourage the newest participants in the congregation to become involved in a specific mission project.
- Initiate ways the newest and youngest participants in church can assume roles of leadership.

The development of small groups has been emphasized as an organization process in congregations through much of Christian history. Educational programming has often been designed around the small group model of learning, with varied outcomes. Kennon Callahan suggests that it takes 12–18 months for a structured small group to form. When it does so, the group will grow to an optimum size of 12–15 participants, stabilize into a closed unit, and survive for the next thirty years. An outsider can seldom enter.[5] Create self-renewing small groups.

The Apostolic Function—Connecting

An apostle is a person who is sent. Unlike the later church, when the apostolate developed into an authoritarian hierarchy, the apostolic function of the church is to move outward from itself into the community of which it is a part and ultimately "to the ends of the earth" (Acts 1:8). Its meaning is inherent in the departing words of the resurrected Christ, "As you are going [participial action], make disciples of all nations [imperative], baptizing and teaching them [imperative] everything I have taught you" (*author's paraphrase of Matthew 28: 19–20*). This is the best summary of the mission of Jesus' followers for the challenging environment of the contemporary congregation.

Connecting is not a program to be implemented; it is a lifestyle of those following Jesus in which they work, play, live, and relate to others. Three primary forms of the outward reach are:

Social Ministry

Churches reach out as they choose to invest their resources of time, energy, and money in service to those in need of the caring meaning of the good news of Jesus Christ. An apostolic community's efforts include feeding the poor, building habitable housing, providing community resources for those in need, sponsoring counseling services, taking care of children, and offering all the ways in which people can be served.

Social Action

The majority of congregations give inadequate attention to those actions that will change the structures of the social order that perpetuate oppression and injustice. These efforts are completely consistent with Jesus' inaugural sermon in Luke 4:16–18: bring the good news to the poor, proclaim liberation to all who are captives of blindness and oppression, and proclaim the Jubilee of God. The church's ministry eliminates perpetual degradation of the land, bondage to debt, and unending imprisonment (Lev. 25).

Evangelism

The apostolic congregation is unapologetic in its readiness to invite the willing into relationship with Jesus Christ.[6] Hopeful congregations are intentional in their willingness to evangelize, not as a threatening message of judgment to those outside the Christian faith, but as an inviting voice of Jesus, "I am the light of the world. Whoever follows me will never walk in darkness but will have the light of life" (Jn. 8:12).

The apostolic function is not separate from the previous three functions described. A going out and a gathering in are essential to the full nature of congregational life. Eddie Hammett calls this "gathering" and "scattering."[7]

Some of the ideas spoken and written by missional church leaders stress the outward movement as the only legitimate function of the church, as though community ministry, evangelism, global mission, and public ministry addressing social justice are the only things that matter. These are important, but they can never happen without an internally strong congregation.

The first three functions of worship, learning, and hospitality are the *attracting* functions of the church. These functions are like magnets that attract people to become a part of the faith community. Growing churches are attractive to outsiders.

The attracting strategy for the church will fail without an equally vibrant *connecting* approach. How can we attract those whom we have not met, served, invited, evangelized, even confronted? We cannot. The calling of all Christians is to live as witnesses of good news in speech and action wherever we find ourselves. Andy Stanley, pastor of the North Point Community Church in Alpharetta, Georgia, has grown a network of megachurches based on making church attractive for the unchurched. The North Point story can be studied with profit by congregations willing to change and embrace a quite different model from the "church for the churched."[8]

The Episcopal Functions—Overseeing

Few of the locally autonomous congregations that comprise the target of this study have bishops in formal roles of church life, though all congregations do have "bishoping" functions. The bishop in the New Testament is an *episcopos* (Greek) or "overseer" with pastoral oversight of the total work of the church. Such a role encompasses the managing or "bishoping" work of the church and includes the organizational tasks essential for meaningful ministry.

One of the serendipities in writing this book occurred when I applied the spellchecker to an early draft. This tool identifies misspelled words and improper grammar, among other functions. The word "bishoping" was identified as a misspelled word, with the suggestion it be replaced with "bar-hopping"! It proves that the contemporary craze for relevance often overlooks tried-and-true wisdom from the past. Or does it? Maybe the true bishop spends time bar-hopping in search of souls to serve.

A different perspective is emphasized here. Bishoping describes the *support* functions of the church. Unfortunately, what *should* be the underpinnings of the church's work often become the all-consuming, energy-draining tasks that "starve" the other needed functions of worship, hospitality, learning, and connecting outreach. Only the most informal cell congregations have little need for addressing the following managing issues that require organizing tasks.

Facilities

Place is important for congregational life. Those on the most innovative and youthful spectrum of life often imagine church without meeting space. Informal conversations can take place at the local coffee shop. Public spaces are available in some communities for study and even worship. The issues of separation of church and state and general resistance to traffic in neighborhoods result in legal pressures on growing cell groups and house churches as they seek to find consistent and useful meeting space. Any successful venture in growing a new congregation will eventually lead to the issue of, "Where do we meet?"

Established congregations have the opposite problem. The Protestant pattern of facilities development from the 1950s to the 1980s was to grow a master "plant" of buildings large enough to incorporate anticipated numbers of new families in the membership. The result was often an overbuilt campus with too much space as the life cycle of the congregation resulted in crowded buildings at the peak of congregational size only to be saddled with excessive maintenance costs as the congregation declined.

Finances

Managing the financial resources of the church is an oversight process. Any but the smallest of congregations need workable, accurate, and legally acceptable practices for raising funds, budgeting their expenditures, and keeping accurate financial records. Additional attention is given to these two managing processes in the next chapter.

Staff

Employees are a support function. The staff exists for accomplishing the primary functions of the church. When they function well, they become essential to the effectiveness of the organization. When they become the center of the church's work, the congregation finds its effectiveness diminished.

The organizing functions of the congregation can be illustrated visually. Figure 11.1 pictures the relationships and flow between each of these functional tasks of congregational work.

Figure 11.1: Functions of the Congregation

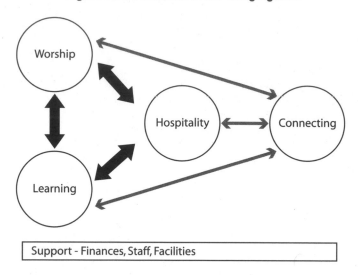

Support - Finances, Staff, Facilities

Organizing Congregations

Organic churches may not be very organic in all areas of their common life. Churches face increasing legal requirements or risks if they do not maintain specific practices and documentation for their work. Incorporation is required in some states for a church to be fully protected from legal actions that could expose each individual member financially for the behavior of one or more members. The Internal Revenue Service is more aggressive in requiring documentation for financial gifts from members who wish to claim a tax deduction. Federal and state governments expect annual reporting of compensation and benefits for all employees, though ministers are usually exempt. Some level of organization is mandatory for wise and effective management.

The leadership challenge is not to design and manage the most finely honed organizational structure possible. It is to assure accurate and appropriate processes that work and require minimal time, energy, and money. Several years ago, Bill Treadwell and I developed a guide designed to assist congregations in developing healthy organizations that were more life-giving than draining.[9]

Landon Whitsitt is a Presbyterian pastor in his first pastorate attempting to apply postmodern approaches to an established church. He writes:

Even though our theology of leadership is sound, we often act in ways quite contrary to it. While we say that we believe God has called each person to mission and ministry, the organizational structures we have created actually discourage people from pursuing their call in favor of the institution's goals. I do not want to suggest that everyone is a natural born leader, but I am suggesting that our organizational structures dramatically underestimate the number of natural leaders sitting in our pews. If we believe that God has called and gifted individual members to engage in certain ministries, what is the most effective way to support the ministry of these individuals in our communities?[10]

Simple Church Structures

Simple church structures fit the small congregation best. At a minimum, simple churches will explore the legal requirement for incorporation in their state and comply if required to do so to protect individual members from legal liability. They will have a clearly written document of guidelines for how decisions are made in the church and who is responsible for implementing them—a set of bylaws. Included should be a description of how the church calls persons to leadership and terminates them in the event of improper behavior or incompetent functioning. A written covenant of work expectations, salary, and benefits should be provided for each person employed by the church to which both employee and congregation agree.

A written annual budget showing anticipated income and expenditures for each year will be presented to the church along with clear responsibility for keeping an accurate account of the funds received and spent.

At a minimum, a pastor and six laypersons can comprise the core of work that guides the simple church structure. The pastor may be a volunteer, or a fulltime or part-time employee. Volunteers lead all other functions:

- The worship leader will work with the pastor in planning worship, lead the musical aspects of worship, and recruit others to assist.
- The hospitality leader will enlist greeters for worship, plan fellowship activities, and seek to build relationships among participants.
- The educator will identify learning interests, develop or purchase curriculum, and assist teachers.
- The connections leader will identify needs for service in the community, keep the congregation informed of service opportunities, and coordinate outreach events.
- The treasurer will manage all financial tasks.
- A trustee or group of trustees will be responsible for legal and facilities issues.

This structure is illustrated in Figure 11.2.

Figure 11.2: Simple Church Organizational Structure

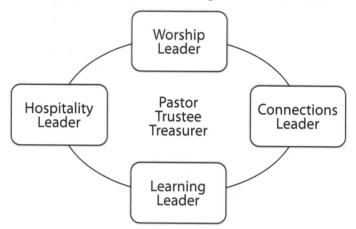

Complex Church Structures

Size drives the complexity of an organization. However simple one wishes a structure to be, essential realities must be addressed. The more formal a structure, the more likely documents will describe expectations, methods of functioning, levels of accountability, and evaluation of outcomes.

Governance

Free Church Congregation. All structures require governance. Someone has to have the authority and responsibility to make decisions for a group. Governance defines *who* can make *what* decisions for a group and *how* the decisions are to be implemented. Theoretically, the ultimate authority and responsibility for governance in the locally autonomous congregation is all of the official members of the congregation. In reality, levels of participation in "church business meetings" are abysmally low—unless a contested action is expected to be controversial. When this happens, the levels of future participation drop significantly.

Reformed Tradition Elders. More and more congregations are adopting elder models of governance from the reformed tradition. In an elder model, even if it is not called such, the congregation elects a small group of leaders to work with the pastor in the governance of the congregation. The group may be an executive committee or elders, but the structure is the same. The tradeoff of this approach vis-à-vis congregational governance is greater efficiency in making decisions, but lower levels of participation in the decisions of what happens in the church.

The majority of autonomous congregations I have observed use a mixture of these two. Governance is still congregational, but nearly all decisions are "filtered" through a process of committees or a council of committee leaders prior to congregation action. This tends to prevent divisive issues from discussion before a whole group until core leaders have come to some consensus.

Complex structures require governing documents that define lines of authority and responsibility for the congregation. Most congregations will develop Articles of Incorporation to establish the legal entity of the church. This step is most important for congregations owning property and employing people. Incorporation offers legal protection from lawsuits against individual members for financial improprieties or improper action by employees or other members. Each state will have unique laws and procedures to be followed. Most will require a Certificate of Formation or Articles of Incorporation to become legally incorporated. A charter sets forth the creeds or statements of faith of the church and specific descriptions of its identity. Bylaws provide the written guidelines for making legal congregational decisions; describe all governing groups and their functions; specify matters such as a quorum for conducting business, the role of officers, and the processes for employment and termination of employees; and management of finances.[11]

Policies and Procedures

Careful attention to decisions that establish guidelines for effective functioning need small groups of thoughtful persons developing recommendations for congregations to consider. A church business session in which important policies are developed from the floor without forethought usually guarantees disaster. At least two policy-making groups are needed in every congregation: finance and personnel. In smaller churches, such work may be done by one group, but the functions are distinct.

Church Budget. A church budget is a policy document. It identifies the priorities most important to the church. It documents available salary and benefits for employees as a group. It specifies the external organizations receiving monetary support. It should indicate shifting priorities within budget categories from year to year.

Personnel Manual. Employees of the congregation will function at higher levels of performance and be protected from improper treatment by members if personnel policies are clearly stated and understood by all employees. A Personnel Manual guides employees by providing:

- job descriptions, including specific work responsibilities, relationships, and supervision one exercises—and the person to whom each employee reports directly;
- processes of employment including application information, references, background checks, and available moving/transition expenses;
- processes of termination including resignation, retirement, or forced termination with stated time frames and benefits associated with each;
- expectations of work such as hours, rules at work, vacations, personal leave, maternity/paternity leave, and holidays;
- description of benefits such as health/dental insurance, retirement contributions, disability insurance, life insurance, tax sheltered medical/child care reimbursement, and eligibility for housing allowance;
- policy statements on employee/parishioner relationships such as sexual harassment;
- methods of evaluation of each employee's performance including any bonus opportunities and any conduct that will bring termination.

This work can be tedious and time-consuming, but it prevents abuse of and by employees.

Ministry Events/Programs

Most congregational work engages the nitty-gritty details of events throughout the year and weekly tasks for engaging the work of the church—ministry. Both ministry staff and volunteers make ministry happen. When planning and thoughtful execution occurs, the outcome can be inspiring, even life-changing. Records of tasks to be completed for each event, the flow of decisions, and budget requirements streamline events repeated from year to year.

Evaluating

Chapter 14 will address more fully suggestions for effective evaluation of the congregation's ministries, volunteers, and employees. Few congregations engage in more than cursory forms of evaluation. Even then, it is often informal. When things go wrong, everyone evaluates, but not necessarily in a helpful way.

Appendix B is a summary chart of each of these organizational dimensions of governance, policy, and ministry action, with visual lines of relationship connecting the parts. A conceptual awareness of the interplay of each of these managing dimensions of church life will enhance the effectiveness of the most complex of congregations.

Organizing Teams

Ask a pastor, "How is your church organized?" "How do you relate to each of the volunteers and employees?" "Do you have documents describing/visualizing the relationships?" The answer would likely resemble corporate structures of two decades ago: a pyramid-shaped diagram with the pastor at the top of the pyramid, a layer of employees supervised by the pastor, with each supervising even more employees or a cadre of volunteers. That system works, but demands extraordinary power and energy from the person at the top. If the pastor sits at the top of this kind of system, the main leader will have neither time nor energy for leading. The pastor will be a manager! Whatever goes wrong at the base of the pyramid eventually ends up in the office of the person at the top.

Control is the primary mechanism of this system. New ideas cannot be implemented without approval from the leader at the top. The bigger the structure, the more difficulty an individual or unit has securing a response of approval from the leader. The system runs on autopilot. The organization survives on order and stability, while the world changes with exponential speed, leaving the congregation behind. The leader feels in charge, however, and leader ego sustains the structure.

Teams can be a corrective to this model. Margaret Wheatley agrees: "We have known for nearly a half century that self-managed teams are far more productive than any other form of organizing. Teams create a clear correlation between participation and productivity. In fact, productivity gains in truly self-managed work environments are at a minimum thirty-five percent higher than in traditionally-managed organizations."[12]

A team structure requires a leader who understands the natural processes of group life. Bruce Tuckman developed a small group process in the 1960s enlarged by others to include each of the following stages.[13] Teams will be more likely to reach the performing stage with success if they understand this process:

- Forming—the team gathers to connect with each other, explore a common direction, and agree on how they will work. Trust emerges as the group thinks, shares, and works together.
- Storming—early in the process, disagreements will form. How the team works through differences of opinion, competing personalities

in the group, and behaviors that derail the process will determine whether the team continues and succeeds.

- Norming—the team comes together around agreed upon goals and processes for achieving them. Harmony describes the team.
- Performing—the team does its job. It is successful in fulfilling its purpose, agreed upon goals, and processes for accomplishing them.
- Deforming/reforming—the group decides whether it accomplished its purpose. If so, it voluntarily concludes it's no longer needed. If new goals or improved approaches to a continuing need are evident, the group reforms, often with changes in the participants.

Volunteer Teams in the Congregation

The primary teams in churches are volunteer teams. Volunteers engage in the tasks of twenty-first–century ministry, or the tasks will not get done. Volunteer teams create opportunities for people to give their gifts, time, and energy to do what each team determines. Core leaders focus on informing congregants of the needs for volunteers, encouraging and inviting their involvement. Congregations that engage in an emphasis on helping participants identify their spiritual gifts described in Chapter 3 will have a natural resource from which to invite people. If congregants do not respond, the work will go undone. That happens in the pyramidal structure also. The difference for the team structure is the blame game played toward the core leaders fits squarely on the shoulders of congregants. No willing volunteers, no work gets done.

Congregation Employees

The second team type consists of the employees of the congregation. The pastor of the pyramidal model selects the staff, delegates tasks, describes how they are to be accomplished, supervises the performances of the employees, and evaluates each on failures and weaknesses. Only four to five employees can be managed effectively by each supervisor. The system becomes a downward flow of decisions from the top, with each level of the pyramid replicating the performance of the pastor at the top. Sally Morganthaler identifies this system as a uniquely male one that women resist. Her more feminine approach stresses flat organizations of equal partners working together:

> In a world weary of hyper individualism, top-down systems, pedestal personalities, and I-win-you-lose dichotomies, the natural feminine resonance with the flattened world—conversation, collaboration, participation, influence, presence, collective intelligence, and

empowerment—has raised the cultural bar for what true leadership is and does.[14]

Staff effectiveness is enlarged if they understand their roles as team leaders and seek to provide effective training in team processes. Staff attention to teams of volunteers in their areas of responsibilities will multiply their energy and accomplish far more ministry than generated by a "lone ranger" approach.[15] They will have to invest in training of team leaders to be successful.

The team approach places both authority and responsibility for performance more equally on each member of the team. This does not release the pastor or "second chair" executive in the corporate church model from ultimate accountability for what happens.[16] Harry Truman was not the only leader with a sign on his desk, "The buck stops here."

Robert Quinn makes assumptions about an effective team that are overstated expectations:

> I define a team as an enthusiastic set of competent people who have clearly-defined roles, associated in a common activity, working cohesively in trusting relationships, and exercising personal discipline and making individual sacrifices for the good of the team. When a team exhibits these characteristics, it performs at levels that exceed toward organizational expectations. The whole is greater than the sum of its parts. There is a high level of cooperative interaction.[17]

I have never seen a team that could fulfill this definition. The terse statement has too many qualifiers: "enthusiastic," "competent," "clear roles," "disciplined," and "sacrificial." A more realistic church staff team would be "a group of Jesus followers willing to work together to accomplish the church's mission, with agreed upon responsibilities for each person's work, seeking to create an environment of open communication with each other." A team is always in process. It is a process of learning how to work together. It is a process of growing toward competency. It is a process of creating trust with each other. It is a process of being led by the Spirit. No team is perfect. Being a part of one that is working excels over any hierarchical structure one can create.

Organizing relates directly to evaluation. An effective organization produces effective outcomes in ministry. The lack of effective outcomes calls for honest evaluation of what we are doing and how. Chapter 14 explores processes of congregational evaluations and a fuller development of team models. The corollary of teams is coaching for evaluation.

Staff Leadership

Larger congregations rise and fall on the quality of the staff leaders employed to engage core leaders in the work of the church. Creating a configuration for staff requires thought, time, and dollars. Failure in this arena is a primary source of congregational conflicts. Failure in staff leadership equals failure for the church. Hopeful congregations engage this process with several principles that will challenge the practice of many contemporary congregations.

Intentional Design

The leadership core dreams the shape of any staff configuration that will enhance God's new order of the Spirit. That is to suggest that the shape of a staff should reflect the priorities for the future of the congregation's life and the resources available now for moving toward them. Visionary staff formation, like visionary congregational movement, imagines where we want to be and how we hope to move toward that vision. Teams of staff leaders can be more vigorous in their intentionality than volunteer teams.

Staff development can be a natural process that moves from the least trained and least costly to the most trained and most costly. Use volunteers for staff roles wherever possible. Many of the support tasks of a church—from answering the telephone to printing, filing, cleaning, repairing, or whatever is needed—can be done by volunteers. As the needs for employed persons grow, imagine a progression that moves sequentially in the following pattern:

- From para-professional part time, to para-professional full time;
- from trained support staff part time, to trained support staff full time;
- from ministerial staff part time, to ministerial staff full time.

Avoid adding ministerial staff without adequate support staff. Too much time is spent in the average church by ministers engaged in routine tasks that rob time for thinking, planning, and relating to people. Lyle Schaller, the dean of church strategists of the past generation, advocated two support staff for each full-time ministerial staff for maximum effectiveness. It is a wonderful idea I have never seen implemented.

Intentionality extends to who and how ministry leaders are employed. Jim Collin's leadership principle of, "If we get the right people on the bus, the right people in the right seats, and the wrong people off the bus, then we'll figure out how to take it someplace great,"[18] applies in part to the church. It is difficult to get the wrong people off the bus in the church, whether employees or volunteers. It makes the decision to get the right people on the bus doubly important. Search processes that seek ministry staff willing to embrace the vision of the church, committed to a missional approach to ministry, possessed of spiritual character, competent in the work that is needed, and committed to work with a disciplined team of followers of Christ can build long-term effective ministries.

Covenants for Staff Teams

Exceptional ministerial teams work in covenant with each other. A written covenant of mutual expectations and relationships will enhance any team's functioning. Jason Byassee asked of associate pastors:

> What do associate pastors want from a senior pastor? The associates invariably mentioned "communication" first. They do not want micromanagement, or a senior pastor constantly glancing over the underlings' shoulders. Instead, associates want clear direction for the areas of ministry over which they have charge, and then they want to be left alone "to make the church's vision a reality" in that area.[19]

Most of the problems of communication identified by staff teams are avoidable if the team works within the framework of a common covenant. What should a covenant include? Let me suggest several items:

- "How will we agree to support each person's spiritual growth? How will we pray for each other?"
- "How will we hold each other accountable to the practice of a weekly Sabbath for ourselves and our families?" Sunday is a workday for ministers and often their families. Overworked and overstressed staff is the bane of effective relationships.
- "How will we assure adequate time to work together on our relationships with each other as well as our common tasks?"
- "What norms will we embrace to assure effective communication with church members about one another?" Triangulation, or the willingness to engage in conversations "about" another without including the other, is a negative reality that staff teams must avoid.[20] "We will not talk about one another except to one another" is a challenging but helpful norm. Write your own norms.
- "How will we support one another's areas of responsibilities—during illness, 'crunch' times, or when problems emerge for which help is needed?" I have worked with one creative staff that created a "sick day bank" in which staff could contribute individual sick days to a chronically ill staff member.

- "How will we play together? Will we include our families in our times of celebration?"

Coaching Staff Teams

Coaching is a growing practice as a process for staff relationships between pastors and associates. The question is whether it will generate improvement in staff functioning or simply be another "fad." Coaching organizations and training programs are springing up like wild flowers.

A difference separates the analogies of coaching from the world of sports as a metaphor for the principles of leading winning organizations and the disciplines of the International Federation of Coaching. Tom Bandy is author of a stimulating, even inspiring book on coaching. His approach makes the coach the center of the action, a team leader who builds a winning team through teaching, inspiring action, and forcing accountability. The leader who builds a winning team is Bandy's understanding of coaching.[21] While I enjoy a winning team, for every winner in athletics there has to be a loser.

The kind of coaching of which I am speaking does not place emphasis on the coach but on a person who enters a coaching relationship seeking growth. The role of the coach is to help the person being coached (PBC) identify strengths and processes for maximizing those strengths. Pastors of medium-sized staffs who seek training in coaching skills can find in this approach one that builds healthy and effective teams. Pastors of larger staffs can lead in the development of resources to employ external coaches to work with employees in developing their strengths.

Ministry coaching needs to be distinguished from other roles of leadership with staff. These include mentoring, or teaching another out of one's personal study and experience. Mentoring is an appropriate commitment for the staff leader with a new employee.

Consulting is more directive. The consultant offers suggestions to another based on expertise developed through personal experience. The consultant *tells* the group or organization what they need to do.

Neither is coaching engaging in counseling. It may be helpful to the counseling process. Coaching is not a therapeutic process that requires specialized training in supporting a client to change emotionally or to address deep-seated insecurities or traumas.

Coaching in its purest form is a nondirective process. The coach asks the PBC powerful questions that allow the coachee to conclude how best to respond for growth. The responsibility for action always lay with the PBC, not the coach. The coach is a facilitator who assists the PBC in identifying passions, strengths, and goals for growing in areas identified by the PBC.

The basic skills required of a coach are summarized in the LEARN model of coaching:

- **L**istening to the agenda of the PBC;
- **E**ncouraging the coachee to identify strengths and potential;
- **A**sking questions that help the PBC achieve clarity;
- **R**esponding with feedback to what is heard;
- **N**egotiating with the PBC actions to be implemented.[22]

Jane Creswell is a unique combination of corporate coach and Jesus disciple. Her seven-fold process of coaching with a Christian foundation will energize and enlarge the values of staffs and congregations. Her "Christ-centered coaching" approach is not unlike a seven-step Christian discipleship process in which individuals are encouraged to grow as followers of Christ with encouragement from a coach. She writes:

> Coaching focuses on promoting discovery. *Christ-Centered* coaching additionally utilizes the power of the Holy Spirit in that discovery process. By helping you focus on the untapped potential within you, a coach can guide you to discover that potential and what needs to be done. The coach won't provide the answer, make decisions for you, or tell you what to do.[23]

Properly done, coaching can be a liberating experience. Daniel Goleman's description of the coaching leader fits well a church staff:

> Coaching leaders help employees identify their unique strengths and weaknesses and tie them to their personal and career aspirations. They encourage employees to establish long-term development goals and help them conceptualize a plan for attaining them. They make agreements with their employees about their role and responsibilities in enacting development plans, and they give plentiful instruction and feedback.[24]

Building the environment for such an approach on a church staff will require understanding and training from the pastor. Employing a professional coach to work with a staff to create the attitude and openness will be a wise direction. Most of the time the pastor can be the coach of the staff, working to develop a team that coaches others in the accomplishment of ministry. A coaching culture that seeks commitment to the church's mission stresses constant encouragement of openness to empowerment and innovation.[25]

Organizing a staff team around the principles of coaching assumes several things about the quality of the team assembled. An inexperienced staff member may need a mentor rather than a coach for the first year of ministry to provide more directive guidance on what needs to be done in the setting. A mentor should assist with understanding the how of accomplishing clear goals.

Some staff may need a consultant to bring expertise and experience to bear on tasks needed for the congregation. A counselor may be more appropriate to address therapeutic issues that need attention. Some staffs may be "simply uncoachable" and need specialized attention from the personnel committee.[26]

A pastor-coach of a ministry staff is quite different from the independent coach who will have less bias in relating to the PBC. The practices of coaching can be an effective way to ensure high levels of commitment on the part of staff to the work they are doing. After all, in a coaching culture the PBC will be the person deciding what he or she needs to be doing and how. The coach simply helps the person come to those conclusions and state them.

12

Resourcing

People do not give to sinking ships. They give to ships that are sailing strong and give every indication of reaching their destination.

J. CLIF CHRISTOPHER [1]

Congregational resourcing is a perpetual concern of congregational leaders. This concern can be all-consuming, or at least the source of significant anxiety. Among the most idolatrous practices of the contemporary church is excessive attention to one dimension of the congregational resources: "How much was the offering last week?" The $ for some congregations is equally as important as a symbol as the cross adorning the sanctuary.

The first challenge of leading in congregational resourcing is a redefinition of the issues. Managing resources gives attention to the larger questions of stewardship as inherent in mission theology.

Redefinition of Issues

A Stewardship of Abundance

- Stewardship in all its dimensions is more a matter of faith than the level of our personal resources.
- God is the Creator of all that is. Any blessings we enjoy are gifts from God's bounty.
- The biblical notion of stewardship is all-encompassing. Every dimension of life is gift.
- The real questions of stewardship concern the choices we make in how we use those gifts.
- We are stewards of the creation. How we treat the planet is a choice rooted in our understanding of God's love of the earth.
- We are stewards of our lives. The choices we make in how we live determine the level of abundance in which we shall live.

> • We are stewards of our financial resources. The ultimate choice God would have us make is to live in the power of enough.

Enough for Everyone

Lynn Miller suggests, "God intends for everyone to have enough—not too little and not too much."[2] That is a revolutionary idea in a consumer-oriented culture. Most Americans are dependent on a capitalist system that is more rooted in the importance of wealth than in dependence on God as the source of all we are and all we have.

The essential meaning of the biblical story stresses the adequacy of God to care for our needs. The essential meaning includes:

- the meaning of God's promise of land and blessings to Abraham and Sarah (Gen. 12:1–3);
- the meaning of the story of God's provision of quail and manna for the wandering Israelites in the desert as they lived daily in dependence on such provision (Ex. 16);
- the meaning of Jesus' teachings of the priority of the kingdom (Mt. 6:33) and the provision of God, as we trust in divine promises (Mt. 6:25–34).

Stewardship is also a matter of finances. The imperative of Jesus in the Great Commission to obey his teachings includes his teachings on money. Jesus taught about wealth, generosity, and trust. As much as one-third of what Jesus taught was on the subject of financial resources.

Principles of Financial Stewardship

The church should be a lighthouse of truth in teaching the principles of financial stewardship if we are to live faithfully in our time of economic challenges. In summary fashion these principles of financial stewardship include:

- The spiritual vitality of our lives—the rightness of our hearts—is the shaping factor in how we live our financial lives (Mt. 6:19–21);
- The management of what we have is a spiritual responsibility (the parable of the dishonest manager) (Lk. 16:1–13);
- Abundance not shared is destructive to self and others (the parable of the rich man and Lazarus) (Lk. 16:19–31);
- Wealth gained by deceit or injustice must be restored to the abused (the story of Zacchaeus) (Lk. 19:1–10);
- Resources invested unwisely will be lost (the parable of the ten pounds) (Lk. 19:11–26);

- The amount given is less important than the sacrifice of giving (the widow's offering) (Lk 21:1–4);
- Deceitful giving is destructive to the meaning of generosity (the story of Ananias and Sapphira) (Acts 5: 1–11).

The Reciprocity Reality

A reciprocal interaction links how churches deal with their financial stewardship and the generosity of their members. Stingy members develop stingy churches, and stingy churches enhance stingy members. Scattered through the Pauline texts of Scripture is an important insight in the importance of financial stewardship for congregations, namely the collection ministry. The model of Paul's interactions with the churches in which he served was first established at the congregation in Antioch. It modeled for a young follower of Jesus, Saul, generosity in its sharing of resources with the church of Jerusalem during a time of famine and poverty. The church in Jerusalem had not yet accepted this Antiochian congregation of Gentile believers into the full fellowship of faith.

On hearing Agabus' prophecies of a major famine, the Antiochian congregation still gathered a collection to send to the mother church in Jerusalem. They developed a practice central to generous Christians through the centuries: "The disciples determined that according to their ability, each would send relief to the believers living in Judea; this they did, sending it to the elders by Barnabas and Saul" (Acts 11:29). When the Apostolic Council in Jerusalem redefined the Christian faith to include Gentiles (Acts 15:1–35), Paul's account of the decision included an agreement to "remember the poor, which was actually what I was eager to do" (Gal. 2:10). Paul established a practice of soliciting an annual offering from the Gentile churches of Asia Minor to be delivered to the Jerusalem church on Pentecost as a symbol of reconciliation between Jews and Gentiles (1 Cor. 16:1–4; 2 Cor. 8:1–8; 2 Cor. 9; Phil. 4:10–20).

Theology of Financial Stewardship

Such a practice gave rise to the most developed theology of financial stewardship in the Early Church, summarized in 2 Cor. 8—9:

- Jesus is the model of generosity: " though he was rich, yet for your sakes he became poor, so that by his poverty you might become rich" (2 Cor. 8:9b);
- Generosity flows from one's abundance, not to impoverish the giver, but to establish balance between rich and poor (2 Cor. 8:12–14);

- Giving is an act of sowing and reaping—bountiful sowing yields bountiful harvest (2 Cor. 9:6);
- Generous offerings are cheerfully given and un-coerced (2 Cor. 9:7);
- Abundance is defined by having enough to share abundantly in "every good work" (2 Cor. 9:8).

The giver is generous in response to God's grace and becomes the recipient of the gratitude of those receiving the benefits of such generosity. Both the giver and the recipient are blessed, and God is glorified (2 Cor. 9:13–15). This is reminiscent of the "thank offering" Moses instituted in Deuteronomy 26:1–11 in recognition of God's gift of the land, whose bountiful harvest provided the resources to praise God in thanksgiving!

The Sense of Systematic Stewardship

Individuals who live within the framework of these values will not be immune from the same economic challenges of those who do not. Have you ever heard a sermon that suggested, "If you tithe to the church, God will bless you with more money than those who do not?" I have, and it is not biblical! Since childhood I have given systematically and generously to my church because that was a faith commitment instilled within me at an early age. My wife and I have continued that commitment throughout the years of our marriage, including the stressful years of low income, high debt, costs of children, and occasional emergencies. We also have fewer material "things" than many we know at similar levels of income who are not generous. We have practiced this discipline individually and collectively for more than sixty years and have yet to be deprived of any necessity important to joyful life. We have been blessed with opportunities of travel, play, and service, as have our children. We have always had "enough," and so we continue to learn to trust that each day of the future will be similar.

Needed: Disciplined Disciples, Not Corporate Donors

Giving is a spiritual discipline. Some of the literature on church stewardship lacks this essential element, with programs patterned after the money-raising techniques of nonprofit organizations that treat people as donors rather than disciples.

The competitive realities in the fund-raising world create a temptation in the contemporary church. J. Clif Christopher makes a compelling argument that the church must treat its members as "donors" in competition with nonprofit organizations. Nonprofits have grown rapidly in number to 1.8

million, with 1,064,000 of these registered as 501 (c) (3) corporations. The competition of these is real, with 320,000 to 370,000 congregations in the U.S. Consequently, the percentage of giving to religious entities has declined from 53 percent of charity dollars in 1985 to 32.8 percent in 2007![3]

I spent seven years in that "donor" world as the president of Shorter College. The number one responsibility I had was to be the CFR of the college—the Chief Fund Raiser. The leader of every donor-based organization takes on that title and function whether they desire it or not. Every marketing technique that can show any success at all is applied in the religious institution world. I sought to learn from other college presidents who were successful fund raisers. I attended national workshops on the topic and worked at it constantly. My task was to assure a trustworthy financial system for the school, make as many friends as possible, become highly visible in the community by assisting other worthy organizations in their fund raising, and thank every donor profusely for every gift received. As a result, the college grew financially from deficit financing to a surplus in funds with salaries increased, old facilities renovated, and new ones constructed. I also barely exceeded the national average for college presidents of five years of tenure. I was exhausted after seven years!

A follower of Jesus Christ is more than a donor. The true disciple has an allegiance to the mission of God in all of its dimensions. Giving is motivated by love for the body of Christ. We do not give to build an institution. We give to serve the world, and that service begins in the lives of those who are a part of our community of faith.

Growing Generous Givers

That is the theological perspective. How do we translate that perspective into the "how" of living generously? You may not agree with the practical suggestions that follow. However, if you do not, will you develop your own practices as a congregation that embodies these principles?

Leading a congregation in generosity is as intentional as growing in faith. It requires intentional attention to a process of education in the meaning of financial stewardship, to assuring a trustworthy system of managing the church's money, and to practicing an unapologetic willingness to offer opportunities for people to give.

Educating for Generosity

The Chief Stewardship Educator of the congregation is the pastor. No place is more significant for an emphasis on the biblical principles of giving than the pulpit. If people never hear from their pastor a challenging word about their support of the ministries of the church through their gifts, they will be less generous. Most stewardship specialists suggest at least four sermons annually addressing the opportunities for growth in giving. "That is too much," you say. Does that not leave forty-eight weeks in the church year for other emphases? Four out of fifty two sermons is a significantly smaller proportion of attention than Jesus gave to the subject.

It is important to include stewardship education in the educational programming for the church. Sunday school classes or small group studies of the biblical teachings on finances will stimulate deeper growth.[4] Increasing numbers of churches are providing classes in financial accountability, which younger families often need to begin managing their debts.[5]

Lay Teaching and Testimony

Equally important in creating a culture of giving is positive attention from the laity about the joy they have experienced in giving. A four-minute testimony from representative laity who are excited by their experience in the church will encourage others to grow. Plan for one at least quarterly. Nothing is more discouraging than to hear in worship from the chair of the Finance Committee, "We are behind on our budget, and we need to dig deeper so we can catch up on paying our bills."

Train the Finance/Stewardship Committee

Sometimes the most important education in this arena is needed in the Finance Committee or Stewardship Committee. Too often these groups function to control risk and avoid asking for too much from the people for fear of offending someone. They may not realize the risk in timidity. These leaders should model enthusiasm for their congregation through their participation and giving. Their role is to *ask* others to join them in that same enthusiasm.

When was the last time the group in your congregation responsible for enlarging financial resources read together a book on how others approach this ministry? What might happen if they read one that suggests practices that would be resisted by the traditions of the congregation? They might reject much of what they read, but they would be introduced to at least one new idea that could be useful in your context. Churches that have structured pledge campaigns could profit from reading the suggestions of Anthony Robinson.[6] Clif Christopher has helpful suggestions for organizing a highly structured approach to asking for gifts. Nelson Searcy[7] will shake up the typical church's approach to giving with an all-encompassing system for enlarging giving commitment.

Enlarge the Financial Resources

Enlarging resources is a product of energy. Every congregation goes through cycles of energy. The energy intensifies in certain seasons of the year, such as Advent and Easter. It lulls during times of vacation in the summer or holiday weekends. When are the seasons of the best attendance and the sense of momentum in your congregation? When are the troughs of apathy?

Every congregation I have known, from the smallest rural congregation to the largest megachurch, will respond to the moment of a particular opportunity above and beyond any pledged or routine gift. A congregation will find the resources it needs because certain people within it love church so much they will dig deeper to help a person in crisis or fund an emergency repair. Most congregations will find whatever funds they need if the roof needs repair or the heating unit breaks down! They will also give over and above regular gifts for the youth mission trip, or to help with a person with emergency needs, or for a special project for which funds are not budgeted. A fundamental difference stands between total income for a church and the amount needed to fund an annual budget. Wise leaders allow for opportunities to arise for the spontaneous outpouring of giving to "over and above" opportunities for the church to be the church.

People give to people, not to programs. Throughout the year during worship let program leaders or special ministry leaders highlight the blessings and results of leading events or ministries so your people will gain more awareness of ways God is working.

Invite energizing community leaders whose ministries are increasing, helped by funds from your church. This will help encourage the congregation.

Have a mission luncheon or dinner that highlights all of the ways in which the church is ministering.

Feature teenagers and children in worship participation with readings of Scripture or testimonies of their experiences in a summer event.

The more people recognize the lives being changed by the church's ministry, the more willing they will be to give, and the better they will understand the impact their giving has on future generations. The backbone of support for church budgets is the cohort of long-time, committed members who give faithfully year after year.

Situational Awareness: Recognize How Various Age Groups Give

Older Adults

Retirees give out of fixed levels of income. Their income is a product of Social Security benefits, interest earned on savings, and dividends earned on investments. Current economic realities have a dramatic impact on their desires to do more. When interest earnings on certificates of deposit are presently at the lowest historic levels, remember retirees and the pressures they face. The pressures for government entitlement reform will likely limit the cost of living adjustments on Social Security in the future. Only the wealthiest have dividend income that may be growing.

Congregations with predominantly elderly participants will live with annual reductions in church income. Energy for innovation will be depressed. Making retires feel guilty for not doing more will only accelerate discouragement.

Retirees may offer the opportunity to develop an emphasis on estate giving, an underdeveloped practice. Wise congregations will have an educational program available for the benefits of including the congregation in personal wills. The legacy of a bequest or endowment directed to fund mission can ensure vitality far beyond the life of the giver. It can also be the life-blood of congregations for the future.

Middle-aged Adults

Employed middle-aged adults are the most viable sources for budget growth in a growing economy. However, those who are lower-middle class and middle class have largely struggled with stagnant increases in income and with growing debt over the past decade. The median wage—half make more, half less—in 2009 was $37 lower than in 2000 and $253 lower than in 2008. In a study of more than 1,300 U.S. counties, median household income grew between 2000 and 2009 in 192 of them, while it declined in more than 1100 of them.[8] For all of the concern we rightly have about our consumerist society, 70 percent of the American economy is dependent on consumer spending, and the consumer is "spent" in most locales of the nation.

Congregations in newer communities with vibrant technology based employment are in settings where strong growth of church resources is likely. This is where the one third of congregations least affected by the recession of 2008-2012 tend to be located.

Young Adults

The congregational dilemma is that young adults under the age of thirty-five need to be the focus of congregational efforts, but are the least likely to give—either from lack of the habit of giving or from the burdens of their debts. These are the years young families are being formed. The binge/debt cycle of the past decade has too many of them with sizeable portions of their incomes committed to a house, autos, furnishings, college loans, and consumer debts. They give out of what is left, and that is little for many young family budgets.

Children

Too little attention is paid to the importance of habits of giving for children. Giving is a lifestyle, and the congregation that teaches its children its importance will see future generations who are generous.

Develop a System for Growing Giving Levels

The simplest means of managing the financial resources of the church is to treat all members the same.

The Traditional System

One system is developed because it requires the least effort. This is usually one of seeking an annual pledge from as many giving units as possible, approving a budget based on slightly more than the pledged amount, distributing offering envelopes to each pledge unit, recording the amount given, sending quarterly records of giving in relation to the pledge, with a final annual report for income tax deduction purposes. This system works and will guarantee stability. It assures meeting a less-than-challenging budget. It also assures little or no growth of resources for enlarging the church's mission. Little growth in the discipline of stewardship for givers is observable.

Alternative Systems

The alternatives require more effort, but they also offer the hope of substantially greater rewards:

Include children in the opportunity for giving. Generosity is learned, and one never begins learning it too soon. Children's sermons can teach the importance of sharing. Sunday classes teach the biblical stories of honoring God with one's gifts, and encouraging children to give along with their parents will help form lifelong habits. Most of the most enduring financial supporters of God's work in the world learned the importance of giving early in life. Any child who has spent five or more years in Christian education and does not know what tithing is has been in a deficient educational program. So, provide separate giving envelopes or banks for children of elementary age with encouragement for them to share proportional to their allowances. Allow children old enough to do so to participate in the collection of tithes and offerings in worship.

Ask nongivers to give. The church is the only membership organization that requires so little to join and maintain membership. The idea of an inactive member should be a misnomer. In reality, vital congregations have higher expectations of their participants, because they are not treated as members but as followers of Jesus. Having one's name on a church roll has little significance. Being a part of a community of faith in Jesus Christ is of eternal importance.

Participants in every congregations face financial stress. In such situations, the amount of the support given is irrelevant. That one give something is not irrelevant. Every congregation has a large number of individuals and families who attend and give nothing financially. For such persons the first step in discipleship growth is to give something, even a small amount, and to begin a process of giving systematically. A weekly contribution of the cost of a coffee latté will generate $182 in a year. Nongivers can do that.

The most systematic way of encouraging giving is to begin with a challenge from the pulpit to support the ministries of the church with a beginning gift of any amount. Once recorded, send a quick "thank you" note to the person, encourage him or her to continue with a description of the multiple ways to give through the church, and offer the gift of personal ministry to the person.[9]

Encourage the occasional giver to give systematically. The average level of attendance for most faithful congregants is now twice monthly. Invite those who are occasional givers to become systematic by asking them to mail gift envelopes when absent. Print giving envelopes with pre-paid postage. Better yet, set up an electronic option for systematic withdrawals from a debit account or credit account. I have some concerns about using credit cards for church gifts, given the levels of debt accumulated by the average family. However, most of the young adults I know buy everything on credit cards to accumulate flight miles for travel. Many pay their monthly bills in full. Few of the students I teach write checks. The younger generations increasingly avoid paper transactions. If you cannot debit or charge on a card or through a cell phone, the transactions do not happen! People who pay monthly bills automatically with an electronic debit will appreciate having this option. It also assures the church systematic income.

Challenge the systematic givers to become tithers. Scripture is clear that a 10 percent gift of one's income is a challenging minimum goal for one's most mature expression of giving. It is a challenge few Christians meet. Only 18 percent of respondents to the U.S. Congregational Life Survey contributed 10 percent or more of their net income to their church.[10] That figure varies among congregations, based largely on the emphasis made by congregational leaders on the importance of tithing. Of the nine congregations I studied in depth in 2010, the percentage of tithers ranged from 18 percent to 47 percent. More than 40 percent of survey respondents in each of the African American congregations were tithers. Their pastors were clear about its importance.

Create opportunities for faithful givers to commit estate gifts for the future mission of the church. Not many churches have foundations, but most denominational groups do. An important part of the congregation's financial system needs to be a regular emphasis through personal contact, letters, or publications encouraging an estate gift in the form of a bequest or charitable annuity or trust.

The Budget as a Missional Document

Developing a congregation's budget can be an exercise in missional thinking. Or, it can simply be an annual review of "tweaking" the dollar amounts for each budget category. Little excitement for enlarged giving will develop from the latter approach.

The economic recession of 2008 forced the reconsideration of budget processes. According to William Enright, executive director of the Lake Institute on Faith & Giving, one third of congregations were affected negatively by the recession, one third maintained their levels of giving, and one third saw little effect in their patterns of giving.[11] Of the ten congregations I studied in 2010 in Atlanta, only one church did not experience a smaller level of income in 2009 than in 2008.

The range of the drop was between 8 and 20 percent. In one megachurch, a major capital campaign initiated in 2008 just as the recession began failed to achieve its goal. Four previous major campaigns had exceeded their goals. Real adjustments had to be made in these churches. The adjustments usually came in the form of reducing the number of employees, reducing the benefits or salary/benefits to staff, or cutting needed resources for internal ministries. It can be "all of the above." Mission project funding is usually the most painful cut for caring congregations, and the last to occur.

Churches vary in how they manage their financial resources. Larger and more programmatic churches must have rather sophisticated practices of managing endowments (which were negatively impacted in the recession), challenging the congregation in its giving, investing excess funds wisely, and exercising moderation in the levels of their debt.[12] The reality of defaults on church mortgages has been reported widely in the press, the most notable being the Crystal Cathedral.

Facing a Darkened Future

Many factors impact the revenue of congregations: the local economy, the shift in the culture toward lower levels of giving to religious charities,[13] the competition from the growing number of faith-based nonprofit ministries, the attitudes toward giving within the congregation, and the effectiveness of leaders in encouraging generosity within the church. No simple answers will solve the financial dilemmas facing churches. Numerous suggestions deserve consideration.

Develop a Culture of Trust

Growing missional resources is impossible in an environment of mistrust. Trust must extend to every aspect of the church, including the character and commitment of the pastor and staff, the lay leadership of the church, and the competency of those who manage financial resources.

The first level of trust in stewardship of finances is with those who collect, deposit, record, and manage the gifts of the congregation. In smaller churches this is often a problem of the lack of knowledge of essential practices for financial accountability. Money is collected and deposited with limited record keeping, and the primary gifts are often in the form of cash. An entrenched treasurer or financial secretary who functions with little supervision or competence will depress the willingness of people to give. If a monthly report of income and expenditures cannot be presented that is transparent and accurate, giving will not grow. Checks and balances such as two signatures on all checks should be a common practice even in the smallest church.

In larger and more complex congregations, computerized record-keeping systems are often so complex that finding competent persons to serve as financial secretaries is difficult and expensive. Such systems require more than a minimal level of knowledge of fund accounting. Improper entry of gifts into accounts or failures to provide regular reports to the giver will poison the well of trust. Errors raise questions as to the trustworthiness of the church itself. A few principles of financial accountability to be practiced in your church are:

Be informed of Internal Revenue Service requirements. One basic requirement to be aware of is what is necessary for givers to claim a tax deduction on their gifts. Too many churches have no idea of what is acceptable. Undocumented cash does not count! A check, an electronic transfer, or cash enclosed in an envelope with the giver's name is an essential requirement. Also, an accurate report to each giver of the amount of her or his gift is important. An accurate quarterly report to each giver that thanks the giver and encourages continued generosity will enlarge trust in the church.

The second requirement of the IRS is the proper recording of all compensation to employees of the congregation. Churches that practice the collection of cash for pastor/staff on anniversary Sundays without deposit to the church and payment of the recipient as income violate this requirement. Any gift that is given with any expectation of service in return is income to the recipient and subject to reporting as income on annual tax returns. Givers of cash gifts to their pastors expect them to visit them in the hospital, pray with them during crises, preach to them weekly, and perform their weddings and funerals. Too many pastors skirt this expectation at great risk of an audit from the IRS either of themselves or the church.

A third requirement of the IRS is proper reporting of all forms of income given to church employees, either in an annual W-2 reporting wages or a Form 1099 reporting honoraria. More will be discussed in budget stewardship below.

Most autonomous congregations receive a report of the current state of the finances at the scheduled business sessions of the congregation. Provide complete information to the church of the income to the church, expenses to date, balances for the budget categories for the year to date, balances in restricted or endowment funds, and deposits in bank accounts with a report of how they are invested. Avoid establishing funds that are not fully reviewed and guided by the finance committee of the church. This is especially problematic when individuals in the church are allowed to establish funds in which they determine how they shall be spent.

Be clear about who has access to giving records. The most generous congregations are those in which a select group, such as chair of the finance committee and the pastor, are aware of the giving practices of the people. Struggling congregations tend to insist on such information being known *only* to the person recording gifts. Yet, growth in generosity requires the encouragement of all congregational disciples to enlarge their commitment in a variety of ways.

This suggestion will be controversial in many congregations and among many pastors. A mistaken notion thinks the amount of one's giving should have no influence in who is selected to serve in key leadership roles or who is challenged to enlarge their commitments. Specialists in stewardship development argue that if there is a relationship between one's spiritual health and one's giving, the pastor should be as aware of this dimension of the person's life as much as knowledge of major illnesses, job losses, family crises, or personal struggles. Giving is an indication of the well-being of the person, so how can one know of the need to respond if there is no knowledge of this aspect of commitment?[14]

Prioritize Expenditures Based on Congregational Mission, Not Programs

The typical church budget is based on programs. The categories of the budget are usually based on the program committee structures of the congregation. There is a line item for each committee, and requests for additional funding form the negotiations for what will get funded each year. In this system every committee asks for more and lobbies within the congregation to keep its requests at the forefront of the finance committee.

A missional budget will be based on the strategic thinking priorities of the congregation as described in Chapter 8. If there is an intentional commitment to the future, priorities in funding make new dreams come to fruition. No missional dream, no missional budget. A missional dream without a missional budget equals no missional accomplishment.

A Mission-based Budget

What would a mission-based budgeting process look like? First, it would be organized around the key functions of the church as described in Chapter 11: worship, learning, hospitality, connecting externally, and administrative support. Include in the budget a description of what has been accomplished for the past year and the goals of the new year. Allocate the actual costs of accomplishing these functions in terms of staff time, facility costs, capital needs, and reserves for future goals.

Staff

Budget planning begins with the costs of congregational ministry. The most valuable and most vulnerable persons in the congregation are the employed staff. Too many churches hold a perception that if the staff desire generous benefits and enjoy possible raises in compensation, they are responsible to assure the growth of the church, or at least growth in the levels of giving of the congregation. That responsibility needs to be more broadly shared among the congregation by committing to an affordable staff structure. It is impossible to employ enough people to do the work of the church; expecting the "hiring" of people to do all ministries is one of our contemporary idolatries.

My examination of congregational budgets shows the total expenditures for staff as a percentage of the budget ranges from 45 percent to as high as 58 percent. Whenever total staff costs exceed 55 percent of the budget, innovations in mission are starved. The best means of generosity for staff is to practice the enlarging of giving described above.

Fixed levels of income equal a loss of resources for the staff for any year in which salaries and benefits do not match the rate of inflation—their compensation is fixed at prior year levels or even reduced. Most ministers have not responded to the call of God for the economic benefits, often volunteering to forgo raises or take cuts to balance the church's budget. I know few laity who volunteer to do so in *their* places of employment.[15]

The most difficult cost factor for staff expenditures is the rise of health insurance costs in excess of the rate of inflation. The rate of increase for health care insurance premiums for the past five years has averaged 6 percent per year, forcing many employers to raise the level of employee contributions or pay higher deductibles. At the same time, incomes have remained essentially fixed, stressing all family budgets.

Providing staff benefits can greatly assist the clergy and staff in experiencing the generosity of the church. Most staff benefits are exempt from income taxes. Churches of median size and larger should include health insurance and retirement benefits in their budget. It is a helpful practice for finance teams to consult with denominational specialists or individuals in financial planning with expertise on clergy finances to ensure adequate benefits. Few laity understand the complexities of tax policies related to clergy because these policies are quite different from those applying to any other profession. I have added a discussion of this important topic with guidance from financial specialist Lamar Barden in Appendix C for leaders who seek additional information on this topic.

Facilities

The second largest expenditure for well-established churches is the costs of operating and maintaining facilities. Excluding debt payments incurred for new building renovations or construction, a typical congregation will spend up to 30 percent of budget for facilities costs, including maintenance, repairs, and utilities. Utility costs in the U.S. have grown from an average of 4 percent annual inflation in the early 2000s to over 12 percent in 2009. Utility inflation is now 10 percent per year.

Congregations should respond to careful utility usage for their commitment to environmental care. But their self-interest will force them to conduct careful energy audits, investing in motion light switches, and meeting in less expensive spaces of their buildings during high costs seasons such as summer in the South and winter in colder climes.

An annual allotment for a reserve fund for deferred maintenance expenses should be considered. Informed laity can project the expected costs of replacement of office equipment, musical instruments, roofs, water heaters, and heating and air conditioning systems. It is far wiser to plan for a systematic replacement of these items than declaring emergencies to fund them when they have failed.

Program Expenses

Resources for worship, fellowship, and education are often the easiest to reduce in times of budget stress. However, they may be the best places to give attention in the budget planning process. Most churches are already too lean in provisions of quality educational literature; expenses for special educational events; provisions of resources to strengthen families, children, and youth; and funding for exciting mission ventures.

Mission Expenditures

Churches often provide a percentage of the budget for mission expenditures ranging from 8 to 20 percent. Some congregations budget as much as 50 percent to mission involvement. Again, mission expenditures are usually a function of the handling of the dollars committed to debt and personnel. The churches that make the most investments in mission expenditures have low levels of debt or no debt and limit the levels of personnel costs to less than 50 percent of the budget.

What Can We Do?

First, most budgeting processes are annual, with too little attention paid to the next three to five years. A key layperson with financial acumen is a marvelous resource if congregations will project a five-year budget scenario of where the congregation needs to move to develop its resources. Leading is an imaginative look at the future. When it comes to dollars, it is not difficult for the well-informed to estimate future needs. Project annual future expectations based on alternative rates of inflation, reasonable increases in compensation, and changes in ministries that will improve efficiency. Efficiency is not the paramount value for the church, but when it comes to money, efficient use of financial resources builds the confidence for people to live out of their generosity rather than anxiety that "we have too little."

Second, effective planning requires careful setting of priorities. Developing an internal consensus about what is most important for the fulfillment of the congregation's vision for the future will allow for the elimination of items that have been fixed in the budget for years whether they matter that much or not. Likewise, new priorities can be developed that can excite and inspire congregants to stronger support. What would happen in your church if one line item were eliminated from your budget each year and another added to take its place? The budget is a mission document. Making the difficult decision to focus on expenditures that enhance participation in the mission of God in the world will be transformative over the years. One can look back over the previous five years and detect energy and commitment when the budget is viewed in terms of its missional impact on the future.

The Stewardship of Facilities

Christian communities are called by God to live as stewards of their congregational assets. These include the people who have made the choice to become a part of a congregation as an observers, participants, or members. Attention and care to each person connected to our community life is the means for kingdom work to be accomplished.

Physical assets also require attention. For most congregations, the most important physical asset consists of their facilities. I have shown previously in this book that owning land and buildings is not essential to being and doing church. But most congregations do.

Contrary to the feelings of many that their facilities are a liability, hopeful leaders think about and act on decisions that will enhance the use and usefulness of church facilities. After all, some group of people constructed them with a vision of a future of ministry in a setting. If that vision is no longer realistic or achievable, the difficult decision of selling the facilities to another congregation or for another use may be the wisest one to make. Short of such a decision, however, much can be done to apply a missional mindset to church buildings.

Maximize Usage

Buildings are largely instrumental; they are not ends unto themselves but means to an end with a value. That end is to fulfill God's mission in a specified locale. Whenever a building is viewed as a possession to be guarded or preserved, it becomes an idol. Naming buildings for persons, whether a pastor or generous giver, makes future changes more difficult. Whenever a building is accorded such a sacred status that it cannot be removed, moved, renewed, or shared, the heart of God's mission is replaced with a false faith.

The first stewardship challenge of facilities is to use them as fully as possible. How many hours per week are your church's facilities actually used? The worship space for most is the most expensive space in a building; it is used two to four hours weekly. Office space is next in order of expense and tends to be the most efficiently used space if utilities are configured wisely. Educational spaces are generally the least expensive and the most vacant of any church buildings; 80 percent of educational space will be used two hours weekly in the average church. Churches that build recreation and fellowship space may seldom use them unless large enough to afford staff to provide programs.

Park Avenue Baptist Church is a renewing congregation in an established urban neighborhood in southeast Atlanta. When Anthony (Tony) Lankford became pastor of the small group of eight senior adults in 2006, its facilities were an albatross of liability. The roof needed repairs, the space configuration was designed for a 1950s congregation, and most of the rooms were dirty and filled with junk. The message of the buildings screamed, "This church is dead!" In fact, when nearby neighbors were asked what they knew of the church, the most frequent response was, "I thought they closed their doors a long time ago."

The first step toward renewal was to maximize the space in the building. The congregation agreed to view its facilities as an asset for use by the community. A grant was received from the Cooperative Baptist Fellowship with which the church was aligned to renovate a section of educational space into housing for other church groups. Youth and mission groups visiting Atlanta for participation in short-term projects now have a low-cost place for overnight lodging. The church also provides an apartment in the building for a seminary couple who manage the space.

The second step was to lease a portion of the building to a local day care ministry. A part of the lease arrangement provided for upgrading the spaces by the ministry. An unused chapel space became home for a Latino congregation. Unused classrooms have been converted into meeting space for community groups. As the church has grown, now to about one hundred participants, worship areas have been reconfigured and renovated. The roof has been repaired. The buildings are now such a beehive of activities throughout the week that the minimal off street parking available to the church is taxed.

Practical Suggestions for Maximizing Space

- Develop new ministries that address needs within a three-mile radius of the facility location if the church has the personnel and finances to do so.
- Lease available spaces to compatible service groups in the community, understanding that sharing space is a constant negotiation of cost sharing, use of supplies, and care for furnishings and equipment.

- Be flexible in using space most affordable for the function and size of the group. A church with a large sanctuary and a modest congregation will be a wise steward of the environment by meeting in a less expensive chapel or fellowship hall for seasons of the year when heating or cooling costs are highest.
- Connect to the people using the space that may not be a part of the worshiping congregation. The hospitality experienced by the outsider may attract a parent or small group participant to attend during worship or bible study.

Think Like an Outsider

The facilities of a congregation are like a magnet—they can attract or repel depending on the direction of the energy field. The attraction factor includes a multitude of elements. The socio-economic environment in which facilities are located shapes how nearby residents will respond. An ostentatious building in a poor neighborhood communicates materialism over care for people. A dilapidated space in a gentrifying urban area will not attract.

Location is an important factor in the potential of a congregation. Think about these questions as you try to imagine the reactions of a person driving past your church's location:

- What is the volume and speed of traffic past our location? How many seconds will the average passerby have to process a visual image of who we are?
- Does the landscaping accenting the buildings hide them or make them more visible? Do the trees, shrubbery, and lawn communicate a sense that these people care about the place they gather? Are there community spaces such as recreational facilities that suggest an invitation to "come and visit"?
- What does our signage communicate about who we are? Are the signs easily legible to a driver passing at 50 miles per hour? 30 mile per hour? 10 miles per hour? Is there a coherent logo, symbol, or inviting word on signage that helps the outsider identify something of our mission?
- How easy or difficult is access and egress into the parking spaces available at our location? Since automobiles are the primary mode of transportation in our society, modern Americans are impatient when it comes to traffic jams and parking difficulties. Such challenges will not be a hindrance to deeply committed members. But a missional congregation thinks about those who may "show up" for worship for the first time. Those people will most likely be unfamiliar with

the facilities and may arrive at the last minute. Getting through the traffic and finding parking can be the first barrier that prevents the opportunity for connection and eventual involvement and leadership. Having clearly marked reserved spaces for guests is a step toward hospitality.

- A key principle: the higher the volume of traffic where facilities are visible, the more important the exterior attractiveness of the landscaping, the architectural features, and the signage that identifies the values of the congregation.

So far, this discussion has focused on the exterior of facilities. Suppose a passerby observes the buildings of the church and decides, "I think I will visit there on Easter Sunday." How delighted you should be. The question is, "Will the visitor want to come back?" The answer to that question will depend on a host of factors.

Since we are talking about the most attended Sunday of the year for most congregations, extra preparation will need to be made to create an atmosphere of hospitality for the unfamiliar. More questions!

- Will there be adequate space to park? Will the guest find such a space readily? Volunteer greeters in parking areas will help.
- Is it obvious to the first-time guest where the congregation gathers? The larger and more imposing the buildings, the more intimidating they will be for the newcomer. If there is not an obvious place for entry from the parking area, visible signage pointing the way will help. A personal touch by a greeter will be even better.
- If the guest is a family with children, directions to nursery or children's areas will be needed. The more comfortable the process of finding one's way, the more likely the guest will return.
- Are the facilities easily accessible for the physically limited? Can one move into worship spaces and find a place in a wheelchair?
- Were the human contacts made naturally, gracefully, and without pressure on the guest?
- Then the most important questions of all! How do we think our guest experienced our congregation? Is he or she likely to return? If so, why or why not?

Manage for Efficiency

In some arenas of church life efficiency is a liability. The management of facilities is not one of them. In this area of church life laity in the congregation who are experts in building construction, maintenance, and organization can use their insights for ministry.

Begin with utilities. Nearly every congregation can find areas of waste that can be eliminated. Inflation in utility costs is an area of potential control.

Sometimes an investment in replacement of windows leaking air; use of the most energy efficient lighting; installing motion switches in educational and rest room facilities; automated thermostats; reconfiguring heating and air conditioning systems into zone usage; installing energy efficient water heaters; and practicing a regular schedule of repair, painting, and modernization will create long-term savings. Managing to maintain an effective program of maintenance when the budgetary resources are strong will help avoid the "catch up" costs when the congregation can least afford them.

If you live in a large city, explore whether a nonprofit ministry called Interfaith Power and Light is available. This ministry focuses on environmentally sensitive actions for all faith groups. They have multiple resources for assisting a congregation complete an energy and environmental usage audit of their facilities and practices. Every dollar saved through efficiency is one more to be spent in people-centered mission actions.

Plan for the Future

The information and processes described in the chapter on dreaming have significant implications for how a congregation thinks about its facilities. New congregations that are at an early stage in their development have an incredible opportunity for tailoring future space to fit the values and mission of God's people in a specific locale. Growing congregations can plan for additions that are functional. Older ones may live with the realities of needing to downsize to meet their future vision of ministry and service.

The Johnson Ferry Baptist Church in Marietta, Georgia, is one of the most efficient churches in developing their facilities that I have studied. This congregation began in the 1980s and has grown from a mission outpost meeting in rented space to a large megachurch of more than 6,000 members. What is impressive is the detailed planning that has resulted in the enlargement of facilities as a series of additions to one major building in which every addition is connected architecturally and functionally to the first one. From a sanctuary with educational space, the master plan has grown to include multiple worship spaces, fellowship space, and educational space in which every level is accessible. One can move from any section of the building to any other with a minimum of difficulty. A host of staff and volunteers is available to assist the movement of new people to the location of the nursery, Sunday school room, or the choice of simultaneous worship experiences. A part of the success of their planning is the result of recruiting staff with organizational skills, including calling an architect by training to lead the administrative staff in their work.

Strategic thinking about facilities calls for an examination of the interaction between multiple factors in the design of space. Davis Byrd is an architect trained in theology who was director of the Church Architecture Department of LifeWay Christian Resources prior to his retirement. Several rules of planning suggested by him are included in the following:

- Understand realistically the land area requirements for fulfilling the congregation's facility dreams. How many acres will be needed to accommodate adequate parking, buildings needed, and future expansion? Local zoning requirements may determine the minimum acreage required for approval of building permits for a church. More than these minimum requirements are usually needed. What is the cost of available land in your community? The greater the population density of your location, the greater the cost of land for construction. This is why most newer megachurches tend to be located in the exurban edges of major cities or rapidly growing communities near large urban areas. Plan for one acre of usable site for every 100–125 people on site at one time.
- Be realistic about the size of worship space in relation to educational and parking space. Plan for 15–17 square feet per person (up to 300 in capacity) or 12–24 square feet per person for more than 300 in capacity.

  I am amazed at the number of congregations who have worship spaces that will seat twice the number of people who can park within a one-block radius of the church. They wonder why their worship space is only half filled! On average, less than two people travel to worship in each car in your parking spaces. Are you planning for half as many parking spaces as seating spaces in your worship facility? If not, are you willing to arrange for satellite parking and provide shuttle buses with volunteers assisting your people with this less convenient way to park? Or, do you have the flexibility and will to provide multiple opportunities for worship and study each week to maximize the use of parking space? Hopeful congregations live with a commitment to multiply the options for how people gather.
- Design educational spaces for ease of configuration and seating. The size of a room, its flexibility in seating, and available equipment shape the level of interaction possible. Educational space constructed

more than two decades ago tends to have fixed room sizes with load bearing walls that make more creative gatherings more difficult. It is much easier to create temporary small spaces out of larger ones than to enlarge small ones. Build flexible and functional spaces that accommodate 20 percent more than you currently need. As you grow beyond that, add new spaces. Plan on 35 square feet per person for preschool space, 25 square feet per person for children, and 12–15 square feet per person for youth and adults. Other areas such as administration, music, fellowship areas, media library, and others will need 30–45 square feet per person in smaller churches and 45-55 square feet in larger ones. Recreation areas require custom sizes depending on the features.

- Prioritize the quality of space. The most important spaces for the missional church are nursery space for babies and educational space for children and youth. Have you ever had the experience I have had of walking through the facilities of an aging and declining congregation and noticing beautifully decorated and furnished rooms for the members most elderly, while the space for children looks fifty years old? Any church whose dream is to minister to contemporary young families should understand that most parents want their children involved in places where the quality of resources is equal to their homes and local schools.

Byrd suggests the planning maxim, "The smallest capacity in space of each of these factors of parking, worship, education, or fellowship areas limits the size of the church." So plan for a physical fit for your potential as a congregation.

Finally, hopeful congregations are careful about the levels of debt they assume for their facilities. Specialists in capital campaigns suggest the cost of facility projects should not exceed four or five times the annual budget income. Generally, a capital campaign of pledges over three years can raise two times the annual budget, unless it is a particularly wealthy congregation. When a campaign is completed, it's total debt for the project should be no larger than three times the annual budget, or a maximum of 30 percent of the annual budget committed to debt service.[16] Personally, I would suggest 10 percent of the total budget in debt retirement is a more realistic percentage if mission involvement is to be primary for the church.

Conclusion

Hopeful congregations are generous congregations. One can approach the important tasks of managing finances as tedious and unfulfilling. But the excitement of participation in a congregation full of generous disciples is itself synergistic to the total ministry of the church. God blesses congregations with vision and the willingness to give to fulfill that vision with the energy of accomplishing kingdom ministries.

13

Mending the Tears of Church Conflict[1]

I assume that God is at work in any and all conflicts in ways that we cannot fully grasp and surely cannot control. Because of this I invite you to join a humble partnership with the power of God.

DAVID R. SAWYER[2]

Change is the most important constant in the shifting sands of contemporary congregational life. Whenever there is change, anxiety levels rise, emotions grow in intensity, and the potential for unhealthy conflict in the church increases. Fortunately, most of the conflict congregations experience is healthy with results of increased energy, greater focus in mission, and growing intimacy among members and participants.[3] Unfortunately, according to the data of the National Congregations Study, "1 in 10 congregations experience what we might call persistent conflict, 1 in 4 congregations experience some sort of conflict over a two-year period, and 2 in 5 experience some sort of conflict over a four-year period."[4]

One's image or metaphor of "church" shapes how one responds to the needs for the work that needs to be done in a given setting. Jesus was clear with his image of a fruitless vine. The vineyard steward needed to prune the branches and burn the dead branches (Jn. 15:2, 6). A contemporary pastor's understanding may be of the church as family requiring therapy for healing. Your image of the church shapes how you will respond to its conflicts.

As you take on the difficult task of leading congregations, consider the image of the church as a beautifully woven tapestry. It has lovely complex patterns and colors. In the center you discover a huge tear in the fabric. You face the difficult task of mending the tapestry's torn threads back together.

The leading process for a congregations torn with emotional, spiritual, and relational splits requires assembling a group of skilled "rug makers," "tailors," or "seamstresses." They will engage in the patchwork process of weaving the tapestry back to wholeness. The evidence of the damage from the tears (weeping is a common reaction to conflict) over the "tear" will remain for those who live through it, but the community of faith can learn to live with repaired fabric.

Ministries done in the settings of congregational conflict are multifaceted, challenging, and complex. Amid the crises of congregational tension, a church leader has no formulas to employ that assure a healthy outcome. No simple rules of engagement can ensure success. Yet, processes of assessment, understanding, care, or decision-making can bring a group of feuding church members to outcomes that restore, rebuild, and even reconcile.[5] These processes can be best understood as *conflict ministry*.

Beginning with Outcomes

One should never underestimate the challenges of conflict. Too much of the literature on this issue proposes simplistic solutions or visionary theological language more designed to sell books with catchy titles than provide realistic guidance to churches in pain. After all, humans are unpredictable, sometimes contrary, occasionally acting out of illness, and now and then demonic.

Knowing one's goal in engaging ministry amid conflict is primary for effective leading. What language shall we employ describing the expectations we communicate in the fray of difference? Many choose the language of *conflict resolution*. This outcome raises the specter of unfulfilled expectations. What happens when leaders promise resolution of conflict and none occurs? The disappointment of promises unfulfilled often enlarges the levels of dissatisfaction and anger. People leave when outcomes disappoint. Most of the conflicts rooted in differences of personality or human preferences cannot be resolved. They require fundamental change by one of the parties to conform to the other. Healthy persons learn how to live together with unresolved differences. Any married person knows that.

Do you prefer the language of *conflict management*? I do not. Quite simply, some conflicts cannot be managed. They are like the tinder grass in a dry forest that, once set aflame, explodes into an uncontrollable fire. There are not enough human resources to control or extinguish them—they have to "burn out." I love the language of *conflict reconciliation*. Again, we overpromise to suggest *we* can bring about reconciliation between individuals or larger groups. Reconciliation can be prayed for, encouraged, and supported. Ultimately reconciliation is the work of *God* in the human hearts of those "set apart" from one another. The most important scripture on conflict processes, Matthew 18:15–19, is a multistep process seeking reconciliation, with the recognition that a protagonist may not "listen" to the faith community, and instead decide to live outside it. There follows an equally important teaching in verses 21–35 on the power of forgiveness. Reconciliation requires *two* persons willing to accept the gift of grace. *One* party of a dispute can only forgive and receive healing, not reconciliation, where there is unwillingness for reconciliation from the other.

An achievable outcome for every form of conflict is simply *conflict conclusion*. The work of the conflict minister is to seek to accomplish each of the outcomes described above with the goal of achieving a conclusion to the issues at hand. When they cannot be resolved, or managed, or reconciled, they can be concluded. Every action the conflict minister takes seeks to bring about an end to the divisions that separate persons. The conclusion that provides the most grace for the largest number is finally the best outcome possible in the hard places of church life.

Processes of Conflict Ministry

Prescriptive solutions for conflict seldom work. The leader caught in the middle of raging conflicts should avoid them. The testimony of professionals who work as consultants or coaches to congregations in conflict report healthy conclusions in roughly two-thirds of the congregations with which they work. Some processes provide a "mental framework" for leaders in congregations. The processes that will be effective in one congregation may not be in another. The effective conflict minister understands the nature of the organizational or organic life of the congregation, the history and value system with which he or she works, and personal preferences for an approach to conflicts.

David Sawyer describes three basic approaches or "keys" to dealing with conflict and seeks to integrate all three into his own suggestions: formal problem solving of organizational stress, effective communication in situations of tension, or family systems theory addressing congregational anxiety.[6] Based on my own work with congregations in conflict, I propose a practical fourfold process as a "mental framework" for attempting the weaving processes in the midst of conflict.

Weaving Through Conflicts

Work Proactively for the Congregation's Health

Effective congregational leading contributes to healthy congregational life, the best form of conflict ministry. Healthy congregations experience their share of tensions, but they are energizing and growth producing. The same events that generate debilitating conflict in the unhealthy congregation may stimulate new initiatives in the healthy one.

Leading is rooted in a theology of the church that stresses God's mission. Churches that are seeking to understand the mission of God in their setting will have a forward-looking vision of what they can do to bring wholeness, healing, and love to their members and neighbors. Mission-focused churches do not have the time to fight.

Leaders of healthy congregations teach the biblical understanding of responding to conflict. Jesus provided a process in Matthew 18:15-16 that is unexcelled for concluding conflict. His teaching stresses the fourfold process of tough talk, tender listening, trusting enlargement, and terminal decision-making. These steps can be applied to most of the issues that divide local churches.

Stimulating and creative worship is a characteristic of churches that deal well with issues of conflict. When the congregation is alive with the presence of the Holy in worship, the issues of difference recede in importance. Healthy congregations work at keeping the relational bonds among members and leaders strong. Insights of Bowen/Friedman's family systems theory on maintaining connection with critics are an essential element of leading for growth toward relational maturity.[7]

Open processes of decision-making are important in keeping momentum in the direction of achieving vision and fulfilling God's mission. Transparent congregations maintain ongoing planning processes. The future is at the forefront of conversations about the church; a vital planning process is a constant in the healthy church.

Finally, conflict is sometimes the result of changes in the external context of the church that "sneak up" on the membership. Monitoring external realities in the shape of shifting demographics, economic changes, and sources of changing values can keep congregations aware of the need to adjust to a changing setting.

Learn to Read Warning Signs

One of the surprises I experience in working with congregations and listening to dozens of conversations with ministers each year is the evidence of conflict developing. "Why could they not see that coming?" is a frequent "aha" to me. In the same way a cautious driver is scanning the highway for warning signs of "construction ahead" or the flashing lights indicating "accident ahead," the wise leader will be attuned to the warning signs of potential difficulties. They are not surprising:

- Declining participation in church activities;
- Reports of "dissatisfaction" in the small group life of the congregation;

- Meetings of committees, ministry groups, task forces that "get off track";
- Evidence of withholding money by members;
- A general sense of anxiety within the fellowship;
- Families leaving the congregation for others in the area;
- Anger in the tone of telephone and e-mail exchanges.

You could likely expand this list from your own observations of developing conflict in the churches of which you have been a part.

Respond Carefully to Conflict Events

Every congregation has within it differences, tensions, irritations, and potential explosions of painful situations. A conceptual framework for how one responds to conflict is a critical component of wise and effective ministry. Each of the keys described above by Sawyer may be effective depending on one's diagnosis of the intensity of the conflict. Family systems approaches, described in Chapter 2, are helpful for leaders to understand developing anxiety and to maintain patience with courage in small and medium-sized congregation with close emotional connections. Larger organizations or highly visible public events require more structured processes of problem solving.

Assessment of Typical Responses

A careful assessment of the preferred styles of response in situations of conflict for the leadership core of the group is helpful. Each of us has a "natural" way of responding to reality. Sometimes our responses add to the intensity of the conflict rather than reducing the tensions associated with it. Speed Leas has developed a most useful tool for evaluating one's preferred conflict management styles. Each of the styles is appropriate for specific situations of conflict, and the wise leader engages issues with the most appropriate response for each situation. His description of the multiple styles can be summarized as follows:

- Support—empathetic responses when one is not a party to the conflict, but encourages participants to seek healthy conclusions.
- Accommodation/Avoidance/Ignoring—may occur at any intensity, but usually make the conflict worse.
- Collaboration—all parties work together for achieving commonly defined outcomes—a "consensus model".
- Persuasion—the effort to convince others to a position by argument, or logical, rational discussion.

- Negotiation/Compromise—a decision in which each party wins something and loses something in the outcome.
- Coercion/Force—the imposition of authority forcing parties to a conclusion. Voting to conclude a conflict is a coercive strategy.[8]

Diagnosis of the Conflict Reality

The actions taken in response to situations of conflict are guided by one's analysis of the realities being faced. Tools for diagnosing the nature of the conflict include a decision about the intensity of the conflict one faces. In my own work with students through the years, the less experienced tend to rank the intensity of conflict much higher than an objective analysis would merit. More experienced leaders often overlook the importance of the growing tear in the fabric of the fellowship until it has become a huge "rip" in the church's life. Remember the emphasis from Chapter 4 on defining reality as important for leadership?

A part of that reality is a diagnosis of the nature and intensity of the conflict being experienced. George Bullard, using the earlier work of Speed Leas, provides a helpful summary of seven levels of conflict intensity.[9]

Figure 13.1: Levels of Conflict Intensity

Intensity

Intentional physical harm to people or congregational facilities

Pursuit of people beyond the congregation

Congregational-wide combat with organizational casualties

Congregational-wide competition with voting

Competition within a group or between groups

Relationship-oriented disagreements over multiple issues

Task-oriented issues with many solutions

Suggestions for Practical Responses

Over the years of observing congregations in conflict, several principles have proven helpful to me. First, recognize that any event can grow to higher levels of intensity. Most congregational leaders can describe the molehill that became a mountain. Even the most seemingly insignificant event can grow to engulf the life of the congregation. A match can ignite a forest fire! A conflict event may begin at low levels of manageable problems and develop into the tsunami that destroys. Alternatively, the first evidence of problems may be more like the unanticipated volcanic explosion that seemingly comes out of nowhere!

Second, work at the lowest levels of conflict intensity possible. Too much attention to lower levels of conflict intensity by leaders may enlarge it. Let those most directly involved collaborate on outcomes that conclude difficulties.

Third, some conflicts need to be accommodated. Conflict is usually a response to change. Allowing change that enhances the mission of God, even though stress in the system is a consequence, is life giving. Learning to embrace the new is healthy. Steinke says, "The first step of change—urgency—is built into mission."[10] Too often mission is stifled because of the fear of healthy conflict.

Fourth, when the going gets tough, call in the cavalry. Outside intervention is often the healthiest response to difficult conflict. Most congregations that practice a polity of local autonomy are reticent to admit they need help. Many outstanding consultants are available who can assist congregations in negotiating their way to a lower level of conflict intensity and forward into a more productive future. No consultant, however, is a magician. The congregation must chart its path forward with wise and Spirit-led decisions.

Fifth, depend on the discerning guidance of the Holy Spirit. The Lord of the church is not its human leaders. A dependency on God and a common searching for God's will should characterize the congregation that truly seeks to find a new way beyond its stresses and differences. When such happens, the new can surely come (2 Cor. 5:17).

Reweave for a New Future

All congregations will face difficult realities at some time in their life cycle of development—whether they are decline, traumatic conflict, irritating setbacks, or the grinding tasks of continuous ministry. Fortunately, congregations are resilient entities capable of healing and renewal. Conflict ministry is not complete until there has been the continuation of the process beyond the events of unpleasant difficulties.

Celebrate Closure

Conflict participants will not forget conflicts. Any congregation effective in attracting new faces into its fellowship must move beyond the pain that has inflicted hurt. There can be no healthier outcome than for the "story" of what happened when the church fought to include the ending of a reweaving of the relationships that were torn.

Some conflicts seem to be ongoing repetitions of old events that never are concluded. The church becomes a fellowship of defensive negativity that is like an ongoing pain that never heals. Very few such negative congregations will attract outsiders. Instead, they will slowly decline into an aging cohort of controlling members.

What can be done to prevent a retearing of the fabric of the congregational tapestry? The church needs to search for a way to cement the conclusion into the psyche/spirit of the congregation. The natural tendency is to pretend the event never occurred or seek to implant it as a secret into the life of the congregation. Like family secrets, they have a way of reappearing in the behaviors of those affected by painful events.

Concluding difficult events may include the worship life of the church. One can create rituals of forgiveness and reconciliation that acknowledge the realities of what happened with celebrations of the presence of God within them. The redemptive story of God's people is one of recognition of sin and failure with seeking a way to move beyond the past.

Bringing closure should involve the small group life of the fellowship. Any conflict of intensity may include the opportunity for the tears of grief for what has happened to be shed in intimate settings. Some churches have employed professional counselors to listen to sharing of the feelings of hurt. Health can emerge from tears of confession and forgiveness.

Some churches may need to revisit previous decisions that carry lingering effects of guilt for those affected. Congregations that terminated a pastor prematurely could invite the pastor and family to return years later for a ceremony of confession and forgiveness. Such events do not undo the hurt, but can bring relief to spouses and children who may feel their family was mistreated by the decisions of the church. These lingering feelings will hinder a church from moving forward into God's best future.

The rules for making decisions may need to be rewritten in the aftermath of conflict. Revisions of bylaws, restructuring of decision-making groups, or reorganization of staff configurations may be needed to prevent a replay of the negative events.

Develop New Leadership

Healthy congregations need to have an expectation of accountability from their leaders. Most of the conflict in congregations is a contest of leadership either within the pastoral team or between the clergy and lay leadership of the congregation. When strongly antagonistic persons are allowed to assume roles of leadership that generate torn fabric, responsible congregations will replace them.[11] Depending on the nature of the conflict, a clear decision is required concerning the ability of the present leadership to continue to be effective.

Leaders following a congregation-wide conflict, especially all who serve in pastoral roles, must be healers and reconcilers in spirit. This will include those who continue to serve, or new personnel called to lead into God's new future.

Finally, the church usually needs to assess how the leadership in the conflict used power. Individuals and groups who used their roles of responsibility to maintain power by controlling persons or processes may not be able to maintain trust within the fellowship. If not, mending requires replacement. Changing how we function may be difficult in reflection on a painful past, but will allow new energy and direction for the future.

Dream a New Vision

A careful study of biblical visions will reveal they were imagined amid desperate realities. Pharaoh's dream interpreted by Joseph envisioned a seven-year plan from God to respond to a coming drought in Egypt (Gen. 41). Isaiah experienced the holy call of God in a time of political uncertainty (Isa. 6—7). Joel dreamed of a universal renewal of God's Spirit for all of God's people during a time of economic uncertainty (Joel 2:28–29; Acts 2:16–21). Mary sang the Magnificat of a vision of a righteous kingdom while dealing with her own pregnancy, which some probably labeled as shameful (Lk. 2:46–55).

A time of renewed hope can characterize faithful congregations following a difficult time. The best time to engage in a discernment process or strategic thinking process for the future of the church may well be in the months following the conclusion of conflict. Such is a time for weaving back the torn threads and rips in the fabric of congregational life.

Conflict events also call into question the calling for many ministers who find the pain more difficult than they can bear. For some, the heartache is so deep that new ways of earning a living are sought even when the calling to minister remains. For others, congregational leadership proves to be a burden they can no longer bear; they are led to noncongregational settings for Christian ministry.

In spite of the tears in the community fabric, God's servants continue to fulfill their vocations serving in the hard places of congregational life. Some ministers, amid conflict no less painful than for others, reaffirm the capacity of God's people to right past wrongs, become agents of healing amid hurt, learn new insights into the ministry of weaving together torn fabric, and discover a deepening of their call to pastoral service.

14

Evaluating

Unless a review results in meaningful conversation, changed behavior, or more effective ministry, it isn't a good use of anyone's time.

JILL M. HUDSON[1]

Research indicates clearly that measurement and feedback are essential to increase efforts to improve performance.

JAMES KOUZES AND BARRY POSNER[2]

Evaluating a congregation or its leaders poses a dilemma for all involved. On the one hand, how are we to improve if we do not know how well we are doing? The other side of the dilemma is the time required to bring to the surface how well we are doing detracts from other agendas.

Let's be honest. Few of us like evaluation. The annual performance review at work may be only a routine to assure a "paper trail" for terminating the least productive. When have you experienced an evaluation that praised your strengths, recognized your accomplishments, and rewarded your performance? We all want that kind of evaluation.

The same is true in most church settings. Clergy bemoan the annual evaluation from their denomination or local personnel committee. Dread and sometimes "fear and trembling" reign supreme. The same groups of the church who want to evaluate employees go into overdrive anger at the suggestion someone should evaluate their work as church members or leaders. Most of the clergy I know would "Amen!" James Hopewell, senior pastor of the Myers Park United Methodist Church in Charlotte, North Carolina. in his response to denominational evaluations: "The kinds of people who raise their hand to become pastors aren't fond of such instruments —to put it bluntly. We do want feedback, and we really crave support. We want to cultivate stellar ministry habits. But what's the best way to do this?"[3]

Why are periodic, formal ministry evaluations so difficult? Let me suggest a variety of reasons:

1. *Because we are under constant evaluation.* Every sermon, every lesson taught, every committee led is evaluated by those who participate with you in them. Such evaluations are usually informal and shared only within the confines of family or close friends. These include cliques of the congregation. The pastor and staff seldom know the content of such evaluations until a crisis of confidence arises and it is too late to correct problems. We know all about these informal evaluation processes, and for clergy they prove to be one of the most difficult parts of the calling. The people who pay our salaries are the people we serve. They see us do our work at every level. It is nearly impossible to hide our failures.

2. *Because there are few external measurements of good ministry.* Congregations have no "manual of good practices" around which to design effective measures of performance. Ministry is so subjective. The informal evaluations by laity are often comparisons with other "successful" congregations that appear from the outside to be accomplishing so much.

3. *Because the true measure of ministry has few quantitative measurements.* How do you measure depth of spiritual sensitivity? What are the objective standards for the quality of care shown for people in need? How do we know we have followed God in our discernment of future strategic thinking? Do we know the kinds of changes occurring in the lives of congregants?

4. *Because effectiveness in those activities that can be measured quantitatively grow from multiple sources.* Success in the measurable criteria of institutional success is a function of life cycle, environmental setting, leadership, strategy, sometimes luck, and the blessings of the Spirit. To credit a pastor or ministry team alone for such successes will last only as long as growth continues. Then who gets the blame for decline in these areas?

5. *Because employees can so easily discount the evaluators.* Evaluations make value judgments about people. How does the chair of the Personnel Committee evaluate the pastor who has walked beside him during his marital infidelities? When the evaluation process moves from a consensus of congregational appraisal to individual assessments, ministers often know too well the struggles and failures of the one evaluating.

None of these objections, however, eliminates the need for evaluating what we are doing. There can be only one real reason for refusing to invest the time, expertise, and expense of evaluation: no accomplishments!

Evaluate the Congregation First

Meaningful evaluation of any individual is rooted in the culture of the seedbed of the Spirit. Imagine a gardener who never examines her plants. Gardens need watering, cultivating, weeding, and fertilizing. So do churches. Kathleen Cahalan writes, "Planning and evaluation are interrelated tasks: plans spell out the work to be done and the goals to be reached; evaluation provides an accurate picture of the work, how goals have been met, and information that can help leaders modify the plan as it moves forward."[4]

Informal Evaluations

Numbers are not sacred. Most of the evaluations within a congregation are feelings, reactions, and intuitions. They may never be recorded as a statistic. No one else in the congregation may share or agree with them.

Congregants find ways to bring to the surface informal evaluations. The inclusion of an open-ended question in a worship folder or a response card participants can answer provide feedback to worship planners. Would it not be helpful to have brief written responses to "What did you find most helpful to you about worship today?" "What suggestions would you offer about today's worship experience that would make it more meaningful to you?" "Was there a particular new insight about your relationship to Christ in worship today?"

When have you ever evaluated a team meeting? A brief discussion at the conclusion of a meeting about how well the group functioned, suggestions for improving future meetings, or future agenda needs builds improvement into future meetings.

The same process works in educational classes, forums, or special events. If the people attending such gatherings have no suggestions for improvement, it is unlikely much energy will be present.

If pastoral leaders can affirm this kind of feedback from all aspects of church life, a culture of openness will grow. The perception that leaders can "hear" informal evaluations without defensiveness will move informal evaluations into a more direct arena of conversation with pastoral leaders. Louis Weeks writes, "Some pastoral staff members say that the most difficult parts of leading are having regular opportunities to hear from others ways in which the work and worship can be improved and practices that inhibit effective care of members and officers, and particularly to pay attention to the voices of those less vocal in the congregation."[5]

A brief week-by-week journal of reaction by leaders of each of the events of the week can be helpful in reflection on needed changes. Solo pastors could profit from sharing journal notes on perceived reactions to the sermon, the worship experience, a funeral, or a parishioner visit with a trusted friend or peer from another church. In multi-staff churches, a brief discussion evaluating each event could be a weekly agenda item. Compile a summary sentence for each week for fifty-two weeks and look back at the cumulative changes made.

Formal Evaluations

Formal evaluations are quantitative. They are easier, too. Any congregation that keeps a record of weekly worship attendance; counts participants in education, fellowship, or mission events; and tracks income each week is engaging in "bottom line" evaluation. How one interprets the trends of such numbers is what is crucial.

I recommend two forms of congregation-wide evaluations. The first is what I would call a "benchmark" evaluation. A cardiologist will not develop a treatment plan for a patient without a complete workup of the physical health of the patient. Congregations need comprehensive measures of their characteristics as a basis from which to make future measures of evaluation.

The best instrument I know for benchmark analysis is the U. S. Congregational Life survey. It is available from www.uscongregations.org. I have used it in a number of congregations. Its value is the numerical summary of responses generated on the characteristics of those responding. Attention to a high level of participation will generate an important point for assessing future ministry. The survey consists of fifty questions that measure levels of personal involvement, spiritual growth, demographic characteristics, levels of support for the church, and theological opinions/perspectives. A computer-generated summary of responses to all questions is provided.

The second value of the survey is the generation of indexes of congregational strengths based on responses. Scales of responses to clusters of questions measure ten congregational strengths. The ten strengths are:

- *Growing Spiritually:* Worshipers are growing in their faith and feel the congregation meets their spiritual needs.
- *Meaningful Worship:* Worshipers evaluate their experience on eight measures of worship quality.

- *Participating in the Congregation:* Worshipers are measured on their levels of attendance, leadership, participation in the work of the church, and levels of financial support.
- *Sense of Belonging:* Worshipers have a strong sense of belonging and say most of their closest friends are a part of the congregation.
- *Caring for Children and Youth:* Worshipers are satisfied with the offerings for children and youth and have children living at home who also attend there.
- *Focusing on the Community:* Worshipers are involved in civic activities, social service, or advocacy, and work to make their community a better place to live.
- *Sharing Faith:* Worshipers are involved in evangelism activities and invite friends or relatives to worship.
- *Welcoming New People:* Worshipers feel the congregation is attracting new people.
- *Empowering Leadership:* Worshipers assess the pastor as open to input from congregants, as a fit for the congregation, as one who inspires others to action, and as one who encourages laity to use their gifts.
- *Looking to the Future:* Worshipers feel committed to the congregation's vision and are excited about the congregation's future.

The third value of this instrument is the comparisons that are possible with similar congregations completing it. All results are made available in printed form, and a computer account is available, through which comparisons with groupings of similar congregations can be made.[6]

The second form of congregation-wide evaluation is more difficult. Congregations that have developed priorities from strategic thinking described in Chapter 8 can design their own processes of measuring effectiveness. Those designs might include a survey of the congregation, a collection of responses to open-ended questions gathered from small groups of the congregation, brief computer-generated surveys individuals can complete online, or an e-mail response design.

Evaluate the Staff Team

Formal staff evaluations abound.[7] If the staff is organized as a team, with coaching as a primary approach to growth as described in Chapter 11, evaluations are designed to fit that model. The coaching process could focus on each staff member identifying his or her goals for spiritual growth, plans for leading in areas of responsibility, and commitments to the team for the coming year. One model of coaching is more directive than the LEARN skills described in Chapter 11. The three authors of *Coaching for Commitment* do not apply their insights to the church. However, their approach to coaching fits how you can do so. Their definition of coaching for commitment is, "a conversation of self-discovery that follows a logical process and leads to superior performance, commitment to sustained growth, and positive relationships."[8] Their approach is performance-based coaching. An outcome in a workplace provides the content of the coaching relationship.

Coaching a church staff through a process of self-evaluation is definitely performance-based coaching. "A performance coaching conversation," write Coe, Zehnder, and Kinlaw, "is defined as one during which you, the coach, confront someone with an issue or problem that needs to be solved. The key point here is that the coach initiates the coaching conversation, and the conversation has a clear purpose."[9]

Accountability is a part of employment. Effective leading includes effective accountability. This kind of coaching allows the most personal process for the employee, shaping the accountability each will give to the lay leadership of the church.

A summary evaluation of progress for each employee will be provided to a personnel team for feedback and encouragement at the end of each year. The personnel team should affirm major strengths and growth. If problems are identified in accountability to the job responsibilities of the staff member, they should be communicated clearly, along with requests for a plan for improvement within a stated time frame. Copies of all written staff evaluations are maintained in a confidential file for each employee in a locked file drawer available only to the Personnel Team.

Missional congregations know where they are going. They communicate not only their mission with clarity, they can demonstrate effectiveness in fulfilling it. What an exciting kind of congregation to serve!

15

Celebrating

Our calling in life is to make music, at first with all that we have, and then when that is no longer possible...to make music with what we have left.

INSPIRED BY ITZHAK PERLMAN

The epigram for this chapter is printed on a small bookmark. It comes from a story of a concert by Itzhak Perlman, the great violinist afflicted with polio. He walks with great difficulty, and setting up for a performance creates a challenge. During a performance at Lincoln Center in 1995, according to the story, a string on his violin broke. Rather than stopping and going through the difficult task of gathering himself, leaving the stage to repair his violin, and returning, he continued to complete a masterful performance on three strings.[1]

The bookmark was written and given to me by long-time friend and pastor, Fred Andrea. It became a theme of his life amid the tragic death of his daughter, Rebecca, from an asthma attack followed four years later by the death of his wife, Dawn. Such losses could have destroyed his passion and direction for ministry. His resilient willingness to celebrate their lives by continuing to give himself in leadership and receive the support of a congregation and community has only enlarged his effectiveness as a pastor.

Celebrating is a leading function. Hopeful congregations live in the gratitude of grace and spend significant energy in expressing that gratitude. The best indicator of congregational health may well be the sense of a celebrative spirit within the life of a congregation. Celebrating includes the passion for achieving excellence in all that is done by core leaders. When the leadership fails, the passion does not fail. The passion continues to work for the best possible result in the midst of the people.

Celebrating is intuitive. At times the last thing a congregation is prepared to experience is the celebrative moment. The intuitive leader also understands the importance of public displays of gratitude for the grace of God, the investment of the people in God's work in their setting, and the individual contributions so essential to the work of the church.

Tipping Points in Congregational Life

Intuitive leadership recognizes the undulating cycles of success and failure, points of significant change, and seasons when everything seems stuck in a rut of ordinariness. The most celebrative moments will accompany those times when momentum is evident because all of the efforts of leading are bearing results.

Intuition is a difficult skill to describe. Intuition is somewhat native to the person rather than a learned response to reality. Intuition is the awareness of reality without a rational or even logical explanation. Intuitive leaders "know" what needs to be done without consulting the policy manual or securing a fiat from an authority figure. They are first-class observers of what is happening, are attuned to the underlying messages being communicated in a system, and spend a lot of their time in listening to what others are saying.

Intuitive managers often think in terms of metaphors, stories, or patterns that capture a central theme or idea. One of these metaphors important for ministry leaders to understand is the concept of the "tipping point" in organizational life.

Malcolm Gladwell wrote a provocative bestselling book on the contagious nature of change.[2] His fundamental thesis is that change is a product of small actions, usually by a small group of people, whose actions bring about a different way of functioning in the social order.

While Gladwell applied his insights largely to mass social movements, especially the impact of tipping points on corporate marketing, reductions in rates of crime, and youth practices such as suicide and smoking, his insights apply to change in congregations as well.

His thesis is: "The Tipping Point is the moment of critical mass, the threshold, the boiling point."[3] His concept is simple. Change occurs like a spreading infection as persons adopt an idea until a certain critical mass is reached in all human communities, however simple or complex. When a sufficient number of people accept the change in process, it reaches its tipping point and will spread like wildfire. Gladwell further asserts that the number of people required for such a tipping point to be reached is quite small in comparison to the rapid change that results from it. He points to the commonly accepted 20/80 rule at work—20 percent of the people do 80 percent of the work. To say it in church parlance, "The minority sets the agenda for the congregation!" They form its core leadership.

Gladwell calls his approach counterintuitive, but I disagree. It requires high levels of intuition to apply his thesis to churches. The intuitive ministry leader reads the signs of developing tipping points, whether in the direction of health or dysfunction. The intuitive leader knows the likely outcome of processes, whereas the purely rational leader can see such realities only by hindsight. Gladwell's framework for understanding tipping points is threefold.

Contagious Change

Change in a given context works like an epidemic. The law of the few works to bring about change in the same way an infection spreads among a group of people. It takes only one passenger with a dangerous disease on an airplane to introduce an epidemic into a whole nation.

Not all persons are "carriers" of change. Gladwell suggests three types of individuals bring about most of the change in any group:

- *mavens* who have a special understanding of what needs to happen,
- *connectors* who have networks of people with whom they communicate the change, and
- *salespersons* who convince others to adopt the change.

Intuitive leaders understand that tipping points work in the direction of both positive and negative change in the church. With her passion for a given mission project, her knowledge of the needs for it, and her energy in motivating a group of people to become involved, a relatively new member of a congregation who is a "missions maven" *can* transform the congregation into a mission organization. One mission trip led by one passionate church member to an orphanage in Guatemala created a tipping point, generating numerous other mission projects that have involved more than a third of that congregation.

The same process can work for unhealthy problems in a congregation. The natural congregational impulse is to resist change, like the natural immunity of the body fights off invading viruses. Conflict occurs when a critical mass of persons unites, either in the new direction of the introduced contagion, or in the forces of immunity allied to resist the virus of change.

It takes just one seriously committed dysfunctional leader to infect the fabric of the group life of a congregation until it becomes a full-blown conflict dividing the entire church. The last thing a healthy church needs is a staff member or key leader who exposes the fellowship to disease with misplaced priorities, unrealistic directions, or questionable/unethical methods of ministry to people.

My own research in a number of congregations reveals a tipping point in the development of health and vitality as well as dis-ease and debilitating conflict. That tipping point is about 15 percent of the active membership of the church.

A permanent undercurrent of criticism, unhappiness, and complaint can be found in the healthiest of congregations. As long as that undercurrent is small, the congregation functions normally and can even grow in size and in all the indicators of health. However, if the size of that group grows to exceed 15 percent of the active participants, conflict results.

Sticky Change

The second idea of Gladwell's work is the concept of stickiness. Stickiness causes a change to resonate within a group and be communicated in such a way that it connects, it "takes hold," and grows. How change is communicated determines whether it will stick; an effective message repeated in a variety of formats is required. We all complain about the repetition of television advertisements, but we can repeat the story line of the TV commercial whether we like it or not.

Long-term pastors understand this concept well. Very often the difference between long-term success in ministry leadership and short-term failure is the ability to repeat one's message until it "sticks." We have all observed congregations with great ideas, visions, and exciting new futures that got nowhere. Other rather routine dreams become transformative because of the application of the plan in the routine procedures of the church's life— calendar, budget, and team processes. One simple idea that gets repeated and adopted can be transformative.

I have conducted class experiments to test the idea that any instruction must be communicated at least seven times to "catch." When I give only verbal instruction on how to identify a class assignment as an e-mail attachment, few do it correctly. At times I write the instruction in the syllabus and do not mention it, about the same number respond correctly. When I write the instructions, announce them, and repeat the guidelines with examples seven times, the entire class will comply. If the message is important enough to merit a response, it is important enough to be restated in multiple media until it takes hold. If it does not "stick," it may not be important.

Postmodern congregations are leading the way in applying this insight in worship. The greater the diversity of "signals" given about the message, the more likely the message is to "take." So worship includes all the senses—art, music, visuals, incense, movement—as well as multiple layers of communication—facts, humor, drama, story, outlines, notes—to get the message to stick in a context of message overload.

Rituals of celebration stick in creating a sense of accomplishment and momentum. Anniversary Sundays, homecomings, recognition of key events and leaders, lunches and dinners, and special musical events root the sense of passion into the common life of the church.

Consider the Context

Gladwell's third emphasis is on context. Some settings encourage the spread of ideas better than others. Gladwell applies this concept to issues like crime, sexually transmitted diseases, and prison settings. To change the incidents of these social ills, one must change the context.

In applying this to the church, intuitive leaders search for the little things that impact how persons will react. Tipping point principles can be applied in three areas.

First, facilities matter. Watch what happens to attendance when the parking coordinator fails to function for two consecutive Sundays, so that it takes an extra ten minutes to get out of the parking lot after worship. Failure will show up in declining participation within three weeks. Likewise, poor maintenance, poor scheduling of spaces, dirty linens in the nursery, inadequate signage, and limited personal direction to various meeting places will infect the frustration level of participants, especially those newest to the fellowship. Negative tipping points will more likely be created by problems in the area of facilities than will positive benefits accrue if everything is properly organized and functioning. Well-run facilities may not create tipping points, but poorly managed ones will. And they will be the wrong kind.

Second, size matters. Much attention has been given to the large church in the past two decades. The large church will remain so only to the degree that it creates an effective small group life in which the possibility of intimacy occurs in gatherings of fewer than fifteen people. The gospel thrives on the intimacy of relationship, prayer, and mutual support. Unless a context is available for the possibility of meaningful intimacy at the small group level, the tipping points will be toward loss and decline rather than growth and health. Management of the small group life also functions on the size principle of 150 stressed by Gladwell. He suggests that the maximum size of a group for knowing each other by name and working together effectively is 150. Sociologists call this a tribal structure composed of several small groups. He is correct. This principle explains the fact that the majority of the churches in the world stagnate at this size level. The largest total group one staff person can serve effectively is 150, with multiple small groups of fifteen. Adequate leadership and support staff are essential in organizing gatherings of the congregation into communities of interaction that do not exceed this number if growth in discipleship and commitment are to be expected.

The large church is a collection of mini-churches. Leaders who think in terms of groupings of 150 for facilities design, parking design, and ministry programming will create positive tipping points.

Third, diversity matters. At the small group level of fifteen intimates, diversity is most difficult. Such groups are likely to reflect a common marital status, age grouping, racial/ethnic makeup, and even geographic similarity. Unless a cross-cultural connection across these commonalities exists at the mini-church level of groupings of 150, the church will become a homogenous expression of one dominant cultural group. This limits the ability to attract the diversity of people in all communities in which large churches are located.

When the context is right and the tipping point principle is observed, dramatic and quick change occurs. It is unbelievable how quickly a congregation can change. An influx of a new ethnic group grows within the congregation and brings suddenly an explosion of change that moves the church to focus on that group. Let a decline cycle go unattended too long, and suddenly the congregation realizes it is aging, declining, and losing income beyond the levels of viability. Or, a new pastor arrives, bringing new worship styles that prove attractive to the unconnected in the community; and growth mushrooms. A group of young adult couples gets formed. Within three years the nursery is at capacity with babies. Tipping points are at work in each scenario. Intuitive church leaders will be on a constant lookout for both observing them and working to create them in the direction of God's vision for the congregation.

Synergetic Gratitude

The celebrating congregation reflects a synergy of gratitude that unites and empowers its sense of belonging. Dennis Voskuil suggests, "Gratitude is a way of life, a disposition, an attitude, a response to the grace of God revealed through Jesus Christ."[4] The hopeful leader displays a constant sense of gratitude for the support and encouragement of the congregation being led. Such actions create concentric circles of gracious responses to the positive sense of God's blessings within the congregation. Gracious leaders enlarge gracious congregations. The consequence is a growing sense of the presence of the Spirit, and there is a reciprocal appreciation of the one who is leading.

Special Recognitions

Gratitude grows from dependency on God and on a mutuality of leaders and followers. Unfortunately, too many congregations live with the dissonance of unappreciated service. Ministry leaders who do not share appreciation for the support and investment of the laity in the work of the church will find themselves living with the burdens of stinginess. A congregation in which no one celebrates the pastor and staff will find itself led by a burned-out core of ministers. A congregation led by a ministry team that can always find a reason for complaining about the lack of responsiveness by the congregation will seldom appreciate its leadership.

Affirm the Followers

A simple "thank you" is a celebration. It may be in the form of a birthday greeting from the pastor to each parishioner, expressing appreciation for the gifts of each. Personal notes of appreciation are never overlooked by a grateful laity. A public expression of appreciation for the servants who prepare a communal meal, the musicians who create a sense of praise and adoration in worship, the teachers of young children who encourage a new generation, and praise for fellow ministers—all contribute to the celebrative ethos of the congregation. The appreciation may be expressed in worship, a newsletter, or in informal meetings. People thrive on recognition and appreciation.

Obviously, celebration may elicit the risk of jealousy from some who feel overlooked or seldom identified. The congregation needs to develop ways of affirming all who are deserving. But reticence to recognize those who contribute because of reactions from a few is not an appropriate response for the grateful congregation.

The flow of gratitude needs to be a two-way direction. Congregations will find their less-than-perfect ministers, which includes all of them, excelling beyond their natural gifts when appreciated. "Clergy," according to Richard Hester and Kelli Walker-Jones, "have one of the most complex and daunting leadership roles of any professional."[5] The role will prove less complex and daunting in congregations that have learned how to affirm the leadership of those they employ.

The African American church has much to teach the rest of the Christian community in this regard. The level of respect and public affirmation for the pastor in this tradition needs to infuse the larger Christian community. A pastor's anniversary is a celebration of leadership. It is also a major source of financial support for Black clergy rooted in a history of low salaries and benefits. White churches have much to learn from African American churches' practice of attention to the contributions of their pastors. Alternatives can be practiced in any congregation, including public recognition of all staff on anniversaries, whether compensation is given or not. An additional day off or a party in honor of the staff will go a long way to enlarge the reservoir of appreciation for effective service.

The contributions of African American congregations to Protestantism is still under- appreciated in the larger fabric of American Christianity. The despair of decline in the vitality of Christian faith in the U.S. does not apply to the thousands of vibrant Black congregations that continue to attract multigenerational members and impact their communities with service in the name of Christ. It is ironic that forty years after the gains of the civil rights movement interaction between these congregations and their Caucasian counterparts occurs so seldom. Partnerships between mono-racial congregations from both traditions can be an opportunity of joint celebration of the accomplishments of each.

Encouragement of Self-Care

Ministry leaders are among the least healthy of any of the professions according to studies of clergy health. Melissa Clodfelter reports, "The Clergy Health Initiative 2008 survey of over 17,000 active North Carolina United Methodist clergy showed their rates of obesity to be about 10 percent higher than other North Carolinians. The same survey revealed clergy rates of high blood pressure and asthma at about four percent higher and diabetes rates at about three percent higher than those of their non-clergy peers."[6]

Sabbath Keeping

Both ministers and congregations share responsibility for improving this overload situation. It begins with a joint commitment to a weekly sabbath. Clergy I know are self-giving and understand the need for response to emergencies, but the schedules of too many ministers are ones of *constant* availability.

The number one variable of effectiveness in both my research and the findings of others who research congregations is longevity. Bryant Wright, the pastor for twenty-eight years of the largest congregation in my sample of ten Atlanta congregations, responded to my question on his work schedule, "Is there a day of the week you don't work?" as follows: "Absolutely, I'm passionate about a weekly sabbath, usually on Tuesday. If not Tuesday, Monday or Wednesday. I'm passionate for the staff having a weekly sabbath that's not just Saturday because all of us who are ministers, if there's stuff you're doing, it's not really a free day."

William Self is another of the persons in my study group. In his eighties, he served as pastor of several large congregations and is passionate about the practice of a sabbath. He writes:

> God has called us to set aside a timeless time for catching our breath and savoring life. We cannot make meaning simply by willing it; we must make space for it by allowing for the working of the unconscious activity of the soul… This is not a day off to wash the car or run errands. Neither is it a day to catch up on office work nor to make that visit that must be made before Sunday. This is a day of personal worship and meditation in addition to the private devotions and prayer we conduct the other six days. For us, the best day for this is after Wednesday and before Sunday.[7]

Suggesting such a practice does not make it an easy practice. Richard Hester and Kelli Walker-Jones worked with interfaith peer groups of clergy for three years in their development of a narrative approach to ministry. One of their questions related to how the individuals in their groups practiced sabbath. For some, the Hester/Walker-Jones group meeting itself became one of the few experiences of such an idea. They write,

> Our clergy participants were in a hurry. They had long to-do lists, and they were pursued by guilt that told them, "You're not doing enough!" They led congregations that were saturated in expectations of production and progress…We found only small narrative fragments that showed that we or the participants had made sabbath a part of the rhythm of our lives…When clergy entered their groups, there were times they experienced sabbath rest. We would say they tasted sabbath. They did not get a full meal of it, but they tasted it.[8]

Congregations led by Sabbath-practicing leaders will experience them as more energetic, healthier, and more filled with the Spirit. That is the admonition of Scripture after all: "Remember the sabbath day, and keep it holy. Six days you shall labor and do all your work. But the seventh day is a sabbath to the LORD your God" (Ex. 20:8–10a). How do clergy who do not practice sabbath teach such a practice to a congregation?

External Support

Self-care can be enhanced by participation in support ventures outside the congregation. Some churches include in the pastor's benefit package a monthly session with a pastoral counselor to process issues of concern in their personal lives or ministry settings. The provision of a personal coach or ministry coach to reflect on issues within the congregation can be renewing and helpful. Participation in a peer group is a growing practice for pastors and staff personnel. Having the encouragement of one to whom you are not accountable for performance can become the source of new insights and the resolve to address congregational issues.

Sabbatical Leave

Most congregations do not provide the resources for their clergy to have a time of extended leave every seven years of ministry. However, as a long time academic who has experienced four such times of escape from the demands of daily tasks, I can attest to the renewal physically, spiritually, and emotionally that is so important to vitality in continuing work.

The resources are growing for external support for clergy sabbaticals through the Louisville Institute. A grant from this organization funded by The Lilly Endowment, Inc., provided the possibility for much of the research and free time to think through the ideas of this book. Explore the requirements at: http://www.louisville-institute.org.

Congregants can be encouragers or resisters to clergy self-care. Those who resist the disciplines of their leaders in taking time away for vacation, preparation, and renewal will find the synergy of celebratory life together lost in their church. Nothing pays greater dividends for the church than healthy, vibrant, and spiritually growing pastoral leaders. The investment in healthy leadership is the best investment a congregation can make for its own hopefulness.

A Concluding Celebration

This final chapter was written on January 16, 2012, the holiday celebrating the legacy of one of the most powerful ministers of our time, Dr. Martin Luther King Jr. I had the privilege of marching with him following a worship service in which he preached at the West Chestnut Street Baptist Church in Louisville, Kentucky, one month before his tragic assassination.

As the group of worshipers moved from the sanctuary to the streets on that March night in 1968 to advocate for open housing policies in the city of Louisville, the streets were lined with young opponents of the march. We sang "We Shall Overcome" arm-in-arm as a prayer for the victory of God's new order of the Spirit. The opponents jeered with racial epitaphs that still ring in my ears as obscenities.

That is the way leadership is. It is always a mixture of the coming order of God's Spirit amid the human resistance to it. The agenda of the civil rights movement is not complete and will never be complete until the coming of our

Lord. But progress has been made because of one who answered the call of God to lead us all as a new Moses in the twentieth century. My prayer is that the leaders of the hopeful congregations of the future will never allow the people who do not yet understand the will of God for the Church to hinder their willingness to keep marching to the tune of God's melodic promise that the new order of the Spirit shall truly come on earth as it is in heaven.

Appendices

A: Leadership Approaches by Psychological Type

ISTJ	Loyalist, responsible, task-oriented, highly productive, and detail-oriented. May be perceived as uncaring, disrespectful in completing tasks.	**ISFJ**	Harmonious team player, steady energy, highly protective of people in his or her care. May be perceived as unwilling to upset equilibrium.
ISTP	Problem solver, hands-on action, quick to act on facts, adept at practical decisions. May be insensitive to team discussion and uninterested in interpersonal relationships.	**ISFP**	Improviser, pragmatic builder of close-knit teams, quiet and quick catalyst for decisions in changing situations. May resist long-range decisions and highly analytic processes.
ESTP	Promoter, pragmatic, risk-taking, quick decision-maker and high motivator of the group, gregarious and social. May resist collaboration and conceptual strategies.	**ESFP**	Performer, highly social, energetic, seeks quick and harmonious decisions with fun. May be restless in conflict situations and resist analytical problem solving.
ESTJ	Supervisor, responsible, productive, organized, decisive, and results-oriented. May produce compliance rather than commitment among supervisees.	**ESFJ**	Unifier, works well with people, warm and social, builds cooperative relationships, attentive to the needs of others. May overlook discontent and fail to achieve full potential of the group.
INFJ	Empathetic collaborator, centered in core values, imaginative and conceptual. May be slow to decide if relationships are threatened.	**INTJ**	Visionary, strong conceptual abilities, able to synthesize vast amounts of information, committed to logical processes. May be resistant to ideas that do not fit the plan.
INFP	Clarifier, idealistic, loyal follower who works well in small groups, seeks to make decisions reflective of personal values. May be slow to act on tough decisions or confront peers, lowering productivity.	**INTP**	Independent, detached theoretical or scientific thinker, able to ask clear questions, quick thinker. May be detached from group processes and require withdrawal to conclude an inward decision.
ENFP	Inspirer, strong motivator, enjoys collaborating in "big picture" solutions, with strong connections to people. May be unwilling to focus on details in implementing a plan.	**ENTP**	Inventor, enjoys complex patterns and interactions, consumes volumes of information, able to work quickly in teams to develop new solutions. May be so focused on personal ideas, emotional needs of followers are ignored.
ENFJ	Networker, attuned to emotional needs, tolerant, appreciative, builds effective support for collaborative goals and plans. May discount diverse opinions and give more attention to relationships than tasks.	**ENTJ**	Strategist, excels at directing others, able to develop comprehensive systems, focuses on results based on objective criteria, gifted public speaker. May be viewed as blunt and demanding, intolerant of views of others.

Compiled by the author from Linda V. Berens, et al., *Quick Guide to the 16 Personality Types in Organizations: Understanding Personality Differences in the Workplace* (Huntington Beach, Calif.: Telos Publications, 2001) and Sondra A. Vansant, *Wired for Conflict: The Role of Personality in Resolving Differences* (Gainesville, Fla.: Center for Applications of Psychological Type, 2003).

B: Complex Congregational Organization Structures

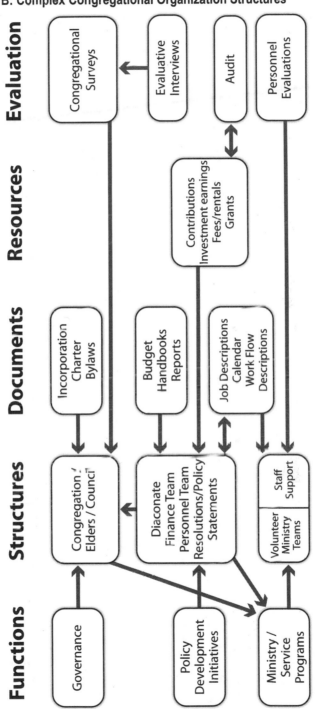

C: Differences in Church Employees

Single Status	Dual Status—self-employed for purpose of housing.
An employee similar to any other organization.	Minister who meets qualifications for a housing allowance and selects the option.
Files W-4 for withholding of income taxes and one-half of Social Security/Medicare.	W-4 is elective. If not filed, minister must pay quarterly estimated taxes and report income on Schedule C. If W-4 is filed, may have income taxes and all SS/Medicare taxes withheld from each pay period.
Earnings reported at end of year on a W-2.	If W-4 not filed, no W-2. All income for the year will be reported on a 1099.
The church withholds all taxes and ½ of SS and MED=7.65%.	If taxes withheld, SS and MED can also be withheld=15.3%.
Church pays 7.65% of SS/MED.	Minister pays all SS/MED=15.3%.
No tax shelter for housing.	Minister pays no income taxes on approved housing allowance that meets IRS requirements.
Church may provide tax exempt benefits:	*Church may provide tax exempt benefits:*
a. Health Ins. Coverage	a. Health Ins. Coverage
b. Life Ins. Coverage	b. Life Ins. Coverage
c. Retirement Contribution	c. Retirement Contribution
d. Reimbursable expenditures	d. Reimbursable expenditures
e. Medical Reimbursement Plan	e. Medical Reimbursement Plan
f. Child Care Reimbursement Plan	f. Child Care Reimbursement Plan
g. Moving Expenses	g. Moving Expenses
Church may provide taxable benefits:	*Church may provide taxable benefits:*
a. Bonuses/Gifts	a. Bonuses/Gifts
b. Club Memberships	b. Club Memberships
	c. Reimb. Of ½ of SS/MED (13th Check)
	d. Home equity allowance if lives in parsonage

Requirements for Dual Status Employee—Housing Allowance

1. The minister must meet IRS qualifications for housing allowance:
    a. "Ministers are individuals who are duly ordained, commissioned, or licensed by a religious body constituting a church or church denomination. They are given the authority to conduct religious worship, perform sacerdotal functions, and administer ordinances or sacraments according to the prescribed tenets and practices of that church or denomination."

"If a church or denomination ordains some ministers and licenses or commissions others, anyone licensed or commissioned must be able to perform substantially all the religious functions of an ordained minister to be treated as a minister for Social Security purposes."

2. The church or designated body must approve at the beginning of each year a statement of housing allowance requested by the minister.

3. The minister with an approved housing allowance may exempt reporting of income for taxes on the smallest of the following:

   a. The amount of housing allowance approved by the church in that calendar year.

   b. The amount of actual costs of housing: mortgage, utilities, repairs, furnishings, equipment, etc.

   c. The amount of the fair market rental value of the housing costs described in number (2).

      In the event the full amount of the housing allowance is not spent in a year, it must be reported as taxable income; if overspent, the housing allowance for that year cannot be increased.

4. The minister must pay the full amount of Social Security/Medicare self-employment taxes on taxable income plus the amount of eligible housing allowance.

Developed by the author in consultation with Dr. Lamar Barden, Peachtree Planning, 500 East Second Street, Rome, GA 30161, 706-500-7469.

Notes

Introduction

[1]Richard L. Hester & Kelli Walker-Jones, *Know Your Story and Lead with It: The Power of Narrative in Clergy Leadership* (Herndon, Va.: The Alban Institute, 2009), 13.

[2]William Butler Yeats, "The Second Coming," *The Classic Hundred Poems*, ed. William Harmon, 2nd ed. (New York: Columbia University Press, 2009), 207.

[3]David T. Olson, *The American Church in Crisis* (Grand Rapids: Zondervan, 2008) documents, from his study of more than 200,000 congregations, rapid decline in attendance and participation in today's churches. Only newer churches, both small and large, are growing.

[4]Brian McLaren, "Seminary Is Not the Problem—the Church Is. What if seminaries became more like entrepreneurial boot camps than shop management schools?" http://www.patheos.com/Resources/Additional-Resources/Seminary-is-Not-the-Problem-the-Church-Is-Brian-McLaren-11-02-2011.html.

[5]Sherwood Lingenfelter, "Defining Institutional Realities: The Myth of the Right Form," *The Three Tasks of Leadership: Worldly Wisdom for Pastoral Leaders*, ed. Eric O. Jacobsen (Grand Rapids: William B. Eerdmans, 2009), 60–61.

[6]The Barna Group has documented the abandonment of these kinds of churches by the young in "Six Reasons Young Christians Leave Church." http://barna.org/teens-next-gen-articles/528-six-reasons-young-christians-leave-church.

[7]Lingenfelter, "Defining Institutional Realities," 67.

Chapter 1

[1]Richard Nelson Bolles, *How to Find Your Mission in Life* (Berkeley, Calif.: Ten Speed Press, 1991, 2000), 11–12.

[2]R. L. Scheef Jr., "Vocation," *The Interpreter's Dictionary of the Bible*, IV, ed. George Arthur Buttrick (New York: Abingdon Press, 1962), 791.

[3]H. Richard Niebuhr, *The Purpose of the Church and Its Ministry: Reflections on the Aims of Theological Education* (New York: Harper and Row, 1956), 64.

[4]R. Paul Stevens, *The Other Six Days: Vocation, Work, and Ministry in Biblical Perspective* (Grand Rapids: William B. Eerdmans, 1999), 80–82.

[5]James W. Fowler, *Becoming Adult, Becoming Christian: Adult Development and Christian Faith* (San Francisco: Jossey-Bass, 2000), 77.

[6]Paul S. Minear, *To Die and Live: Christ's Resurrection and Christian Vocation* (New York: The Seabury Press, 1977), 8.

[7]Parker Palmer, *Let Your Life Speak* (San Francisco: Jossey-Bass, 2000), 10.

[8]Barbara J. Essex, *Women in the Bible* (Cleveland: The Pilgrim Press, 2001), 40.

[9]Gregg Lavoy, *Callings: Finding and Following an Authentic Life* (New York: Harmony Books, 1997), 279.

[10]Stevens, *The Other Six Days*, 159.

[11]Victor Hunter, *Desert Hearts and Healing Fountains: Gaining Pastoral and Vocational Clarity* (St. Louis: Chalice Press, 2003), 28–33, suggests the tradition of vows of ordination provides a compass for pastors amid the desert experience of ministry. Hunter provides descriptions of ordination vows in various traditions. There is no comparable tradition in most locally autonomous congregations.

[12]Palmer, *Let Your Life Speak*, 78.

[13]The issue of sexual abuse is present in all congregational polities. Hierarchical and connectional groups have established procedures for dealing with them in ways autonomous congregations do not. I often ask the question of Baptist ordaining councils how one is "unordained." Few have ever considered the question.

[14]Courtney Wilder, "Workers in the Kingdom," *Sightings* 10 (May 2007). A publication of the Martin Marty Center, University of Chicago Divinity School, Chicago.

[15]Andrew Strieber, "Whistling While You Work: The 10 Most Satisfying Careers," http://www.careercast.com/jobs-rated/whistling-while-you-work-10-most-satisfying-careers.

[16]William Self, "Tears and Lifeblood…," *Christian Century* 128/7 (April 2011), 5.

[17]Palmer, *Let Your Life Speak*, 25.

[18]Larry L. McSwain and Kay Wilson Shurden, *Call Waiting: God's Invitation to Youth* (Valley Forge: Judson Press, 2005).

Chapter 2

[1]James M. Kouzes and Barry Z. Posner, *The Leadership Challenge*, 3rd ed. (San Francisco: Jossey-Bass, 2002), 390–91.

[2]Note in the bibliography the works of Murray Bowen, Edwin H. Freidman, Ronald W. Richardson, and Peter L. Steinke for further study of their insights.

[3]Ronald W. Richardson, *Becoming a Healthier Pastor: Family Systems Theory and the Pastor's Own Family* (Minneapolis: Fortress Press, 2005) stimulates thinking about one's family genogram and associated dynamics. Israel Galindo, Elaine Boomer, and Don Reagan, *A Family Genogram Workbook* (Richmond, Va. : Israel Galindo Educational Consultants, 2006) is a helpful workbook for constructing a paper genogram. A detailed family genogram can also be developed at http://www.genopro.com/genogram/. For a descriptive application in the minister's life and congregation see James Lamkin, "Systems Theory and Congregational Leadership: Leaves from an Alchemist's Journal," *Review and Expositor* 102, no. 3 (Summer 2005): 461–89.

[4]Ronald W. Richardson, *Creating a Healthier Church: Family Systems Theory, Leadership and Congregational Life* (Minneapolis: Fortress Press, 1996), 144–57.

[5]Both extroverts and introverts can be effective in ministry if they balance their natural preferences with willingness to engage persons who are different. Adam S. McHugh, *Introverts in the Church: Finding Our Place in an Extroverted Culture* (Downers Grove, Ill.: IVP Books, 2009) provides guidance for understanding this group of "quiet" and "internal" people.

[6]This summary is drawn primarily from descriptions in http://www.personalitypathways.com/. A bibliography of resources can be found at this website as well.

[7]Geil Browning, *Emergenetics®: Tap into the New Science of Success* (San Francisco: HarperCollins e-books, 2010), Kindle edition, chap. 3.

[8]The Pastoral Institute is a major resource for congregational planning and training as well as counseling services, http://www.pilink.org. A leadership retreat utilizing the Emergenetics® process can be a significant learning experience in building leading teams.

[9]Browning, *Emergenetics®*. The Emergenetics instrument and training resources are available from multiple organizations. Primary is Emergenetics® International, http://emergenetics.com. An introduction to the concepts of the instrument can be found at http://www.insightfulendeavors.com.

[10]See http://www.enneagraminstitute.com/ .

[11]Howard Gardner, *Intelligence Reframed: Multiple Intelligences for the 21ˢᵗ Century* (New York: Basic Books, 1999), 47–66.

[12]Daniel Goleman, *Emotional Intelligence* (New York: Bantam Books, 1995) and Daniel Goleman, Richard E. Boyatzis, and Annie McKee, *Primal Leadership: The Power of Emotional Intelligence* (Boston: Harvard Business School Press, 2002).

[13]Daniel Goleman, *Leadership: The Power of Emotional Intelligence* (Northhampton, Mass.: More Than Sound, 2011), Kindle edition, chap. 4.

[14]Ibid.

[15]Ibid.

[16]Ibid.

[17]Ibid., chap. 5.

[18]M. Craig Barnes, *The Pastor as Minor Poet: Texts and Subtexts in the Ministerial Life* (Grand Rapids: William. B. Eerdmans, 2009), 4.

[19]Ibid., 5.

[20]Lamkin, "Systems Theory and Congregational Leadership," 476.

[21]Alan J. Roxburgh and Fred Romanuk, *The Missional Leader: Equipping Your Church to Reach a Changing World* (San Francisco: Jossey-Bass, 2006), 127.

[22]Jackson W. Carroll, *God's Potters: Pastoral Leadership and the Shaping of Congregations* (Grand Rapids: William B. Eerdmans Publishing Co., 2006), 152.

[23]Kouzes and Posner, *Leadership Challenge*, 33.

[24]Ibid., 48.

[25]Israel Galindo, *The Hidden Lives of Congregations: Discerning Church Dynamics* (Herndon, Va.: The Alban Institute, 2005), 51–56, identifies five dynamics of congregations that are interrelated—systemic anxiety, energy, organizing, controlling, and relational dynamics.

Chapter 3

[1]Robert D. Dale, *Seeds for the Future: Growing Organic Leaders for Living Churches* (St. Louis: Lake Hickory Resources, 2005), 52.

[2]Anthony B. Robinson, *Changing the Conversation: A Third Way for Congregations* (Grand Rapids: William. B. Eerdmans, 2008), 99.

[3]Brother Lawrence, *The Practice of the Presence of God: The Best Rule of a Holy Life* (Gloucester, U.K.: Dodo Press, 2007), Kindle edition.

[4]N. Graham Standish, *Humble Leadership: Being Radically Open to God's Guidance and Grace* (Herndon, Va.: The Alban Institute, 2007), 142.

[5]Ibid., 142–55.

[6]M. Craig Barnes, *The Pastor as Minor Poet: Texts and Subtext in the Ministerial Life* (Grand Rapids: Wm. B. Eerdmans, 2009), 49.

[7]Standish, *Humble Leadership,* 15.

[8]Urban T. Holmes III, *Spirituality for Ministry* (Harrisburg, Pa.: Morehouse Publishing, 1982, 2002), 5–6.

[9]Corinne Ware, *Discover Your Spiritual Type: A Guide to Individual and Congregational Growth* (Bethesda, Md.: An Alban Institute Publication, 1995). Her categories are drawn from Urban T. Holmes III, *A History of Spirituality: An Analytical Introduction* (New York: Seabury Press, 1980).

[10]Henri J. M. Nouwen, *Making All Things New: An Invitation to the Spiritual Life* (San Francisco: HarperSanFrancisco, 1981), 57.

[11]The phrase appears in several of his writings, but most notably, T. S. Eliot, "The Love Song of J. Alfred Prufrock," *Collected Poems, 1909-1962* (New York: Harcourt, Brace, Jovanovich, 1991), 3–7.

[12]Holmes, *Spirituality for Ministry,* 35.

[13]Ibid., 36–49.

[14]Joseph shared his collection of books for the group to examine. They included: Henry T. Blackaby and Claude V. King, *Experiencing God: How to Live the Full Adventure of Knowing and Doing the Will of God* (Nashville: Broadman & Holman Publishers, 1994); Timothy C. Geoffrion, *The Spirit-Led Leader: Nine Leadership Practices and Soul Principles* (Herndon, Va.: The Alban Institute, 2005); Celia Allison Hahn, *Uncovering Your Church's Hidden Spirit* (Bethesda, Md.: The Alban Institute, 2001); Urban T. Holmes III, *Spirituality for Ministry* (Harrisburg, Pa.: Morehouse Publishing, 1982, 2002); Herb Miller, *Connecting with God: 14 Ways Churches Can Help People Grow Spiritually* (Nashville: Abingdon Press, 1994); Carolyn Coon Mowchan and Damian Anthony Vraniak, *Connecting with God in a Disconnected World: A Guide for Spiritual Growth and Renewal* (Minneapolis: Augsburg Fortress, 2003); and Corrine Ware, *Connecting to God: Nurturing Spirituality through Small Groups* (Bethesda, Md.: The Alban Institute, 1997), *Discover Your Spiritual Type: A Guide to Individual and Congregational Growth* (Bethesda, Md.: The Alban Institute, 1995), and *Saint Benedict on the Freeway: A Rule of Life for the 21st Century* (Nashville: Abingdon Press, 2001).

[15]Several such inventories can be found on the Internet. The Spiritual Gifts Inventory used was developed by the United Methodist Church. It is easy to complete and has helpful educational resources for study of spiritual gifts. http://www.umc.org/site/c.lwL4KnN1LtH/b.1355371/k.9501/Spiritual_Gifts.htm.

[16]From Ware, *Discover Your Spiritual Type,* 107.

Chapter 4

[1]Mark Lou Branson, "Gratitude as Access to Meaning," *The Three Tasks of Leadership: Worldly Wisdom for Pastoral Leaders,* ed. Eric O. Jacobsen (Grand Rapids: William B. Eerdmans, 2008), 153.

[2]Cf. Max Depree, *Leadership Is an Art (* New York: Doubleday, 1989), 9. He also explores the art of leadership in *Leadership Jazz* (New York: Doubleday, 1992).

[3]Jim Somerville, pastor of the First Baptist Church, Richmond, Virginia, uses the apt metaphor of shifting sands in his leading congregations to understand the impact of change on their ministries. "When the Sand Castle Crumbles: Why Is My Church Dying, and What Can I Do About It?" http://jimsomerville.wordpress.com/.

[4]Leadership thinkers who recognize these limits are Jim Collins, *Good to Great: Why Some Companies*

Make the Leap…and Other's Don't (New York: HarperBusiness, 2001) with his rejection of charismatic approaches to corporate leadership and his application to the nonprofit world in *Good to Great and the Social Sectors* (Boulder, Colo.: Jim Collins, 2005). Ronald A. Heifetz and Marty Linsky, *Leadership on the Line: Staying Alive through the Dangers of Leading* (Boston: Harvard Business School Press, 2002) is a business-related work that applies well to congregational leadership.

[5]Alan J. Roxburgh and Fred Romanuk, *The Missional Leader: Equipping Your Church to Reach a Changing World* (San Francisco: Jossey-Bass, 2006), 122.

[6]These are only a few of the many images of the church in the New Testament. Paul S. Minear, *Images of the Church in the New Testament* (Philadelphia: The Westminster Press, 1960) documented ninety-six metaphors for the church in the New Testament.

[7]Robert L. Kelley, *The Power of Followership: How to Create Leaders People Want* (New York: Doubleday/Currency, 1992), 46.

[8]Ibid., 20–21.

[9]Ibid., 202.

[10]George W. Bullard Jr., *Pursuing the Full Kingdom Potential of Your Congregation* (St. Louis: Lake Hickory Resources, 2005), 44.

[11]Ibid., 42–53

[12]Adam Hamilton, *Leading Beyond the Walls: Developing Congregations with a Heart for the Unchurched* (Nashville: Abingdon Press, 2002), 59.

[13]Kelley, *The Power of Followership*, 34.

[14]James M. Kouzes and Barry Z. Posner, *The Leadership Challenge*, 3rd ed. (San Francisco: Jossey-Bass, 2002), 50.

[15]Walt Wright, "Introduction: Mentor to Mentor," *The Three Tasks of Leadership: Worldly Wisdom for Pastoral Leaders*, ed. Eric O. Jacobsen (Grand Rapids, William B. Eerdmans, 2009), 2–3.

[16]Daniel Goleman, *Leadership: The Power of Emotional Intelligence* (Northhampton, Mass.: More Than Sound, 2011), Kindle edition, chap. 4.

[17]Kouzes and Posner, *The Leadership Challenge*, 31–32.

[18]Ibid., 116.

[19]Jackson W. Carroll, *God's Potters: Pastoral Leadership and the Shaping of Congregations* (Grand Rapids: William B. Eerdmans, 2006), 134–35. Figure 4.2 from page 135.

[20]Ibid., 137.

[21]Ibid., 81.

[22]Robert LaRochelle, *Part-Time Pastor, Full-Time Church* (Cleveland: Pilgrim Press, 2010).

[23]Collins, *Good to Great*, 41–64. Churches can practice this idea of who is placed in leadership roles. However, Collins also emphasizes getting the wrong people off the bus. Accomplishing that task is more difficult in the church. Too many churches put the wrong people on the bus as they employ ministers or enlist lay leadership.

[24]Louis B. Weeks, *All for God's Glory: Redeeming Church Scutwork* (Herndon, Va.: The Alban Institute, 2000).

[25]Kouzes and Posner, *The Leadership Challenge*, 190.

[26]Ibid., 162.

Chapter 5

[1]Ryan Bolger, "Following Jesus into Culture: Emerging Church as Social Movement, *An Emergent Manifesto of Hope*, eds. Doug Pagitt and Tony Jones (Grand Rapids: Baker Books, 2007), 133.

[2]Howard W. Stone and James O. Duke, *How to Think Theologically*, 2nd ed. (Minneapolis: Fortress Press, 2006), 13–20.

[3]Cf. Karl Ludwig Schmidt, "βασίλεία," *Theological Dictionary of the New Testament*, ed. Gerhard Kittel, trans. Geoffrey W. Bromiley, vol. 1 (Grand Rapids: William B. Eerdmans, 1964), 579–90.

[4]Evelyn Jensen, "Women's Issues in Context," *The Good News of the Kingdom: Mission Theology for the Third Millenium*, ed. Charles Van Engen, Dean S. Gilliland, and Paul Pierson (Maryknoll, N.Y.: Orbis Books, 1993), 213–18.

[5]Brian D. McLaren, *Everything Must Change: Jesus, Global Crises, and a Revolution of Hope* (Nashville: Thomas Nelson, 2007), 99. This is his transliteration of Mk. 1:14.

[6]Ibid., 131–33, 189–99, calls this dimension *God's sacred ecosystem* with a passionate call for Christians to challenge the religion of "theocapitalism."

[7]Christopher J. H. Wright, *The Mission of God: Unlocking the Bible's Grand Narrative* (Downers

Grove, Ill.: IVP Academic, 2006), 189.

[8]Lesslie Newbigin, *The Open Secret: An Introduction to the Theology of Mission*, rev. ed. (Grand Rapids: William B. Eerdmans, 1978, 1995), 73.

[9]Wright, *Mission of God*, 249–51.

[10]David J. Bosch, *Transforming Mission: Paradigm Shifts in Theology of Mission* (Maryknoll, N.Y.: Orbis Books, 1991), 32.

[11]Johannes Verkuhl, "The Biblical Notion of Kingdom: Test of Validity for Theology of Religion," *The Good News of the Kingdom: Mission Theology for the Third Millenium*, ed. Charles Van Engen, Dean S. Gilliland, and Paul Pierson (Maryknoll, N.Y.: Orbis Books, 1993), 72.

[12]Wright, *Mission of God*, 299.

[13]Douglas John Hall, *The Cross in Our Context: Jesus and the Suffering World* (Minneapolis: Fortress Press, 2003), 38.

[14]Newbigin, *The Open Secret*, 35.

[15]Hall, *The Cross*, 183.

[16]Barry Harvey, "The Church as a Company of Nomads," *Christian Reflection: A Series in Faith and Ethics*, 34 (Waco: Baylor University, 2010), 13.

[17]Newbigin, *The Open Secret*, 69–70.

[18]McLaren, *Change*, 128–130, describes these commitments as participation in the "Divine Peace Insurgency," "God's Unterror Movement," a "New Global Love Economy," and "God's Sacred Ecosystem."

[19]Bosch, *Transforming Mission*, 390.

[20]Newbigin, *The Open Secret*, 53–54.

[21]Craig Van Gelder, *The Ministry of the Missional Church: A Community Led by the Spirit* (Grand Rapids: Baker Books, 2007), 93.

[22]David J. Bosch, *Believing in the Future: Toward a Missiology of Western Culture* (Valley Forge, Pa.: Trinity Press International, 1995), 59.

Chapter 6

[1]Erwin Raphael McManus, "The Global Intersection," *The Church in Emerging Culture: Five Perspectives*, ed. Leonard Sweet (El Cajon, Calif.: emergentYS 2003), 237.

[2]*Merriam-Webster's Collegiate Dictionary, 11th ed.* (Springfield, Mass.: Merriam-Webster, 2005),1345.

[3]Robert Bellah, "Religious Evolution," *Beyond Belief: Essays on Religion in a Post-Traditionalist World* (Berkeley: University of California Press, 1991), 20–51.

[4]Phyllis Tickle, *The Great Emergence: How Christianity Is Changing and Why* (Grand Rapids: Baker Books, 2008).

[5]Ibid., 19–31.

[6]Stanley J. Grenz, *A Primer on Postmodernism* (Grand Rapids: Eerdmans, 1996), 2.

[7]Ibid., 8.

[8] Ibid., 168.

[9]Charles Kenny, "TV Will Save the World: In a lot of places, it's the next big thing," *Time* 175/11 (March 22, 2011): 54, estimates two-thirds of households globally will have a TV by 2013.

[10]Thomas L. Friedman, *The World Is Flat: A Brief History of the Twenty-first Century* (New York: Farrar, Straus and Giroux, 2005), 10–11, where he calls this change Globalization 3.0. His ten forces that flattened the world should be required reading for all contemporary leaders. His sequel, *Hot, Flat, and Crowded: Why We Need a Green Revolution and How It Can Renew America* (New York: Farrar, Straus and Giroux, 2008) is equally provocative.

[11]Friedman, *The World Is Flat*, 201.

[12]Scott Thumma and Dave Travis, *Beyond Megachurch Myths: What We Can Learn From America's Largest Churches* (New York: John Wiley and Sons, 2007), 14.

[13]Matt Rosenberg, "Current World Population and World Population Growth Since the Year One," *About.com*, January 1, 2012, http://geography.about.com/od/obtainpopulationdata/a/worldpopulation.htm (accessed January 24, 2012).

[14]"Largest Cities in the World," *WorldAtlas*, http://www.worldatlas.com/citypops.htm.

[15]"How We Compiled the 2010 Index," *Foreign Policy.com*, August 18, 2010. http://www.foreignpolicy.com/articles/2010/08/18/global_cities_index_methodology.

[16]*Foreign Policy.com*, http://www.foreignpolicy.com/articles/2010/08/11/the_global_cities_index_2010.

[17]Pew Research Center, "91.7%—Minorities Account for Nearly All U.S. Population Growth," http://pewresearch.org/databank/dailynumber/?NumberID=1225. A small number of other minorities brings the total to 100 percent.

[18]Diana L. Eck, *A New Religious America: How a "Christian Country" Has Become the World's Most Religiously Diverse Nation* (New York: HarperCollins, 2001), 4.

[19]Steven Johnson, *Where Good Ideas Come From: The Natural History of Innovation* (New York: Riverhead Books, 2010), 53.

[20]This concept is developed in Warren G. Bennis and Robert J. Thomas, *Geeks and Geezers: How Era, Values and Defining Moments Shape Leaders* (Boston: Harvard Business School Press, 2002) and Jackson W. Carroll and Wade Clark Roof, *Bridging Divided Worlds: Generational Cultures in Congregations* (San Francisco: Jossey-Bass, 2002).

[21]Paul Taylor and Scott Keeter, eds., *Millennials: A Portrait of Generation Next* (Philadelphia: Pew Research Center, 2010), 1–10. http://pewresearch.org/millennials/. Analysis of the "Greatest Generation" is not included in this superb research resource.

[22]Robert D. Putnam and David E. Campbell, *Amazing Grace: How Religion Divides and Unites Us* (New York: Simon and Schuster, 2010), 2–7.

[23]Taylor and Keeter, *Millennials,* 77–81.

[24]Summarized from ibid., Chapter 9, 100–109. These findings are generally consistent with the research of the Barna Research Group in Gabe Lyons and Dave Kinnaman, *unChristian: What a New Generation Really Thinks about Christianity…and Why It Matters* (Grand Rapids: Baker Books, 2007), Kindle edition, chapter 1. They report, "There are about twenty-four million outsiders [outside the church] in this country who are ages sixteen to twenty-nine." Most of these are "dechurched" rather than unchurched.

[25]Anthony Robinson, *Changing the Conversation: A Third Way for Congregations* (Grand Rapids: William B. Eerdmans Publishing Co., 2008), 26.

Chapter 7

[1]R. Stephen Warner, "The Place of the Congregation in the Contemporary American Religious Configuration," *American Congregations: New Perspectives in the Study of Congregations,* ed. James P. Wind and James W. Lewis, vol. 2 (Chicago: The University of Chicago Press, 1994), 54.

[2]Anthony B. Robinson, *Changing the Conversation: A Third Way for Congregations* (Grand Rapids: William B. Eerdmans, 2008), 7–8, describes congregations as open-set, bounded-set, or centered-set. The open-set is what I am calling "fuzzy" with few boundaries, while the bounded-set is rigid in its expectations. The centered-set congregation has a clearly defined mission and set of values defining its identity.

[3]Arlin J. Rothage, *Sizing Up a Congregation for New Member Ministry* (New York: Seabury, n.d.).

[4]Israel Galindo, *The Hidden Lives of Congregations: Discerning Church Dynamics* (Herndon, Va.: The Alban Institute, 2004).

[5]James Hopewell, *Congregation: Stories and Structures,* ed. Barbara G. Wheeler (Philadelphia: Fortress Press, 1987).

[6]David Roozen, William McKinney, and Jackson W. Carroll, *Varieties of Religious Presence: Mission in Public Life* (New York: The Pilgrim Press, 1984).

[7]Penny Edgell Becker, *Congregations in Conflict: Cultural Models of Local Religious Life* (New York: Cambridge University Press, 1999).

[8]Nancy Tatom Ammerman with Arthur E. Farnsley, et al., *Congregation and Community* (New Brunswick: Rutgers University Press, 1997).

[9]Wayne A. Meeks, *The First Urban Christians: The Social World of the Apostle Paul,* 2nd ed. (New Haven: Yale University Press, 2003), 74–107.

[10]Lisa Miller, "House of Worship: Finding spirituality at home," *Newsweek* (January 11, 2010): 31.

[11]Cynthia Woolever and Deborah Bruce, *A Field Guide to U.S. Congregations: Who's Going Where and Why* (Louisville: Westminster John Knox Press, 2002), 24, Figure 3.1.

[12]Jackson W. Carroll with Becky R. McMillan. *God's Potters: Pastoral Leadership and the Shaping of Congregations* (Grand Rapids: William B. Eerdmans, 2006), 63, Figure 3.1.

[13]Ibid., 81.

[14]Ibid., 80.

[15]Ronald W. Richardson, *Creating a Healthier Church: Family Systems Theory, Leadership, and Congregational Life* (Minneapolis: Fortress Press, 1996), 101–113.

[16]Carroll, *God's Potters*, 64.

[17]Edgar W. Mills and John P. Koval, *Stress in Ministry* (New York: IDOC, 1971).

[18]Carroll, *God's Potters*, 153.

[19]Ibid., 148.

[20]*Merriam-Webster's Collegiate Dictionary*, 11th ed. (Springfield, Mass.: Merriam-Webster, 2005), 407.

[21]Scot McKnight, "Five Streams of Emerging Church: Key elements of the most controversial and misunderstood movement in the church today" *Christianity Today* (February 2007): 35–39.

[22]Explore the bibliography for works by Brian D. McLaren, Donald Miller, and Rob Bell for contributions on this theological revision.

[23]Barry Taylor, "Converting Christianity: The End and Beginning of Faith," *An Emergent Manifesto of Hope*, ed. Doug Pagitt and Tony Jones (Grand Rapids: Baker Books, 2007), 170.

[24]Carroll, *God's Potters*, 102, Table 4.1.

[25]Scott Thumma and Dave Travis, *Beyond Megachurch Myths: What We Can Learn from America's Largest Churches* (San Francisco: John Wiley & Sons, 2007), 6.

[26]Ibid., a brief summary of Table 2.3, which develops more fully the characteristics of each type, 32–35.

[27]Ibid., 5.

[28]Ibid., 6, citing Mark Chaves, *Congregations in America* (Cambridge, Mass.: Harvard University Press, 2004), 18.

[29]Ibid., 14–15, 182–83.

[30]Cynthia Woolever and Deborah Bruce, *Leadership That Fits Your Church: What Kind of Pastor for What Kind of Congregation* (St. Louis: Chalice Press, 2012) provides data that helps a congregation identify key factors in pastoral fit.

Chapter 8

[1]Robert D. Dale, *Seeds for the Future: Growing Organic Leaders for Living Churches* (St. Louis: Lake Hickory Resources, 2005), 42.

[2]Diana Butler Bass, *The Practicing Congregation: Imagining a New Old Church* (Herndon, Va.: The Alban Institute, 2004), 5–6. Urban T. Holmes III emphasized the idea of pastoral imagination in *Ministry and Imagination* (New York: Seabury Press, 1976), and Craig Dykstra, "The Pastoral Imagination," *Initiatives in Religion* (Spring 1–2, 2001): 15, has popularized it in funding projects of The Lilly Endowment, Inc.

[3]Steven Johnson, *Where Good Ideas Come From: The Natural History of Innovation* (New York: Riverhead Books, 2010), 59.

[4]Ibid., 10.

[5]Ronald W. Johnson, *From the Outside In* (St. Louis: Lake Hickory Resources, 2006) develops helpful suggestions for enlarging awareness of the ministry context.

[6]Dale, *Seeds for the Future*, 44.

[7]Jackson W. Carroll, *God's Potters: Pastoral Leadership and the Shaping of Congregations* (Grand Rapids: William B. Eerdmans, 2006), 153–54.

[8]Malcolm Gladwell, *Outliers: The Story of Success* (New York: Little Brown and Company, 2008), 40.

[9]Robert J. Sternberg, *Successful Intelligence: How Practical and Creative Intelligence Determine Success in Life* (New York: Plume, 1997), quoted in ibid., 101.

[10]Gilbert R. Rendle, *Leading Change in the Congregation: Spiritual and Organizational Tools for Leaders* (Herndon, Va.: The Alban Institute, 1998) could be read with profit by core leaders prior to initiating a change process.

[11]Robet D. Dale, *To Dream Again* (Nashville: Broadman Press, 1981).

[12]George W. Bullard Jr., *Pursuing the Full Kingdom Potential of Your Congregation* (St. Louis: Lake Hickory Resources, 2005).

[13]Israel Galindo, *The Hidden Lives of Congregations: Discerning Church Dynamics* (Herndon, Va.: The Alban Institute, 2004).

[14]Energy and control are two of the five system dynamics in congregations emphasized in ibid., 51–56.

[15]Carl S. Dudley and Nancy T. Ammerman, *Congregations in Transition: A Guide for Analyzing, Assessing, and Adapting in Changing Communities* (San Francisco: Jossey-Bass, 2002).

¹⁶Jim Herrington, Mike Bonem, and James H. Furr, *Leading Congregational Change: A Practical Guide for the Transformational Journey* (San Francisco: Jossey-Bass Publishers, 2000). A companion workbook is also available.

¹⁷Lovett H. Weems Jr., *Take the Next Step: Leading Lasting Change in the Church* (Nashville: Abingdon Press, 2003).

¹⁸Bullard, *Full Kingdom Potential.*

¹⁹Gil Rendle and Alice Mann, *Holy Conversations: Strategic Planning as a Spiritual Practice for Congregations* (Herndon, Va.: The Alban Institute, 2003).

²⁰Sue Annis Hammond, *The Thin Book of® Appreciative Inquiry*, 2nd ed. (Bend, Oreg.: Thin Book Publishing, 1996), Kindle edition, section 5.

²¹David Cooperrider and his associates at Case Western Reserve University are credited with first developing the process as an application of the "appreciative eye" in art to business settings. Ibid., section 2.

²²Ibid., section 3.

²³Ibid., location 167.

²⁴This 4-D process has been summarized in my language from David L. Cooperrider and Diana Whitney, "A Positive Revolution in Change: Appreciative Inquiry" (Draft), Appreciative Inquiry Commons, 7–14 http://appreciativeinquiry.case.edu/uploads/whatisai.pdf and Jane Logan, "Appreciative Inquiry," Association Xpertise Inc. (AXI) January 2004, http://www.axi.ca/tca/jan2004/facilitationrole_1.shtml.

²⁵Luther K. Snow, *The Power of Asset Mapping: How Your Congregation Can Act on Its Gifts* (Herndon, Va.: The Alban Institute, 2004).

²⁶Cooperrider and Whitney, "A Positive Revolution," 8.

²⁷Dale, *Seeds for the Future*, 129.

Chapter 9

¹Thomas Moore, *Care of the Soul: A Guide for Cultivating Depth and Sacredness in Everyday Life* (New York: HarperPerennial, 1992), xv.

²E. Brooks Holifield, *God's Ambassadors: A History of the Christian Clergy in America* (Grand Rapids: William B. Eerdmans, 2007), 13, includes 1 Corinthians 12:28; Philippians 1:1; 1 Corinthians 11:5; Romans 16:1; 1 Timothy 5:3 and acknowledges the historical debates of whether they describe "offices" or functional responsibilities in the early Church.

³Charles J. Scalise, "Defining the Reality of Your Role: Historical Contexts and Theological Models of Christian Leadership," *The Three Tasks of Leadership: Worldly Wisdom for Pastoral Leaders*, ed. Eric O. Jacobsen (Grand Rapids: William B. Eerdmans, 2009), 28.

⁴Ibid., 36–45. A fuller development of his approach can be found in Charles J. Scalise, *Bridging the Gap: Connecting What You Learned in Seminary with What You Find in the Congregation* (Nashville: Abingdon Press, 2003).

⁵Marvin A. McMickle, *Caring Pastors, Caring People: Equipping Your Church for Pastoral Care* (Valley Forge: Judson Press, 2011), 46–47.

⁶*Merriam-Webster's Collegiate Dictionary*, 11ᵗʰ ed. (Springfield, Mass.: Merriam-Webster, 2005), 253.

⁷McMickle, *Caring Pastors, Caring People*, 27–31.

⁸E. Brooks Holifield, *A History of Pastoral Care in America: From Salvation to Self-Realization* (Nashville: Abingdon Press, 1983), 17.

⁹Ibid., 18–25. These theological differences shaped varied approaches to the spiritual growth process in each of the traditions.

¹⁰Richard Baxter, *The Reformed Pastor*, ed. William Brown (Carlisle, Pa.: The Banner of Truth Trust, [1656], 1997), 87–110.

¹¹E. Brooks Holifield, "Toward a History of American Congregations," *American Congregations: New Perspectives in the Study of Congregations*, ed. James P. Wind and James W. Lewis, vol. 2 (Chicago: The University of Chicago Press, 1994), 43–47, in which he describes the participatory congregation as an organization offering programs meeting needs defined by the members.

¹²Wayne E. Oates, *The Christian Pastor* (Philadelphia: Westminster Press, [1951], 1982), 190–218, for the traditional levels, and 219–60 for a description of the "deeper" levels.

¹³William H. Willimon, *Pastor: The Theology and Practice of Ordained Ministry* (Nashville: Abingdon Press, 2002), 101, suggests Hiltner "moved from a theological mode into the therapeutic mode" in his *Preface to Pastoral Theology* (Nashville: Abingdon Press, 1979, reprint of 1956 edition). Seward

Hiltner, *Ferment in the Ministry* (Nashville: Abingdon Press, 1969), included shepherding as one of his nine functional images of ministry.

¹⁴Willimon, *Pastor*, 95.

¹⁵Holifield, *History of Pastoral Care*, 307–13, 342–48.

¹⁶McMickle, *Caring Pastors, Caring People*, 6.

¹⁷ Moore, *Care of the Soul*, 225.

¹⁸Clearly my Baptist tradition of the symbolic nature of the Lord's Supper is evident in my language. More sacramental traditions need not experience a greater sense of the presence of the risen Lord in the supper, however.

¹⁹ M. Craig Barnes, *The Pastor as Minor Poet: Texts and Subtexts in the Ministerial Life* (Grand Rapids: William. B. Eerdmans, 2009), 113.

²⁰I have drawn these metaphors from the powerful insights of Christine M. Smith, *Preaching as Weeping, Confession, and Resistance* (Louisville: Westminster/John Knox Press, 1992). Hers is a challenging style addressing issues of handicappism, ageism, sexism, heterosexism, white racism, and classism.

²¹Harry Emerson Fosdick, *The Living of These Days: An Autobiography* (New York: Harper & Row, 1956), quoted in Harry Emerson Fosdick, "Learning to Preach," *Pastor: A Reader for Ordained Ministry*, ed. William H. Willimon (Nashville: Abingdon Press, 2002), 145–46.

²²John R. Claypool, *The Preaching Event* (Waco: Word Books, 1980), 86.

²³Ibid., 106–107. The sermon is in John R. Claypool, *Tracks of a Fellow Struggler: How to Handle Grief* (Waco: Word Books, 1974), 65–83. I was present for the sermon, and its power was memorable. The honesty of his anger at God for the death his daughter was more than some in the congregation could understand.

²⁴Thomas G. Long, *Accompany Them with Singing—The Christian Funeral* (Louisville: Westminster John Knox Press, 2009) calls for the recovery of a body-centered tradition of funeral drama that reclaims traditional Christian meanings.

²⁵Charles Qualls, *Divorce Ministry: A Guidebook* (Macon: Smyth & Helwys Publishing Incorporated, 2011) is a practical guide for developing a ministry to divorced persons.

²⁶ McMickle, *Caring Pastors, Caring People*, 99.

²⁷Thomas C. Oden, *Pastoral Theology: Essentials of Ministry* (San Francisco: HarperSanFrancisco, 1983), 88, quoted in Barnes, *Pastor as Minor Poet*, 61.

²⁸Robert M. Franklin, *Crisis in the Village: Restoring Hope in African American Communities* (Minneapolis: Fortress Press, 2007), 160–64.

²⁹Robert D. Lupton, *Return Flight: Community Development Through Reneighboring Our Cities* (Atlanta: FCS Urban Ministries, 1993, 1997).

³⁰Robert D. Lupton, *Compassion, Justice and the Christian Life: Rethinking Ministry to the Poor* (Ventura, Calif. : Regal Books, 2007), 31.

³¹Larry L. McSwain, *Old Louisville: A Challenge, An Opportunity* (Louisville: Urban Studies Center, University of Louisville, 1969).

Chapter 10

¹ Adam Hamilton, *Leading Beyond the Walls: Developing Congregations with a Heart for the Unchurched* (Nashville: Abingdon Press, 2002), 91.

² William L. Self, *Surviving the Stained-Glass Jungle* (Macon: Mercer University Press, 2011), 56–57.

³ St. John Chrysostom: *Six Books on the Priesthood*, trans. Graham Neville (London: SPCK, 1964) quoted in St. Chrysostom, "Temptations of the Teacher," *Pastor: A Reader for Ordained Ministry*, ed. William H. Willimon (Nashville: Abingdon Press, 2002), 124.

⁴ Harry Emerson Fosdick, *The Living of These Days: An Autobiography* (New York: Harper & Row, 1956) quoted in Harry Emerson Fosdick, "Learning to Preach," *Pastor: A Reader for Ordained Ministry*, ed. William H. Willimon (Nashville: Abingdon Press, 2002), 142.

⁵William E. Hull, *Strategic Preaching: The Role of the Pulpit in Pastoral Leadership* (St. Louis: Chalice Press, 2006), 12.

⁶Landon Whitsitt, *Open Source Church: Making Room for the Wisdom of All* (Herndon, Va.: The Alban Institute, 2011), Kindle edition, chap. 2.

⁷James Gustafson, *Treasure in Earthen Vessels: The Church as a Human Community* (New York: Harper, 1961).

⁸Leonora Tubbs Tisdale, *Preaching as Local Theology and Folk Art* (Minneapolis: Fortress Press, 2007), 58.

[9] M. Craig Barnes, *The Pastor as Minor Poet: Texts and Subtexts in the Ministerial Life* (Grand Rapids: William B. Eerdmans, 2009), 75–76.

[10] Ibid., 80.

[11] Ibid., 136.

[12] Hull, *Strategic Preaching*, 78.

[13] James Lamkin, "Recalling That Which Is Not Yet," a sermon preached at Northside Drive Baptist Church, Atlanta, Georgia, December 18, 2011.

[14] Hull, *Strategic Preaching*, 101–110, gives a masterful example of a sermon on the ministry of Jesus to children, addressing the need for a capital campaign for enlarging children's ministries areas of church facilities.

[15] Hamilton, *Leading Beyond the Walls*, 79.

[16] Ibid., 90.

Chapter 11

[1] Rob Bell, "From Structure to Spirit and Back," *Faith & Leadership*, http://www.faithandleadership.com/ multimedia/rob-bell-structure-to-spirit, 11/12/2010.

[2] Anthony Robinson, *Changing the Conversation: A Third Way for Congregations* (Grand Rapids: William B. Eerdmans, 2008), 139.

[3] Thomas G. Long, *Beyond the Worship Wars: Building Vital and Faithful Worship* (Bethesda, Md.: The Alban Institute, 2001) adopts this language because it is so descriptive of the conflict congregants create by making personal worship preferences primary.

[4] Joseph R. Myers, *Organic Community: Creating a Place where People Connect Naturally* (Grand Rapids: Baker Books, 2007), 42–44.

[5] Kennon Callahan, *Twelve Keys to an Effective Church* (San Francisco: Harper & Row, 1983), 35–40.

[6] Martha Grace Reese, *Unbinding the Gospel: Real Life Evangelism* (St. Louis: Chalice Press, 2008) will stimulate readers to participate personally in the faith-sharing adventure of evangelism.

[7] Edward H. Hammett, *The Gathered and Scattered Church: Equipping Believers for the 21ˢᵗ Century* (Macon: Smyth & Helwys, 1999).

[8] Andy Stanley, *Deep and Wide: Creating Churches Unchurched People Love to Attend* (Grand Rapids: Zondervan, 2012).

[9] William C. Treadwell Jr. and Larry L. McSwain, *Church Organizations Alive!* (Nashville: Broadman Press, 1987).

[10] Landon Whitsitt, *Open Source Church: Making Room for the Wisdom of All* (Herndon, Va.: The Alban Institute, 2011), Kindle edition, chap. 2.

[11] "Keeping Your Church Out of Court," 3rd ed., produced by the Christian Life Commission of the Baptist General Convention of Texas, is a CD of legal descriptions and sample documents developed by attorneys of Bourland, Wall & Wenzel in Fort Worth, Texas. It may be purchased for a modest price from http://christianlifecommission.com.

[12] Margaret Wheatley, "Goodbye, Command and Control," *Leader to Leader* (July 1997): 1, quoted in Sally Morgenthaler, "Leadership in a Flattened World: Grassroots Culture and the Demise of the CEO Model," *An Emergent Manifesto of Hope*, ed. Doug Pagitt and Tony Jones (Grand Rapids: Baker Books, 2007), 178.

[13] Bruce Tuckman, "Developmental Sequence in Small Groups," *Psychological Bulletin* 63, no. 6 (1965): 384–99.

[14] Morgenthaler, "Leadership in a Flattened World," 187–88.

[15] For resources that fit congregations, see Patrick M. Lencioni, *The Five Dysfunctions of a Team: A Leadership Fable* (San Francisco: Jossey-Bass, 2002), and George Cladis, *Leading the Team-Based Church: How Pastors and Church Staffs Can Grow Together into a Powerful Fellowship of Leaders* (San Francisco: Jossey-Bass, 1999).

[16] Mike Bonem and Roger Patterson, *Leading from the Second Chair: Serving Your Church, Fulfilling Your Role, and Realizing Your Dreams* (San Francisco: Jossey-Bass, 2005).

[17] Robert L. Quinn, *Deep Change: Discovering the Leader Within* (San Francisco: Jossey-Bass, 1996), 161.

[18] Jim Collins, *Good to Great: Why Some Companies Make the Leap...and Others Don't* (New York: HarperBusiness, 2001), 41.

[19] Jason Byassee, "Team Players: What do associate pastors want?" *Christian Century* (January 24, 2006): 18.

[20] Triangulation applies to all relationships. See Ronald W. Richardson, *Creating a Healthier*

Church: Family Systems Theory, Leadership and Congregational Life (Minneapolis: Fortress Press, 1996), 114–30, for a good description of how to avoid it.

[21]Thomas G. Bandy, *Coaching Change: Breaking Down Resistance, Building Up Hope,* (Nashville: Abingdon Press, 2000).

[22]Edward H. Hammett and James R. Pierce with Stephen DeVane, *Making Shifts without Making Waves: A Coach Approach to Soulful Leadership* (St. Louis: Chalice Press, 2009), 33, describes these more fully and explores multiple dimensions of leadership coaching.

[23]Jane Creswell, *Christ-Centered Coaching: 7 Benefits for Ministry Leaders* (St. Louis: Chalice Press, 2006), 13.

[24]Daniel Goleman, *Leadership: The Power of Emotional Intelligence* (Northampton, Mass.: More Than Sound LLC, 2011), Kindle edition, chap. 4.

[25]Cindy Coe, Amy Zehnder, and Dennis Kinlaw, *Coaching for Commitment: Achieving Superior Performance from Individuals and Teams,* 3rd ed. (San Francisco: John Wiley & Sons, 2008), 199. See their list of qualities of a coaching for commitment culture.

[26]Ibid., 43–52.

Chapter 12

[1]J. Clif Christopher, *Not Your Parents' Offering Plate: A New Vision for Financial Stewardship* (Nashville: Abingdon Press, 2008), 28.

[2]Lynn Miller, *The Power of Enough: Finding Contentment,* 2nd ed. (Goshen, Ind.: MMA® Stewardship Solutions, 2003, 2007).

[3]Christopher, *Not Your Parents' Offering Plate,* 1–3, citing statistics from Giving USA Foundation™/ *Giving USA 2007.*

[4]Randy Alcorn, *Money, Possessions, and Eternity* (Carol Stream, Ill.: Tyndale House Publishing, 2003), is a significant resource for education, though the book is quite long, detailed, and somewhat legalistic. Miller, *The Power of Enough,* is a manageable resource I have used in a Church school class and found most helpful.

[5]Financial Peace University (http://www.daverramsey.com/fpu/home/); Crown Financial Ministries (http://www.crown.org/); Master Your Money (http://www.masteryourmoney. org/); Good Sense (http://www.goodsenseministry.com/); and Abundant Living (http://www. abundantlivingministry.org/ministrypartners.aspx).

[6]Anthony B. Robinson, *Stewardship for Vital Congregations* (Cleveland: The Pilgrim Press, 2011).

[7]Nelson Searcy with Jennifer Dykes Henson, *Maximize: How to Develop Extravagant Givers in Your Church* (Grand Rapids: Baker Books, 2010).

[8]Alex Tanzi, "U.S. Median Household Income Changes by County, From 2000 to 2009," Bloomberg.com, December 14, 2010. www.bloomberg.com/news/2010-12-14/u-s-median-household-income-change-from-2000-by-county-table-.html.

[9]Each of the primary resources mentioned in this chapter offer more suggestions than space allows in this text. Searcy, *Maximize,* 61–74, has the most developed approach, while Christopher, *Not Your Parents' Offering Plate,* 33–41, segments giving groups for letters to congregants.

[10]Cynthia Woolever and Deborah Bruce, *A Field Guide to U.S. Congregations: Who's Going Where and Why,* 2d ed. (Louisville: Westminster John Knox Press, 2010), 65.

[11]William G. Enright, "Money is like a vital sign," *Faith and Leadership,* July 5, 2011, www. faithandleadership.com/qa/william-g-enright-money-vital-sign?page=full&print=true.

[12]Ibid. Enright identifies endowment earnings and level of debt as the two most significant triggers of decline during the recession. He suggests debt repayments in excess of 4–5 percent of operational budgets are negative for financial health.

[13]Ibid. From 1970 to 1995, roughly half of charitable giving was to religious entities; since 1995 it has dropped to one third.

[14]Louis Weeks, *All for God's Glory: Redeeming Church Scutwork* (Herndon, Va.: The Alban Institute, 2008) offers compelling arguments for the pastor knowing the giving record of individual congregants.

[15]Jackson W. Carroll, *God's Potters: Pastoral Leadership and the Shaping of Congregations* (Grand Rapids: William B. Eerdmans, 2006), 173–74, reported that dissatisfaction with salary and benefits was the most important source of dissatisfaction in ministry, and those who felt it were more likely to report spousal resentment of the family's finances.

[16]Ruben Swint, "Let's Do the Math," http://columbiapartnership.typepad/the_columbia_ partnership/2011/06/lets-do-th-math.html.

Chapter 13

[1]An earlier form of this chapter was published in Larry L. McSwain, "Mending the Tears of Church Conflict," *NACBA Ledger* 30/1 (Spring 2011): 6–8.

[2]David R. Sawyer, *Hope in Conflict: Discovering Wisdom in Congregational Turmoil* (Cleveland: The Pilgrim Press, 2007), 8.

[3]George W. Bullard Jr., *Every Congregation Needs a Little Conflict* (St. Louis: Chalice Press, 2008) is an excellent resource for dealing with both healthy and unhealthy conflict.

[4]Mark Chaves, "How Common Is Congregational Conflict?" Call and Response Blog, *Faith & Leadership*, February 25, 2009. http://www.faithandleadership.com/blog/02-25-2009/mark-chaves-how-common-congregational-conflict .

[5]Hugh F. Halverstadt, *Managing Church Conflict* (Louisville: Westminster/John Knox Press, 1991) offers the most detailed systematic process for addressing conflict.

[6] Sawyer, *Hope in Conflict,* 16–21.

[7]Note in the bibliography the works of Murray Bowen, Edwin H. Freidman, Ronald W. Richardson, and Peter L. Steinke for further study of their insights.

[8]Speed Leas, *Discover Your Conflict Management Style* (Washington, D.C.: Alban Institute, 1998). I have worked with dozens of clergy and ministerial students over the years using this assessment. Overwhelmingly their preferred styles are Persuasion, Support, Avoidance, or Collaboration—each is best used in low levels of conflict intensity. Negotiation and Coercion/Force are more appropriate to higher levels of conflict.

[9]Bullard, *Every Congregation Needs a Little Conflict.* His summary chart on page 17 integrates levels of conflict with strategies of response and diagnoses of win-lose realities. It is a useful framework for the conflict minister.

[10]Peter L. Steinke, *A Door Set Open: Grounding Change in Mission and Hope* (Herndon, Va.: The Alban Institute, 2010), 78.

[11]Kenneth C. Hauk, *Antagonists in the Church: How to Identify and Deal with Destructive Conflict* (Minneapolis: Augsburg Publishing House, 1988).

Chapter 14

[1]Jill M. Hudson, *When Better Isn't Enough: Evaluation Tools for the 21ˢᵗ-Century Church* (Herndon, Va.: The Alban Institute, 2004), 24.

[2]James M. Kouzes and Barry Z. Posner, *The Leadership Challenge,* 3rd ed. (San Francisco: Jossey-Bass, 2002), 84.

[3]James Howell, "Evaluation Anxiety," http://www.faithandleadership.com/blog/08-03-2011/james-howell-evaluation-anxiety? utm_source=newsletter&utm_medium=headline&utm_campaign=NI_feature.

[4]Kathleen A. Cahalan, *Projects That Matter: Successful Planning and Evaluation for Religious Organizations* (Bethesda, Md.: The Alban Institute, 2003), xv.

[5]Louis Weeks, *All for God's Glory: Redeeming Church Scutwork* (Herndon, Va.: The Alban Institute, 2008), 71.

[6]Cynthia Woolever and Deborah Bruce, *Beyond the Ordinary: Ten Strengths of U. S. Congregations* (Louisville: Westminster John Knox Press, 2004).

[7]Hudson, *When Better Isn't Enough,* provides instruments for personnel committee evaluations of staff, with self-evaluation forms for pastors, associate pastors, and volunteers. Her criteria will not fit all congregations, however.

[8]Cindy Coe, Amy Zehnder, and Dennis Kinlaw, *Coaching for Commitment: Achieving Superior Performance from Individuals and Teams,* 3rd ed. (San Francisco: John Wiley & Sons, 2008), 8.

[9]Ibid., 150.

Chapter 15

[1]There is debate whether the concert ever occurred. The story has inspired many, however, and is included in Wayne Dosick, *When Life Hurts: A Personal Journey from Adversity to Renewal* (New York: Ulysses Press, 1999).

[2]Malcolm Gladwell, *The Tipping Point: How Little Things Can Make a Difference* (New York: Little, Brown and Company, 2000, 2002). This material found here is adapted from Larry L. McSwain, "Tipping Points in Congregational Life," *Net Results,* XXVII/3 (May/June 2006): 6–7, and, "Recognize the 'tipping points' in your ministry," *Church Executive* 7/3 (March 2008): 38–40.

[3]Gladwell, *Tipping Point,* 12.

[4]Dennis N. Voskuil, "The Grateful Pastor," *The Three Tasks of Leadership: Worldly Wisdom for Pastoral Leaders,* ed. Eric O. Jacobsen (Grand Rapids: William B. Eerdmans, 2009), 181.

[5]Richard L. Hester and Kelli Walker-Jones, *Know Your Story and Lead with It: The Power of Narrative in Clergy Leadership* (Herndon, Va.: The Alban Institute, 2009), 6.

[6]Melissa Clodfelter, "Numbers Don't Lie: The Truth About Clergy Health," *Door Posts: The Newsletter of the Center for Congregational Health,* vol. 02-062011 (June 2011).

[7]William L. Self, *Surviving the Stained-Glass Jungle* (Macon: Mercer University Press, 2011), 45.

[8]Hester and Walker-Jones, *Know Your Story,* 80–81.

Bibliography

Books, Chapters, and Articles

Alcorn, Randy. *Money, Possessions, and Eternity*. Carol Stream, Ill.: Tyndale House Publishing, 2003.

Ammerman, Nancy Tatom, with Arthur E. Farnsley II, et al. *Congregation and Community*. New Brunswick, N.J.: Rutgers University Press, 1997.

Bandy, Thomas G. *Coaching Change: Breaking Down Resistance, Building Up Hope*. Nashville: Abingdon Press, 2000.

Baptist General Convention of Texas, Christian Life Commission, "Keeping Your Church Out of Court." Third edition, http://christianlifecommission.com.

Barna Group. "Six Reasons Young Christians Leave Church." http://barna.org/teens-next-gen-articles/528-six-reasons-young-christians-leave-church.

Barnes, M. Craig. *The Pastor as Minor Poet: Texts and Subtexts in the Ministerial Life*. Grand Rapids: William B. Eerdmans, 2009.

Barrett, Lois Y., et al., eds. *Treasure in Clay Jars: Patterns in Missional Faithfulness*. Grand Rapids: William B. Eerdmans, 2003.

Bass, Diana Butler. *Christianity for the Rest of Us*. San Francisco: HarperSanFrancisco, 2006.

———. *The Practicing Congregation: Imagining a New Old Church*. Herndon, Va.: Alban Institute, 2004.

———. *Strength for the Journey: A Pilgrimage of Faith in Community*. San Francisco: Jossey-Bass, 2002.

Bass, Diana Butler, and Joseph Stewart-Sickling. *From Nomads to Pilgrims: Stories from Practicing Congregations*. Herndon, Va.: Alban Institute, 2006.

Baxter, Richard. *The Reformed Pastor*. Edited by William Brown. Carlisle, Pa.: The Banner of Truth Trust, 1997 [1656].

Becker, Penny. *Congregations in Conflict: Cultural Models of Local Religious Life*. New York: Cambridge University Press, 1999.

Bell, Rob. *Love Wins: A Book about Heaven, Hell, and the Fate of Every Person Who Ever Lived*. New York: HarperOne, 2011.

———. *Velvet Elvis: Repainting the Christian Faith*. Grand Rapids: Zondervan, 2006.

Bellah, Robert. "Religious Evolution," in *Beyond Belief: Essays on Religion in a Post-Traditionalist World*. Berkeley: University of California Press, 1991, 20–51.

Bennis, Warren G., and Robert J. Thomas. *Geeks & Geezers: How Era, Values, and Defining Moments Shape Leaders*. Boston: Harvard Business School Press, 2002.

Berens, Linda, Sue Cooper, Linda K. Ernst, Charles R. Martin, Steve Myers, Dario Nardi, Roger R. Pearman, Marci Segal, and Melissa A. Smith.

Quick Guide to the 16 Personality Types in Organizations: Understanding Personality Differences in the Workplace. Huntington Beach, Calif,: Telos Publications, 2001.

Blackaby, Henry T., and Claude V. King, *Experiencing God: How to Live the Full Adventure of Knowing and Doing the Will of God.* Nashville: Broadman and Holman, 1994.

Bolger, Ryan. "Following Jesus into Culture: Emerging Church as Social Movement," in *An Emergent Manifesto of Hope.* Edited by Doug Pagitt and Tony Jones. Grand Rapids: Baker Books, 2007, 132–139.

Bolles, Richard N. *How to Find Your Mission in Life.* 1991. Revised, Berkeley, Calif.: Ten Speed Press, 2000.

Bonem, Mike, and Roger Patterson. *Leading from the Second Chair: Serving Your Church, Fulfilling Your Role, and Realizing Your Dreams.* San Francisco: Jossey-Bass, 2005.

Bosch, David J. *Believing in the Future: Toward a Missiology of Western Culture.* Valley Forge, Pa.: Trinity Press International, 1995.

——. *Transforming Mission: Paradigm Shifts in Theology of Mission.* Maryknoll, N.Y.: Orbis Books, 1991.

Bowen, Murray. *Family Therapy in Clinical Practice.* New York, N. Y.: Jason Aronson, Inc., 1993.

Branson, Mark Lou. "Gratitude as Access to Meaning," in *The Three Tasks of Leadership: Worldly Wisdom for Pastoral Leaders.* Edited by Eric O. Jacobsen. Grand Rapids: William B. Eerdmans, 2008.

Branson, Mark Lou, and Juan F. Martínez. *Churches, Cultures & Leadership: A Practical Theology of Congregations and Ethnicities.* Downers Grove, Ill.: IVP Academic, 2011.

Browning, Geil. *Emergenetics®: Tap into the New Science of Success.* San Francisco: HarperCollins e-books, 2010. Kindle edition.

Bullard, Jr., George W. *Every Congregation Needs a Little Conflict.* St. Louis: Chalice Press, 2008.

——. *Pursuing the Full Kingdom Potential of Your Congregation.* St. Louis: Lake Hickory Resources, 2005.

Byassee, Jason. "Team Players: What do associate pastors want?" *Christian Century* (January 24, 2006): 18–22.

Cahalan, Kathleen A. *Projects That Matter: Successful Planning & Evaluation for Religious Organizations.* Bethesda, Md.: The Alban Institute, 2003.

Callahan, Kennon. *Twelve Keys to an Effective Church.* San Francisco: Harper & Row, 1983.

Carroll, Jackson W., with Becky R. McMillan. *God's Potters: Pastoral Leadership and the Shaping of Congregations.* Grand Rapids: William B. Eerdmans, 2006.

Carroll, Jackson W., and Wade Clark Roof. *Bridging Divided Worlds: Generational Cultures in Congregations.* San Francisco: Jossey-Bass, 2002.

Chaves, Mark. *Congregations in America.* Cambridge: Harvard University Press, 2004.

Christopher, J. Clif. *Not Your Parents' Offering Plate: A New Vision for Financial Stewardship.* Nashville: Abingdon Press, 2008.

Cladis, George. *Leading the Team-Based Church: How Pastors and Church Staffs Can Grow Together into a Powerful Fellowship of Leaders.* San Francisco: Jossey-Bass, 1999.

Claypool, John R. *The Preaching Event.* Waco, Tex.: Word Books, 1980.

———. *Tracks of a Fellow Struggler: How to Handle Grief.* Waco, Tex.: Word Books, 1974.

Clodfelter, Melissa. "Numbers Don't Lie: The Truth About Clergy Health." *Door Posts: The Newsletter of the Center for Congregational Health.* Vol. 02-062011 (June 2011).

Coe, Cindy, Amy Zehnder, and Dennis Kinlaw. *Coaching for Commitment: Achieving Superior Performance from Individuals and Teams.* 3rd ed. San Francisco: John Wiley & Sons, 2008.

Collins, Jim. *Good to Great: Why Some Companies Make the Leap...and Other's Don't.* New York: HarperBusiness, 2001.

———. *Good to Great and the Social Sectors.* Boulder, Colo.: Jim Collins, 2005.

Creswell, Jane. *Christ-Centered Coaching: 7 Benefits for Ministry Leaders.* St. Louis: Chalice Press, 2006.

Dale, Robert. *Leadership in a Changing Church: Charting the Shape of the River.* Nashville: Abingdon Press, 1998.

———. *Seeds for the Future.* St. Louis: Lake Hickory Resources, 2005.

———. *To Dream Again.* Nashville: Broadman Press, 1981.

DePree, Max. *Leadership Is an Art.* New York: Doubleday, 1989.

———. *Leadership Jazz.* New York: Doubleday/Currency, 1992.

De Young, Curtiss, et al. *United by Faith: The Multiracial Congregation as an Answer to the Problem of Race.* New York: Oxford University Press, 2003.

Dosick, Wayne. *When Life Hurts: A Personal Journey from Adversity to Renewal.* New York: Ulysses Press, 1999.

Dyrness, William A. "The Reality of Your Context: Fundamental Elements and Multicultural Leadership," in *The Three Tasks of Leadership: Worldly Wisdom for Pastoral Leaders.* Edited by Eric O. Jacobsen. Grand Rapids: William B. Eerdmans Publishing Company, 2009.

Dudley, Carl S., and Nancy T. Ammerman. *Congregations in Transition: A Guide for Analyzing, Assessing, and Adapting in Changing Communities.* San Francisco: Jossey-Bass, 2002.

Dykstra, Craig. "The Pastoral Imagination," *Initiatives in Religion* (Spring, 1-2, 2001): 15.

Eck, Diana. *A New Religious America: How a "Christian Country" Has Become the World's Most Religiously Diverse Nation.* New York: HarperCollins, 2001.

Eliot, T. S. "The Love Song of J. Alfred Prufrock," *Collected Poems, 1909-1962*. New York: Harcourt, Brace Jovanovich, 1991.

Ellingson, Stephen. *The Megachurch and the Mainline: Remaking Religious Tradition in the Twenty-First Century.* Chicago: The University of Chicago Press, 2007.

Essex, Barbara J. *Women in the Bible*. Cleveland: The Pilgrim Press, 2001.

Fosdick, Harry Emerson. *The Living of These Days: An Autobiography*. New York: Harper & Row, 1956, quoted in Harry Emerson Fosdick, "Learning to Preach," in *Pastor: A Reader for Ordained Ministry*. Edited by William H. Willimon. Nashville: Abingdon Press, 2002.

Fowler, James W. *Becoming Adult, Becoming Christian: Adult Development and Christian Faith*. San Francisco: Jossey-Bass, 2000.

Franklin, Robert M. *Crisis in the Village: Restoring Hope in African American Communities*. Minneapolis: Fortress Press, 2007.

Friedman, Edwin H. *A Failure of Nerve: Leadership in the Age of the Quick Fix*. Edited by Margaret M. Treadwell and Edward W. Beal. 1999. Reprint. New York: Seabury Books, 2007.

———. *Generation to Generation: Family Process in Church and Synagogue*. New York: Guilford Press, 1985.

Friedman, Thomas L. *Hot, Flat, and Crowded: Why We Need a Green Revolution and How It Can Renew America*. New York: Farrar, Straus and Giroux, 2008.

———. *The World Is Flat: A Brief History of the Twenty-first Century*. New York: Farrar, Straus and Giroux, 2005.

Galindo, Israel. *The Hidden Lives of Congregations: Discerning Church Dynamics*. Herndon, Va.: The Alban Institute, 2004.

Galindo, Israel, Elaine Boomer, and Don Reagan. *A Family Genogram Workbook*. Richmond, Va.: Israel Galindo Educational Consultants, 2006.

Gardner, Howard. *Intelligence Reframed: Multiple Intelligences for the 21st Century*. New York: Basic Books, 1999.

Geoffrion, Timothy C. *The Spirit-Led Leader: Nine Leadership Practices and Soul Principles*. Herndon, Va.: The Alban Institute, 2005.

Gladwell, Malcolm. *Outliers: The Story of Success*. New York: Little, Brown, and Company, 2008.

———. *The Tipping Point: How Little Things Can Make a Big Difference*. 2000. Reprint. New York: Little, Brown, and Company, 2002.

Goleman, Daniel. *Emotional Intelligence*. New York: Bantam Books, 1995.

———. *Leadership: The Power of Emotional Intelligence*. Northhampton, Mass.: More Than Sound, 2011. Digital edition.

Goleman, Daniel, Richard E. Boyatzis, and Annie McKee. *Primal Leadership: The Power of Emotional Intelligence*. Boston: Harvard Business School Press, 2002.

Goodman, Denise W. *Congregational Fitness: Healthy Practices for Layfolk*. Bethesda, Md.: The Alban Institute, 2000.

Greer, Robert C. *Mapping Postmodernism: A Survey of Christian Options*. Downers Grove, Ill.: InterVarsity Press, 2003.

Grenz, Stanley J. *A Primer on Postmodernism*. Grand Rapids: William B. Eerdmans, 1996.

Gustafson, James. *Treasure in Earthen Vessels: The Church as a Human Community*. New York: Harper, 1961.

Hadaway, C. Kirk. *Behold I Do a New Thing: Transforming Communities of Faith*. Cleveland: The Pilgrim Press, 2001.

Hahn, Celia Allison. *Uncovering Your Church's Hidden Spirit*. Bethesda, Md.: The Alban Institute, 2001.

Hall, Douglas John. *The Cross in Our Context: Jesus and the Suffering World*. Minneapolis: Fortress Press, 2003.

Halverstadt, Hugh F. *Managing Church Conflict*. Louisville: Westminster/John Knox Press, 1991.

Hamilton, Adam. *Leading Beyond the Walls: Developing Congregations with a Heart for the Unchurched*. Nashville: Abingdon Press, 2002.

Hammett, Edward H. *The Gathered and Scattered Church: Equipping Believers for the 21st Century*. Macon: Smyth & Helwys, 1999.

Hammett, Edward H., and James R. Pierce with Stephen DeVane. *Making Shifts without Making Waves: A Coach Approach to Soulful Leadership*. St. Louis: Chalice Press, 2009.

Hammond, Sue Annis. *The Thin Book of® Appreciative Inquiry*. 2nd ed. Bend, Oreg.: Thin Book Publishing Co., 1996. Kindle edition.

Harvey, Barry. "The Church as a Company of Nomads," *Christian Reflection* (34). Waco: The Center for Christian Ethics at Baylor University, 2010, 11–18.

Hauk, Kenneth C. *Antagonists in the Church: How to Identify and Deal with Destructive Conflict*. Minneapolis: Augsburg Publishing House, 1988

Herrington, Jim, Mike Bonem, and James H. Furr. *Leading Congregational Change: A Practical Guide for the Transformational Journey*. San Francisco: Jossey-Bass, 2000.

Heifetz, Ronald A., and Marty Linsky. *Leadership on the Line: Staying Alive through the Dangers of Leading*. Boston: Harvard Business School Press, 2002.

Hester, Richard L., and Kelli Walker-Jones. *Know Your Story and Lead with It: The Power of Narrative in Clergy Leadership*. Herndon, Va.: The Alban Institute, 2009.

Hiltner, Seward. *The Christian Shepherd: Some Aspects of Pastoral Care*. Nashville: Abingdon Press, 1959.

——. *Ferment in the Ministry*. Nashville: Abingdon Press, 1969.

——. *Preface to Pastoral Theology*. 1956. Reprint. Nashville: Abingdon Press, 1979.

Holifield, E. Brooks. *God's Ambassadors: A History of the Christian Clergy in America*.

Grand Rapids: William B. Eerdmans, 2007.

———. *A History of Pastoral Care in America: From Salvation to Self-Realization.* Nashville: Abingdon Press, 1983.

———. "Toward a History of American Congregations," in *American Congregations: New Perspectives in the Study of Congregations,* Vol. 2. Edited by James P. Wind and James W. Lewis. Chicago: The University of Chicago Press, 1994.

Holmes III, Urban T. *A History of Spirituality: An Analytical Introduction.* New York: Seabury Press, 1980.

———. *Ministry and Imagination.* New York: Seabury Press, 1976.

———. *Spirituality for Ministry.* 1982. Reprint. Harrisburg, Pa.: Morehouse Publishing, 2002.

Hopewell, James F. *Congregation: Stories and Structures.* Edited by Barbara G. Wheeler. Philadelphia: Fortress Press, 1987.

Hudson, Jill M. *When Better Isn't Enough: Evaluation Tools for the 21st-Century Church.* Herndon, Va.: The Alban Institute, 2004.

Hull, William E. *Strategic Preaching: The Role of the Pulpit in Pastoral Leadership.* St. Louis: Chalice Press, 2006.

Hunter, Victor. *Desert Hearts and Healing Fountains: Gaining Pastoral and Vocational Clarity.* St. Louis: Chalice Press, 2003.

Jensen, Evelyn. "Women's Issues in Context," in *The Good News of the Kingdom: Mission Theology for the Third Millenium.* Edited by Charles Van Engen, Dean S. Gilliland, and Paul Pierson Maryknoll: Orbis Books, 1993.

Johnson, Ronald W. *From the Outside In: Connecting to the Community Around You.* St. Louis: Lake Hickory Resources, 2006.

Johnson, Steven. *Where Good Ideas Come From: The Natural History of Innovation.* New York: Riverhead Books, 2010.

Jones, L. Gregory, and Kevin R. Armstrong. *Resurrecting Excellence: Shaping Faithful Christian Ministry.* Grand Rapids: William B. Eerdmans, 2006.

Kelley, Robert L. *The Power of Followership: How to Create Leaders People Want.* New York: Doubleday/Currency, 1992.

Kenny, Charles. "TV Will Save the World: In a lot of places, it's the next big thing," *Time* 175/11 (March 22, 2011): 54.

Kouzes, James M., and Barry Z. Posner, editors. *Christian Reflections on the Leadership Challenge.* San Francisco: Jossey-Bass, 2004.

Kouzes, James M., and Barry Z. Posner. *The Leadership Challenge.* 3rd ed. San Francisco: Jossey-Bass, 2002.

Leas, Speed. *Discover Your Conflict Management Style.* Washington, D.C.: Alban Institute, 1998.

Lamkin, James. "Recalling That Which Is Not Yet," a sermon preached at Northside Drive Baptist Church, Atlanta, Georgia, December 18, 2011.

———. "Systems Theory and Congregational Leadership: Leaves from an Alchemist's Journal." *Review and Expositor,* 102 (Summer 2005): 461–89.

LaRochelle, Robert. *Part-Time Pastor, Full-Time Church.* Cleveland: Pilgrim Press, 2010.

Lavoy, Gregg. *Callings: Finding and Following an Authentic Life*. New York: Harmony Books, 1997.

Lawrence, Brother. *The Practice of the Presence of God: The Best Rule of a Holy Life*. Gloucester, U.K.: Dodo Press, 2007. Kindle edition.

Lencioni, Patrick M. *The Five Dysfunctions of a Team: A Leadership Fable*. San Francisco: Jossey-Bass, 2002.

Lingenfelter, Sherwood. "Defining Institutional Realities: The Myth of the Right Form," in *The Three Tasks of Leadership: Worldly Wisdom for Pastoral Leaders*. Edited by Eric O. Jacobsen. Grand Rapids, William B. Eerdmans Publishing Company, 2009.

Long, Thomas G. *Accompany Them with Singing—The Christian Funeral*. Louisville: Westminster John Knox Press, 2009.

———. *Beyond the Worship Wars: Building Vital and Faithful Worship*. Bethesda, Md.: The Alban Institute, 2001.

Lupton, Robert D. *Compassion, Justice and the Christian Life: Rethinking Ministry to the Poor*. Ventura, Calif.: Regal Books, 2007.

———. *Return Flight: Community Development Through Reneighboring Our Cities*. 1993. Reprint. Atlanta: FCS Urban Ministries, 1997.

Lyons, Gabe, and Dave Kinnaman, *unChristian: What a New Generation Really Thinks about Christianity and Why It Matters*. Grand Rapids: Baker Books, 2007. Kindle edition.

McHugh, Adam S. *Introverts in the Church: Finding Our Place in an Extroverted Culture*. Downers Grove, Ill.: IVP Books, 2009.

McKnight, Scot. "Five Streams of Emerging Church: Key elements of the most controversial and misunderstood movement in the church today," *Christianity Today* (February, 2007): 35–39.

McLaren, Brian B. *Everything Must Change: Jesus, Global Crises, and a Revolution of Hope*. Nashville: Thomas Nelson, 2007.

———. *A Generous Orthodoxy*. Grand Rapids: Zondervan Youth Specialties, 2006.

———. *The Story We Find Ourselves In: Further Adventures of a New Kind of Christian*. San Francisco: Jossey-Bass, 2003.

McKinney, Lori-Ellen. *Getting to Amen: Eight Strategies for Managing Conflict in the African American Church*. Valley Forge, Pa.: Judson Press, 2005.

McManus, Erwin Raphael. "The Global Intersection," in *The Church in Emerging Culture: Five Perspectives*. Edited by Leonard Sweet. El Cajon, Calif.: emergentYS, 2000.

McMickle, Marvin A. *Caring Pastors, Caring People: Equipping Your Church for Pastoral Care*. Valley Forge, Pa.: Judson Press, 2011.

McSwain, Larry L., and Kay Wilson Shurden. *Call Waiting: God's Invitation to Youth*. Valley Forge, Pa.: Judson Press, 2005.

McSwain, Larry L., and William C. Treadwell. *Church Organizations Alive!* Nashville: Broadman Press, 1987.

McSwain, Larry L. "Mending the Tears of Church Conflict," *NACBA Ledger* 30/1 (Spring 2011): 6–8.

———. *Old Louisville: A Challenge, An Opportunity*. Louisville: Urban Studies Center, University of Louisville, 1969.

———. "Recognize the "tipping points' in your ministry," *Church Executive* 7/3 (March 2008): 38–40.

———. "Tipping Points in Congregational Life," *Net Results*, 27/3 (May/June 2006), 6-7.

Meeks, Wayne A. *The First Urban Christians: The Social World of the Apostle Paul*. 2nd ed. New Haven: Yale University Press, 2003.

Melander, Rochelle. *A Generous Presence: Spiritual Leadership and the Art of Coaching*. Herndon, Va.: The Alban Institute, 2006.

Merriam-Webster's Collegiate Dictionary, 11th ed. Springfield, Ma.: Merriam-Webster, Incorporated, 2005.

Merritt, Carol Howard. *Reframing Hope: Vital Ministry in a New Generation*. Herndon, Va.: The Alban Institute, 2010.

———. *Tribal Church: Ministering to the Missing Generation*. Herndon, Va.: The Alban Institute, 2007.

Miller, Herb. *Connecting with God: 14 Ways Churches Can Help People Grow Spiritually*. Nashville: Abingdon Press, 1994.

Miller, Lisa. "House of Worship: Finding spirituality at home," *Newsweek*, January 11, 2010, 31.

Miller, Lynn. *The Power of Enough: Finding Contentment*. 2003. Reprint. Goshen, Ind.: MMA® Stewardship Solutions, 2007.

Miller, Donald. *Blue Like Jazz: Nonreligious Thoughts on Christian Spirituality*. Nashville: Thomas Nelson, 2003.

Mills, Edgar W., and John P. Koval. *Stress in Ministry*. New York: IDOC, 1971.

Minatrea, Milfred. *Shaped by God's Heart: The Passion and Practices of Missional Churches*. San Francisco: Jossey-Bass, 2004.

Minear, Paul S. *Images of the Church in the New Testament*. Philadelphia: The Westminster Press, 1960.

———. *To Die and Live: Christ's Resurrection and Christian Vocation*. New York: The Seabury Press, 1977.

Moore, Thomas. *Care of the Soul: A Guide for Cultivating Depth and Sacredness in Everyday Life*. New York: HarperPerennial, 1992.

Morgenthaler, Sally. "Leadership in a Flattened World: Grassroots Culture and the Demise of the CEO Model," in *An Emergent Manifesto of Hope*. Edited by Doug Pagitt and Tony Jones. Grand Rapids: Baker Books, 2007.

Mowchan, Carolyn Coon, and Damian Anthony Vraniak. *Connecting with God in a Disconnected World: A Guide for Spiritual Growth and Renewal*. Minneapolis: Augsburg Fortress, 2003.

Myers, Joseph R. *Organic Community: Creating a Place Where People Naturally Connect*. Grand Rapids: Baker Books, 2007.

Nessen, Craig L. *Beyond Maintenance to Mission: A Theology of the Congregation*. Minneapolis: Fortress Press, 1999.

Newbigin, Lesslie. *Signs Amid the Rubble: The Purposes of God in Human History.* Edited by Geoffrey Wainwright. Grand Rapids: William B. Eerdmans, 2003.

———. *The Open Secret: An Introduction to the Theology of Mission.* Rev. ed.. Grand Rapids: William B. Eerdmans, 1995.

Niebuhr, H. Richard. *The Purpose of the Church and Its Ministry: Reflections on the Aims of Theological Education.* New York: Harper and Row, 1956.

Njiru, Paul Kariuki. *Charism and the Holy Spirit's Activity in the Body of Christ: An Exegetical-Theological Study of 1 Corinthians 12,4-11 and Romans 12,6-8.* Roma: Editrice Pontificai Università Gregoriana, 2002.

Nouwen, Henri J. M. *Making All Things New: An Invitation to the Spiritual Life.* San Francisco: HarperSanFrancisco, 1981.

Oates, Wayne E. *The Christian Pastor.* 1951. Reprint. Philadelphia: Westminster Press, 1982.

Oden, Thomas C. *Pastoral Theology: Essentials of Ministry.* San Francisco: HarperSanFrancisco, 1983.

Olson, David T. *The American Church in Crisis.* Grand Rapids: Zondervan, 2008.

Ortberg, Nancy. "Ministry Implications of Service," in *The Three Tasks of Leadership.* Edited by Eric O. Jacobsen. Grand Rapids: William B. Eerdmans, 2009.

Ott, E. Stanley. *Transform Your Church with Ministry Teams.* Grand Rapids: William B. Eerdmans, 2004.

Palmer, Parker. *Let Your Life Speak.* San Francisco: Jossey-Bass, 2000.

Putnam, Robert D., and David E. Campbell. *American Grace: How Religion Divides and Unites Us.* New York: Simon & Schuster, 2010.

Qualls, Charles. *Divorce Ministry: A Guidebook.* Macon: Smyth & Helwys, 2011.

Quinn, Robert L. *Deep Change: Discovering the Leader Within.* San Francisco: Jossey-Bass, 1996.

Reese, Martha Grace. 2nd ed. *Unbinding the Gospel: Real Life Evangelism.* St. Louis: Chalice Press, 2008.

Rendle, Gilbert R. *Leading Change in the Congregation: Spiritual and Organizational Tools for Leaders.* Herndon, Va.: The Alban Institute, Inc., 1998.

Rendle, Gil, and Alice Mann. *Holy Conversations: Strategic Planning as a Spiritual Practice for Congregations.* Herndon, Va.: The Alban Institute, 2003.

Richardson, Ronald W. *Becoming a Healthier Pastor: Family Systems Theory and the Pastor's Own Family.* Minneapolis: Fortress Press, 2005.

———. *Creating a Healthier Church: Family Systems Theory, Leadership and Congregational Life.* Minneapolis: Fortress Press, 1996.

Robinson, Anthony B. *Changing the Conversation: A Third Way for Congregations.* Grand Rapids: William B. Eerdmans, 2008.

———. *Stewardship for Vital Congregations.* Cleveland: The Pilgrim Press, 2011.

———. *Transforming Congregational Culture.* Grand Rapids: William B. Eerdmans, 2003.

Roozen, David, William McKinney, and Jackson W. Carroll, *Varieties of Religious Presence: Mission in Public Life*. New York: The Pilgrim Press, 1984.

Rothage, Arlin J. *Sizing Up a Congregation for New Member Ministry*. New York: Seabury, n. d.

Roxburgh, Alan J., and Fred Romanuk. *The Missional Leader: Equipping Your Church to Reach a Changing World*. San Francisco: Jossey-Bass, 2006.

St. John Chrysostom, "Temptations of the Teacher," in *Pastor: A Reader for Ordained Ministry*. Edited by William H. Willimon. Nashville: Abingdon Press, 2002.

———.*Six Books on the Priesthood*. Translated by Graham Neville. London: SPCK, 1964. Sawyer, David R. *Hope in Conflict: Discovering Wisdom in Congregational Turmoil*. Cleveland: Pilgrim Press, 2007.

Scalise, Charles J. *Bridging the Gap: Connecting What You Learned in Seminary with What You Find in the Congregation*. Nashville: Abingdon Press, 2003.

———. "Defining the Reality of Your Role: Historical Contexts and Theological Models of Christian Leadership," in *The Three Tasks of Leadership: Worldly Wisdom for Pastoral Leaders*. Edited by Eric O. Jacobsen. Grand Rapids: William B. Eerdmans, 2009.

Scazzero, Peter. *The Emotionally Healthy Church: A Strategy for Discipleship that Actually Changes Lives*. Grand Rapids: Zondervan, 2003.

Scheef, Jr., R. L. "Vocation," in *The Interpreter's Dictionary of the Bible*, IV. Edited by George Arthur Buttrick. New York: Abingdon Press, 1962.

Schmidt, Karl Ludwig. "βασίλεία," in *Theological Dictionary of the New Testament*. Edited by Gerhard Kittel. Translated by Geoffrey W. Bromiley. Vol. 1. Grand Rapids: William B. Eerdmans Publishing Co., 1964.

Searcy, Nelson, with Jennifer Dykes Henson. *Maximize: How to Develop Extravagant Givers in Your Church*. Grand Rapids: Baker Books, 2010.

Self, William L. *Surviving the Stained Glass Jungle*. Macon, Ga.: Mercer University Press, 2011.

———. "Tears and Lifeblood...," *Christian Century* 128/7 (April 2011): 5.

Sisk, Ronald D. *The Competent Pastor: Skills and Self-Knowledge for Serving Well*. Herndon, Va.: The Alban Institute, 2005.

Smith, Christine M. *Preaching as Weeping, Confession, and Resistance*. Louisville: Westminster/John Knox Press, 1992.

Snow, Luther K. *The Power of Asset Mapping: How Your Congregation Can Act on Its Gifts*. Herndon, Va.: The Alban Institute, 2004.

Standish, N. Graham. *Humble Leadership: Being Radically Open to God's Guidance and Grace*. Herndon, Va.: The Alban Institute, 2007.

Stanley, Andy. *Deep and Wide: Creating Churches Unchurched People Love to Attend*. Grand Rapids: Zondervan, 2012.

Steinke, Peter L. *Congregational Leadership in Anxious Times: Being Calm and Courageous No Matter What*. Herndon, Va.: The Alban Institute, 2006.

———. *A Door Set Open: Grounding Change in Mission and Hope*. Herndon, Va.: The

Alban Institute, 2010.

———. *Healthy Congregations: A Systems Approach.* 1996. Reprint. Herndon, Va.: The Alban Institute, 2006.

Sternberg, Robert. *Successful Intelligence: How Practical and Creative Intelligence Determine Success in Life.* New York: Plume, 1997.

Stevens, R. Paul. *The Other Six Days: Vocation, Work, and Ministry in Biblical Perspective.* Grand Rapids: William B. Eerdmans, 1999.

Stone, Howard W., and James O. Duke. *How to Think Theologically.* 2nd. ed. Minneapolis: Fortress Press, 2006.

Taylor, Barry. "Converting Christianity: The End of the Beginning of Faith," in *An Emergent Manifesto of Hope.* Edited by Doug Pagitt and Tony Jones. Grand Rapids: Baker Books, 2007.

Thumma, Scott, and Dave Travis. *Beyond Megachurch Myths: What We Can Learn from America's Largest Churches.* San Francisco: Jossey-Bass, 2007.

Tickle, Phyllis. *The Great Emergence: How Christianity Is Changing and Why.* Grand Rapids: Baker Books, 2008.

Tisdale, Leonora Tubbs. *Preaching as Local Theology and Folk Art.* Minneapolis: Fortress Press, 2007.

Treadwell, Jr., William C., and Larry L. McSwain. *Church Organizations Alive!* Nashville: Broadman Press, 1987.

Tuckman, Bruce, "Developmental sequence in small groups," *Psychological Bulletin* 63, no. 6 (1965): 384–99.

Van Gelder, Craig. *The Essence of the Church: A Community Created by the Spirit.* Grand Rapids: Baker Books, 2000.

———. *The Ministry of the Missional Church: A Community Led by the Spirit.* Grand Rapids: Baker Books, 2007.

Vansant, Sondra A. *Wired for Conflict: The Role of Personality in Resolving Differences.* Gainesville, Fla.: Center for Applications of Psychological Type, 2003.

Verkuyl, Johannes. "The Biblical Notion of Kingdom: Test of Validity for Theology of Religion," in *The Good News of the Kingdom: Mission Theology for the Third Millenium.* Edited by Charles Van Engen, Dean S. Gilliland, and Paul Pierson. Maryknoll, N.Y.: Orbis Books, 1993.

Voskuil, Dennis N. "The Grateful Pastor," in *The Three Tasks of Leadership: Worldly Wisdom for Pastoral Leaders.* Edited by Eric O. Jacobsen. Grand Rapids: William B. Eerdmans, 2009.

Ward, Graham. "Postmodern Theology," in *The Modern Theologians.* Edited by David F. Ford. 2nd ed. Malden, Ma.: Blackwell, 1998.

Ware, Corrine. *Connecting to God: Nurturing Spirituality through Small Groups.* Bethesda, Md.: The Alban Institute, 1997.

———. *Discover Your Spiritual Type: A Guide to Individual and Congregational Growth.* Bethesdah, Md. The Alban Institute, 1995.

———. *Saint Benedict on the Freeway: A Rule of Life for the 21st Century.* Nashville: Abingdon Press, 2001.

Warner, R. Stephen, "The Place of the Congregation in the Contemporary American Religious Configuration," *American Congregations: New Perspectives in the Study of Congregations*, Vol. 2. Edited by James P. Wind and James W. Lewis. Chicago: The University of Chicago Press, 1994.

Weeks, Louis B. *All for God's Glory: Redeeming Church Scutwork*. Herndon, Va.: The Alban Institute, 2008.

Weems, Jr., Lovett H. *Take the Next Step: Leading Lasting Change in the Church*. Nashville: Abingdon Press, 2003.

Wheatley, Margaret. "Goodbye, command and control," *Leader to Leader* (July 1997): 1.

Whitsitt, Landon. *Open Source Church: Making Room for the Wisdom of All*. Herndon, Va.: The Alban Institute, 2011. Kindle edition.

Wilder, Courtney. "Workers in the Kingdom," *Sightings* 10 (May 2007). A publication of the Martin Marty Center, University of Chicago Divinity School, Chicago.

Willimon, William H. *Pastor: The Theology and Practice of Ordained Ministry*. Nashville: Abingdon Press, 2002.

Woolever, Cynthia, and Deborah Bruce. *Beyond the Ordinary: 10 Strengths of U. S. Congregations*. Louisville: Westminster John Knox Press, 2004.

——. *A Field Guide to U. S. Congregations: Who's Going Where and Why*. Louisville: Westminster John Knox Press, 2002.

——. *A Field Guide to U.S. Congregations: Who's Going Where and Why*. 2nd ed.. Louisville: Westminster John Knox Press, 2010.

——. *Leadership That Fits Your Church: What Kind of Pastor for What Kind of Congregation*. St. Louis: Chalice Press, 2012.

——. *Places of Promise: Finding Strength in Your Congregation's Location*. Louisville: Westminster John Knox Press, 2008.

Wright, Christopher J. H. *The Mission of God: Unlocking the Bible's Grand Narrative*. Downers Grove, Ill.: IVP Academic, 2006.

Wright, Walt. "Introduction: Mentor to Mentor," in *The Three Tasks of Leadership: Worldly Wisdom for Pastoral Leaders*. Edited by Eric O. Jacobsen. Grand Rapids: William B. Eerdmans, 2009.

Yancey, George. *One Body, One Spirit: Principles of Successful Multiracial Churches*. Downers Grove, Ill.: InterVarsity Press, 2003.

Yeats, William Butler. "The Second Coming," in *The Classic Hundred Poems*. Edited by William Harmon. 2nd ed. New York: Columbia University Press, 2009.

Electronic Resources

Abundant Living. http://abundantlivingministry.org/.

Bell, Rob. "From structure to Spirit and back," *Faith & Leadership*, http://www.faithandleadership.com/multimedia/rob-bell-structure-spirit-and-back.

Bridge Vision Web Ministries. http://bridgevision.me.

Center for Congregational Health. http://www.healthychurch.org.

Chaves, Mark. "How Common Is Congregational Conflict?" Call and Response Blog. *Faith & Leadership*, February 25, 2009. http://www.faithandleadership.com/blog/02-25-2009/mark-chaves-how-common-congregational-conflict.

Christian Pathway. www.christianpathway.com.

The Columbia Partnership. http://www.thecolumbiapartnership.org.

Cooperrider, David L., and Diana Whitney. "A Positive Revolution in Change: Appreciative Inquiry" (Draft). Appreciative Inquiry Commons, 7–14. http://appreciativeinquiry.case.edu/uploads/whatisai.pdf.

Crown Ministries. http://www.crown.org/.

Emergenetics® International. http://emergenetics.com.

The Enneagram Institute. http:// www.enneagraminstitute.com.

Enright, William G. "Money is like a vital sign," *Faith & Leadership*, July 5, 2011. http://www.faithandleadership.com/qa/william-g-enright-money-vital-sign?page=full&print=true.

E-Zekial.com. http://e-zekial.com.

Faith Lab. http://www.thefaithlab.com/.

Financial Peace University. http://www.daverramsey.com/fpu/home/.

Flavors: The Digital You. http://flavors.me.

ForeignPolicy.com., http://www.foreignpolicy.com/articles/2010/08/11 the_global_cities_index_2010.

GenoPro. http://www.genopro.com/genogram/.

Hartford Institute for Religion Research. http://hirr.hartsem.edu/leadership/consultants.html.

"How We Compiled the 2010 Index," Foreign Policy.com, August 18, 2010. http://www.foreignpolicy.com/articles/2010/08/18/global_cities_index_methodology.

Howell, James. "Evaluation Anxiety." http://www.faithandleadership.com/blog/08-03-2011/james-howell-evaluation-anxiety?utm_source=newsletter&utm_medium=headline&utm_campaign=NI_feature.

Insightful Endeavors International. http://www.insightfulendeavors.com.

"Largest Cities in the World." WorldAtlas. http://www.worldatlas.com/citypops.htm.

Logan, Jane. "Appreciative Inquiry," Association Xpertise Inc. (AXI) January 2004. http://www.axi.ca/tca/jan2004/facilitationrole_1.shtml

The Louisville Institute. http://www.louisville-institute.org.

McLaren, Brian. "Seminary Is Not the Problem—the Church Is. What if seminaries became more like entrepreneurial boot camps than shop management schools?" http://www.patheos.com/Resources/Additional-Resources/Seminary-Is-Not-the-Problem-the-Church-Is-Brian-McLaren-11-02-2011.html.

"91.7%—Minorities Account for Nearly All U.S. Population Growth," Pew

Research Center. http://pewresearch.org/databank/dailynumber/?
NumberID=1225.

Personality Pathways. http://www.personalitypathways.com/

Pastoral Institute. http://www.pilink.org.

Pinnacle Leadership Associates. http://pinnaclelead.com.

PRIZM. http://www.tetrad.com/demographics/usa/claritas/prizmne.html.

Rosenberg, Matt. "Current World Population and World Population Growth Since the Year One," About.com, May 11, 2011, http://geography. about.com/od/obtainpopulationdata/a/worldpopulation.htm.

Somerville, Jim. "When the Sand Castle Crumbles: Why Is My Church Dying, and What Can I Do About It?" http://jimsomerville.wordpress.com.

Stephen Ministry. http://www.stephenministries.org/stephenministry/ default.cfm/917.

Strieber, Andrew. "Whistling While You Work: The 10 Most Satisfying Careers," http://www.careercast.com/jobs-rated/whistling-while-you-work-10-most-satisfying-careers.

Swint, Ruben. "Let's Do the Math," http://columbiapartnership.typepad/ the_columbia_partnership/2011/06/lets-do-th-math.html.

Tanzi, Alex. "U.S. Median Household Income Changes by County, From 2000 to 2009," Bloomberg.com, December 14, 2010. http://www.bloomberg. com/news/2010-12-14/u-s-median-household-income-change-from-2000-by-county-table-.html.

Taylor, Paul, and Scott Keeter, editors. *Millennials: A Portrait of Generation Next.* Philadelphia: Pew Research Center, 2010. http://pewresearch.org/ millennials/.

Teleometrics International. http://www.teleometrics.com/programs/part Number_ 1010I/info.html.

United Methodist Church /Spiritual Gifts Inventory http://www.umc.org/ site/c.lwL4KnN1LtH/b.1355371/k.9501/Spiritual_Gifts.htm.

United States Census. http://factfinder2.census.gov/faces/nav/jsf/pages/ index.xhtml.

Willow Creek Association/Stewardship. http://www.goodsenseministry.com.